BERNARD BERENSON

AESTHETICS
AND HISTORY
IN THE
VISUAL ARTS

N70
B48a

PANTHEON

N 70
B 48 a

Τὰ μὲν γὰρ ὑπὸ τῶν τεχνῶν γενόμενα, τὸ εὖ ἔχει ἐν αὐτοῖς, ἀρκεῖ οὖν αὐτά πος ἔχοντα γενέσθαι.

"Works of art have their merit in themselves so that it is enough if they are produced having a certain quality of their own."

ARISTOTLE: *Nicomachean Ethics*, II, IV, 3

"The sounding cataract
Haunted me like a passion; the tall rock,
The mountain, and the deep and gloomy wood,
Their colours and their forms, were then to me
An appetite; a feeling and a love,
That had no need of a remoter charm,
By thought supplied, nor any interest
Unborrowed from the eye."

WORDSWORTH: *Tintern Abbey*

"Ceux qui n'aiment pas beaucoup la peinture en elle-même, attachent une grande importance aux sujets des tableaux."

MME. DE STAËL: *De l'Allemagne*, II, 158 – 1820

"Almost everything that sets us above savages has come to us from the shores of the Mediterranean."

SAMUEL JOHNSON

Acknowledgment of permission to reproduce their photographs is made to the following firms:

	Plates:
Alinari, Florence	7, 14, 17, 19, 22, 23
Anderson, Rome	3, 8, 10, 11, 15, 18, 20, 21
Croci, Rimini	24
Giraudon, Paris	2, 12
Photo Marburg	5
Reusch, Munich	13
Soprintendenza, Florence	4

CONTENTS

LIST OF ILLUSTRATIONS

PREFACE

I was at a loss what title to give to the pages that follow. In the seventeenth century one could take a paragraph for a title and so convey an idea of a book's contents. Nowadays it must be brief, and one cannot launch out into something like this: "My adventures as an art taster, thinker, and writer, as connoisseur, critic, and historian." So I thought of "My Approach to Art Theory and Art History," of "Theory and History in the Fine Arts," of "Enjoyment of Figure Arts and History," of "Experience and History in the Figure Arts." Least unsatisfactory seemed "Appreciation and History in the Figure Arts," as appreciation comprises enjoyment with intelligent reflection, and even the deeper pondering that may deserve the epithet "intellectual." Nevertheless, and despite the fear of trespassing on the preserves of the incorporated schoolmen, I have settled on Aesthetics and History in the Visual Arts.

I was years writing this essay. It was finished in the autumn of 1941. Before a clean copy could be typed, Italy declared war against us and I had no way of getting the manuscript over. I laid it aside; and private reasons prevented my taking it up again till the summer of 1947, when I gave it a final revision. The reader must not be surprised if he comes across states of mind, or references to events, that go back ten years or more.

INTRODUCTION

THE IDEA of this approach to art theory and art history in the field of visual representation is to restate certain notions which have lain behind a career of many years. I have published books and articles, but, except one on the rudiments of connoisseurship, dating from the beginning of my activities, I have written almost nothing about the assumptions and convictions that have shaped and directed my work.

There are many approaches to the history of art—as many, perhaps, as there are individual students. We are blessed with treatise after treatise on the subject: technical, metaphysical, mathematical, biographical, theological, psycho-analytical, etc., etc. After nearly sixty years of preparation I may venture to speak of my way of facing the subject.

When I was young I cherished the hope of writing about all the arts as a personal adventure, not only about the visual arts but of music and literature as well. It was a hope too glamorous to outlast the inexperience of youth. The visual arts absorbed me to the exclusion of the others. Even then I had to narrow down and concentrate on a couple of centuries of Italian painting. Yet as an amateur—I would prefer the word "lover"—I have lived in many other realms of visual art, in all times and all climes.

It is not the business of art theory or art history to teach the practice of an art. They are not called upon to give training in the craft of painting, of sculpture, or of architecture, although they may stimulate and inspire the artist who sometimes hides in the craftsman. The purpose of art theory and

history should be to reveal the successive phases of what people in their time have been offered to enjoy and appreciate;
and how this enjoyment, and appreciation, waxed and waned
through intervening ages; then whether we still enjoy and
appreciate the same works, and, if we do, whether for the
same reason. Furthermore, the business of art history is to
recount what were the aspirations and ideals to which art
gave permanent as well as passing form.

The theory and history of art as I have tried to pursue
them are concerned with the work of art as it affects the
spectator, the listener, the enjoyer, and not its maker, unless
he too becomes an enjoyer.

Creative genius is a fascinating subject for study or, to be
more accurate, for meditation and guessing. I have nothing
against genial guessing in any field. Indeed, I wonder at
times whether the most suggestive translation of *In initio
erat verbum* would not be "In the beginning was the guess."
So I am not averse to fancies about the ultimate nature of
art and its origin, or to speculations regarding the artist and
his activities. I might even have guesses of my own to offer,
if I had the leisure. I would, however, insist with myself, as I
do with others, on keeping the artist and the work of art
in separate compartments.

It could be argued that no little of the sterility of art
theory, and the unsatisfactoriness of art history, from late
antiquity to our own day, is due to the failure to state at the
outset whether one is thinking from the point of view of the
producer of the work of art, or of its consumer. If Benedetto
Croce, the most authoritative of contemporary writers on
aesthetics, had kept in mind this distinction would he say
as he does in *Per una Poetica Moderna* (written in 1922 and
reprinted in *Nuovi Saggi di Estetica*) that "*l'opera d'arte è
sempre un atto spirituale*"? Perhaps not. The work of art is
the *product* of the mind's activity, but not that activity itself.

From the creator's point of view copies, reproductions, and

imitations may not count; although it is hard to imagine how, without them, his creations would get known to any but the few who could afford access to them; or how his style could become diffused so as to exert a wide influence. Not many masterpieces of Greek sculpture would be known to-day and none of Greek painting. Moreover, what is the finished statue that we enjoy? Is it its intuitive creator's spontaneous and instantaneous creation? In the case of bronze, the preferred Greek material, the statue was a cast, and where marble was concerned it was a copy, made probably, but not certainly, and seldom entirely, by the creator himself after his laboriously contrived model. In painting, the spontaneously created product is more often than not a scrawl that has no closer relation to the elaborated Sistine ceiling by Michelangelo or the Sistine Madonna by Raphael than the product of that most intuitive and spontaneous of all creative acts, the human embryo, has to the grown man of genius.

I am free to inquire what a work of art means to me and has been to me. It has been my life's work to "live" the work of art, to turn it over and over on my mental palate, to brood, to dream over it; and then in the hope of getting to understand it better I have written about it. As consumer of the art product I have the right to do all that. As I am neither figure artist, nor architect, nor musician, I have no certain right to speak of the producer. I am in the position of most critics, philosophers, and scholars. We have enjoyed experiencing the creative process in the art of words only with the logical result that writers on art seldom have in mind any of the arts except the verbal ones.

To take more interest in the artist than in his art is an effect of our hero-worshipping tendency, and, through the hero, of our masked self-worshipping instincts. We must resist these, and I for my part have never thought of writing on art except as an experience, personal, individual, but not private, not capricious, not self-assertive. "I do not love thee,

Dr. Fell, The reason why I cannot tell" is not criticism, no matter how many variations you play on the theme, how well you orchestrate it, how beguilingly you write about it.

There may be no absolute in art, but so long as we stand, grasp, breathe, and react to temperature, for so long will there be fixed although oscillating relations between these functions and the demands they make on the work of art, on painting particularly. There is in fact a relative absolute in art which is determined by our psycho-physiological condition and our mental preparation.

Everything we are aware of, every faintest change within us that reaches consciousness and affects it, is of the mind, is mental. The business of art, as of all creative activities, is to extend the horizons of consciousness not only in width and depth, but in height as well. Art lies in that mental region, for it is based on processes within us that manifest themselves in consciousness. What is under the threshold of consciousness belongs to physiology and not to aesthetics, art theory, or art history.

It will be my endeavour to make myself and my readers more aware, more conscious of the potentialities and qualities of this world of art, this realm of ideated satisfactions. I cannot insist too much on the proposition that it is the prevalence of ideated satisfactions over actual ones that is important for art as distinct from material, technique, and so-called natural shapes.

Thanks to the weaning of the work of art from its begetter, we can uphold with many aestheticians, Benedetto Croce at their head, the instinctiveness, spontaneity, and consequent irresponsibility of the artist in the act of conceiving. He indulges in the free play of his gifts and has nothing else in his head; certainly no idea of teaching or preaching.

There is no better example of intuitive spontaneity than the brilliant talker, the wit, who is stimulated and inspired by his listeners. Almost unconscious and even surprised to hear what comes out of his own mouth, he utters the winged word, the unforgettable phrase that amuses many, stings others, and deeply offends a few. The wit, the verbal clown, is suspected of a deliberate desire to poke fun, or to offend. That is seldom his intention. Nor, as is often imagined, does he act primarily through vanity, to show off, to solicit admiration. Like every other artist, he welcomes and enjoys applause, but the most determining reason for his action is: that under certain circumstances he cannot resist the impulse to talk brilliantly, even when vaguely aware that he may give offence, and draw down upon himself the vindictive displeasure of his listeners. No amount of whippings cured the mediaeval court jester. The producer cannot help producing nor the consumer receiving it according to his humour, regardless of the producer's intentions.

So it is with each and every work of art. The moment it is created the creation is weaned from the creator. It cannot avoid giving satisfaction or dissatisfaction; and it cannot help exercising influence, seeing how prone we are, willynilly, to imitate what we see and to be affected by what we hear. Certain works of art are like plants that produce gorgeous flowers, while secreting deadly poisons. The artist is free and irresponsible, but his creation may be more dangerous than these plants. Seeing and hearing them induces definite reactions in our make-up; whereas the poison in the plant has to be extracted and distilled before it can do mischief. We cannot ignore the effect, good or evil, of the art product on the mind and even on the character of the spectator or the audience, for it cannot avoid serving as a model or pattern. We only need point to our cinema products. Not only did their presentation of American morals help to make Europeans believe that we were too dissolute to make war, but it has persuaded Asiatics that our boasted civilization is, but for machines, inferior to theirs.

I too speak again and again of the "artist," but only in the

way in which I use the first person singular. When I say "I"
it is with no intention of speaking of myself, of my ego. It is
a grammatical necessity avoidable only by circumlocutions
that draw attention to the ego. It is more modest than these,
because it warns the listener that the statement we are about
to make is merely personal, no matter with what arguments
we bolster it up. As surely as there is a mathematics, a chem-
istry, an astronomy, a geology as distinct from mathema-
ticians, etc., etc., so there is art as distinct from individual
artists. Art in the sense here implied is the body of impersonal tradition and practices which, like the Treasures of
Merit in the Catholic Church, are at the disposal of everybody who accepts the terms and conditions of a certain technique in order to practise it.

So I speak of the artist when I mean the creative energy
that produces art, and when I refer to the artistic personality,
it is never the civic, social personality of the individual producer. I do not inquire what was in this individual's mind
while in the act—we may say the spasm—of creating. We are
more humbly and profitably engaged in trying to understand
the nature of art-creating energy as an activity of the mind.
Of this, although with fear and trembling, we may venture
to speak and at times we may narrow it down and shape it
into distinct figures that can be identified with historical
personalities, like Phidias and Polygnotus, Raphael and
Dürer.

Giordano Bruno in *Della Causa, Principio ed Uno* says:
"He who sees the portrait of Helen does not see Apelles:
but he sees only the result of the work which comes from the
merit and genius of Apelles. The work is certainly an effect
of the accident and circumstances of the substance of that
man, who as to his absolute essence is not in the least
known."

No doubt the artist has the first glimpse of his design, be
it poem or romance, be it painting, sculpture, or architecture,

or a musical composition, as if through a lightning rift in a cloud. His task both as artist and as craftsman is to implement this flash and to fix it for himself and for others. He has to be master of a mind and a will capable of holding fast to the vision, determined to defend it against the narrowing and distorting resistance of his materials and the limitations of his craft. "On the long road from the eye through the arm to the pencil how much is lost!" exclaimed the painter in Lessing's *Emilia Galotti*.

The artist has his idea in a flash. What the flash will present or reveal is the result not only of the gifts that he brought with him at birth, but of all that he has absorbed from his surroundings and experience: from his "conditioning," his education, his parents, his companions, his love affairs, reading, and travels—in short, his entire existence up to the moment of creative ecstasy, in which he has the vision of the work of art he is to produce.

But there is nothing peculiar to the artist in this, and it is just as true of every inventive activity, every discovery. Ideas occur to the scholar, the scientist, the mathematician, the inventor, in a similar moment of creative energy with the same cry of *Eureka*. The only difference is that to the artist the vision comes in the terms of his material and technique, while to the others the idea results from their subject matter, and has to be submitted to its austere and searching control.

The critic and historian of the work of art, partaking of both the artist's and the scholar's activities, should start with being as intuitive toward it, enjoying it as spontaneously, and with as little deliberation, as its creator who first conceived it. After which only is he called upon to analyze and interpret, to trace and account for its effects, moral and cultural as well as artistic.

I speak of enjoying the work of art. To avoid misunderstanding let me say that I use the verb to "enjoy" in no hedonistic sense but as people speak of "enjoying bad health." Likewise the word "pleasure" where I use it should be taken as referring to ideated sensations only, never to actual ones. By "actual" I mean the opposite of "ideated," "ideal," and all derivations from the same stem. I mean what is frequently if not universally designated as "real." That word I cannot apply to anything and everything that happens to happen, but only to what fits in and harmonizes with our pattern of the whole, with our cosmos, with the universe of the mind wherein art constitutes a kingdom of its own.

This kingdom is a world by itself subsisting on actuality. It offers us, when exhausted by the effort to detach ourselves from the confusion and buzz of the actual, the rest and refreshment we crave before we take wing and soar to the region of concepts, of abstractions, of pure mathematics. It is a realm where reactions of physical pleasure or pain cannot take place, as neither can cross its frontiers without leaving behind every active principle. It is a realm beyond physical sensation, yet it remains a realm that cannot help serving as model for, and inspiration to, the actual. It is the realm of ideated sensations, about which more will be said later.

Another separation I would insist upon is that between form and content—or, in terms I have always used, between "decoration" and "illustration." By "illustration" I do not mean the reproduction of shapes, whether of objects without or of images within the mind. By "illustration" I mean an independent and not a merely reproducing art; I mean an art that represents whatever it has to represent with shapes hammered out, and perfected during the search for tactile values and movement in advantageous arrangement.

Without the necessary fiction of a sharp division between decoration and illustration, discussion about the ethical and cultural effects of the work of art remains so confused and confusing as to be unprofitable.

Form and content, or in my terms decoration and illustration, are one; but to understand the work of art, and through understanding to return to it with ever greater enjoyment, we must split up the atom of the experience, in our case the visual experience. All thinking, and analytic thinking in particular is, as compared with experience, a fictitious process directed by our imperative urge to understand, and through understanding to enhance experience. Thinking is never more than trying to inscribe within a circle the polygon that comes nearest to coinciding with it.

When dealing with art history, the divorce between decoration and illustration is even more imperative. Art history is too much given to using illustration in the most ordinary sense of the word, namely, as the reproduction of any and every shape, no matter how little transmuted by form. Wherefore history has dealt almost exclusively with what visual art reproduced rather than with what it was by itself. Thus historians will speak of the presence in late Hellenistic compositions of a given kind of dress as proof of Sassanian influence, although the form, even if degenerate, remains untouched; or point to Mongolian pigtails and bits of Chinese textiles in Trecento pictures as proofs of Chinese inspiration, although the Tuscan forms are in no way affected. Or they will assert that Romanesque and Gothic architecture owed a debt to the Arabs, whereas the borrowings were confined to merely ornamental elements; for genuinely Arabic mosques never got beyond the crypts of our mediaeval churches, the rest being colour and picturesqueness. I am surprised that these same historians have thus far failed to comment on the numberless Turkey carpets in Italian, Netherlandish, and Hispanic paintings of the last decades of the fifteenth and the earlier decades of the sixteenth century and have not yet ascribed to the Ottomans a proportionate influence on Western European painting.

As a matter of fact, there is no record or other trace in the Christian world of the presence of a Muslim or Mongol

artist, whereas Giovanni da Pian del Carpino found at Kara-
korum a Russian artificer who fashioned for the Great Khan
of Tartary a throne of ivory and gold. We may be sure it
was in the Byzantine style of the time, the middle of the
thirteenth century. William of Rubruk a few years later discovered in the same city a Parisian goldsmith, named
Buchier, who worked for the same Khan as well as for the
Nestorian Christians, whom he supplied with sacred vessels
in the "French" (that is to say the Gothic) style.

I began this essay with the idea of a brief introduction,
little more than a preface, to a book on "Decline and Recovery in the Figure Arts." I wanted to avoid writing in
axioms and aphorisms as I used to. I wrote that way in
reaction against the purple splendours glistening with the
sublime irrelevances of Ruskin, or against the dreary long-
drawn dullness of Cavalcaselle. But axioms are tabloids, in
the original sense of the word, and just as the digestive appa-
ratus cannot thrive on these concentrated extracts alone, the
mind cannot be fed with axioms only. The mind as well as
the intestine requires bulk.

I fear I am not good at supplying it. I am not a dialecti-
cian; I have no gift for developing an argument with abundance of words and instances. So what I have done is to put
down whatever happened to come into my head as I medi-
tated on art theory and art history. The pages which follow
are the result. They are anything but systematic and scientific. They are a pell-mell of stray thoughts, desultory thinking aloud, generalizations, reminiscences, confessions, but
they may have one thing to recommend them. They exhibit
the cross section, as it were, of a mind that for half a century
and more has been dwelling upon art problems of many
kinds, not only historical but aesthetical; endeavouring to
the utmost of its limitations to discover along which of vari-

ous uncertain paths one may hit upon a road leading to the goal.

Whether what has been admitted in this essay is worth while it is hard for me to judge. I have put down what I have said over and over again in talk with all and sundry. What may sound trite to myself may not be so to a larger public than is reached by table-talk. And besides, *qui dit lieu commun dit vérité encore.* Commonplaces—philosophical ones particularly, serving as bases for standards of values—must be continually restated in the light of the present hour, and its vocabulary. When the hour is past they are forgotten until they reappear as paradoxes that have to be preached, and fought for, until they become commonplaces once more. These of mine have oozed from experience; and as I have read little on art theory and aesthetics, and that little when I was either too young to understand or too old to be influenced, the probability that every word, every phrase here written has been said numberless times before would but confirm my belief that certain minds enjoying like preparation, in contact with like materials, will come to like conclusions. I have just spoken of being too old to be influenced by others. Yet I must not ignore the anonymous debt one owes to what one has not read, which nevertheless one breathes in with the air that envelops the subject over which one is pondering.

The trouble with some art writings, and most so-called aesthetics and treatises on art in the abstract, is that they seldom if ever betray that the author has "lived" the work of art. They are the outcome of reading and cogitation. They remind one of those voluminous and tangled bills of fare presented in Paris restaurants for greenhorns to puzzle over until in despair they cry out, "Give me something to eat, any darned thing." The authors of the numerous discourses now appearing on theories of beauty seem to forget the purpose of their deep delving. Their interest is not in the individual work of art, but in the metaphysical system of which aesthetics is but a coda to which it is attached, I sometimes think, as a tin can to a cat's tail.

Although neither philosopher nor theologian, I am by no means sure that I have not fallen into the same ditch, and that some of my more abstract statements are not merely the rattle of the dangling tin can. It is so hard to say anything that amounts to more than verbalism or even verbiage, the moment one leaves the concrete and abandons the attempt to analyze and to interpret. It is not only to ordinary life and to politics that Talleyrand's famous observation applies: *Si nous nous expliquons nous cesserons de nous entendre*— If we go on explaining we shall cease to understand one another. It is so easy to launch into the void of philosophizing about art as a dialectical postulate that even my sixty years of living in the closest intimacy with architecture, painting, and sculpture may not have made me immune.

Every real work of art is already a simplification and interpretation. To simplify it yet further, and to interpret it more penetratingly or subtly, may reduce it to a concept. It is that concept which the critic imposes on his readers, whereas he ought to help them to "live" the work of art.

The more controversial part of this essay is directed against a movement to subvert humanistic values which was headed by Professor Strzygowski. This Attila of art history seems to have had in the last thirty years of his life the same bitter hatred of all that Mediterranean civilization implies which inspired the Hunnish barbarian whom his Christian contemporaries called "the scourge of God." He ended by persuading his followers that nothing good could come from the Aegean and from the South. Only in the North was there art, and that art was Aryan and Germanic, owing nothing to races tainted with Negroid blood as were Greeks and Semites. So with Professor Strzygowski racialism began to preach its anti-humanistic gospel, long before the word "Nazism" was as much as imagined, and while its chiefs were still children.

It is distressing to recognize that this prophet of aniconic art, with his pathological horror of the nude or indeed of the draped human figure, has had more influence in France, England, and America than in Germany itself. There, studies connected with the classical centuries and the few following them are as yet almost unaffected by racialism and Septentrionalism, with their constellations of absurdities in every field. Italy too has remained untouched by this infection.

In German lands Strzygowski's devastating doctrines made less headway than might have been expected in view of their attractiveness to the contemporary German soul, and of the propaganda made in their favour by the institute founded for that purpose and carried on by the Professor himself and his devoted Viennese followers. The teaching of another Viennese professor with another Slav name has had much more vogue and, although far less alarming, calls for a word of warning.

Max Dvořák advocated the study of art as *Geistesgeschichte* —history of the mind, of the soul, of the spirit (it takes all these epithets to give the equivalent of the German word *Geist* or the Italian word *spirito*). He was not satisfied with teaching that the arts of visual representation could be legitimately and profitably employed to illustrate and complete the kind of history he had in mind. They were by themselves an adequate source for the composing of such a history.

But not only are they not adequate when taken each separately: I doubt whether all the arts put together, including *Dichtung*—poetry, whether in verse or not—can offer a satisfactory history of a period; for its political aspects and all scientific and philosophical thought must be included. How relatively remote are Babylon and Memphis compared with Athens and Jerusalem! Athens furnished an ample *Geistesgeschichte* in the written word, parallel with its visual arts, and at least on their level. As for Jerusalem, with the *Geist* of what other community are we so well acquainted through the word alone?—for it produced no visual art that we can trace. On the other hand, no one would guess that the height of the Baroque and the triumphs of Rococo ran parallel with the ages of geometry and rationalism, exemplified by Galileo, Descartes, and Voltaire.

The arts are subject to accidents in the sense of disasters as well as accidents in the sense of unexpected events. The visual arts in particular are subject to difficulties at times unsurmountable, presented by inadequate or defective technique, by poor or obdurate materials; or else the failure of a genius to appear to open a new vein, or a poor man-crop, unfit to be trained as successors to the aging artists, may land us where we are today. Thus, the visual artists of our last years have produced merely distorted comments and fantastic interpretations of their predecessors, or have drifted rudderless while pretending to originality. The most advanced take to purely geometrical diagrams which a hypnotized public admires as "abstract art."

Yet during the same recent years, literature, science, and thought have suffered little despite alarming symptoms of infantilism. If future writers on the *Geistesgeschichte* of the decades between 1920 and 1940 were to base themselves on the fine arts of those twenty years, their account would be not only inadequate but absurd. What creations of the fine arts in America during those years can hold their own with the novels and stories of Hemingway, of Faulkner or Thomas Wolfe, or with such creations as Steinbeck's *Tortilla Flat* and *Grapes of Wrath*? So it was no doubt again and again in the past. What a gulf, to take but one instance, between the philosophy and theology of our fourth and fifth centuries A.D. and the visual arts of those generations! Not even in the mosaics recently discovered in the courtyard of St. John's at Damascus does one find the equivalent of what is conveyed by the following passage from St. John Chrysostom written about 400 A.D.: "When you look at gleaming buildings, and the aspect of colonnades allures your eye, then turn at once to the vault of heaven and to the spacious meadows where herds graze at the water's edge. Who does not despise all the creations of art, when at dawn in the stillness of his heart he admires the rising sun as it sheds its golden light over the earth; or when resting by a spring in the deep grass or under the dark shade of thick-leaved trees he feasts his eye on the far distance vanishing in the haze." From the visual arts of India how little could we guess the value of its epics, its drama, its wisdom, not to speak of a philosophy next only to the Greek in originality!

To come down the centuries, look at the Elizabethan age in England with, on the one side, its glorious array of poets and playwrights, and, on the other, its pitiable products in the figure arts; or Germany between 1770 and 1830, when in music, literature, and philosophy it revealed its soul—and what a soul!—as never before or since, and compare it with the humble achievements of its sculpture and painting during the same decades. Then take Russia from Gogol to Gorki. What achievement remotely comparable can the graphic arts of that mysterious people show in the same period of years? Finally let me cite the case of Japan at the end of our tenth century. Lady Murasaki in her *Tale of Genji* has left a picture of life (lived, to be sure, "above the clouds," as she herself says) of a subtlety, of a refinement, and at the same time of a genuineness of delicate human feeling, never surpassed in the world's literature. Nothing in the graphic arts of Japan contemporary with Lady Murasaki or later (including many attempts to illustrate her masterpiece) so much as suggest a visual equivalent.

A heresy, antedating both the others, was started by another Viennese professor, Franz Wickhoff. Disregarding what eighteen hundred centuries of wind and weather, sun, rain, and frost have done to the noble reliefs in the Arch of Titus—the last great achievement of ancient art—and seeing them in their present condition with outlines half effaced, modelling blurred, and a general effect of vagueness, Wickhoff jumped to the conclusion that they were done by "impressionists," who deliberately intended them to look the way they do now. His thesis had a great success, perhaps because of the word "impressionistic," which was then in the air, and was taken by his followers to signify not at all what it meant to the Parisian painters of more than sixty years ago, but anything sketchy, dashed off, free and easy, and indifferent to correct drawing and modelling. This notion led somehow to the contention that there was no such thing as decline in art, but only changes of taste, one phase following another with deliberate preference for the latest flowering mode of presentation and notation.

This view, based on a candid ignorance of the specific, the decorative elements in the work of art, still holds sway among most writers on the centuries we are about to study—centuries, by the way, that were never before considered worthy of the archaeologist's attention, but have now become fashionable.

Some readers may accuse me of ignoring the individuality of regional schools and of seeing Greek shapes and the influence of Greek form in all the artifacts of more recent antiquity from every part of the ancient world.

I confess to being by temperament disposed to discern the One so clearly in the Many that from the point of view taken in this essay the differences do not strike me as important. In actual experience the differences are not without interest. Yet in art as form and not as content (in my own

1. Late Hellenistic Mosaic. Great Mosque, Damascus.

2. Byzantine Dish. Salle d'Apollon, Louvre, Paris.

terms as "decoration" and not "illustration") the shapes
imposed by Hellenistic form in every part of the world
known to late antiquity are so obviously dominant, so taken
for granted, that people felt called upon to make claims for
their own province of a certain independence and originality.
These claims at first were modest and justified, until the rise
of nationalism led them to become exaggerated beyond fact
and reason. They are in essence a return to the archaic community from which the Greeks, the Jews, and the Romans
converging into Christianity tried to save our world. They
failed because it was being constantly besieged from every
side, and finally was invaded by un-advanced, lawless tribes
of barbarians. Defence absorbed more and more of the available energies and stored-up wealth of the community, until
at last the vast Roman state collapsed and broke up. The
remnants drifted back to totalitarianism, hoping to survive
by the concentration of all energies on one purpose. For
similar reasons the Church also became totalitarian, and with
more pronounced pretensions than our world has known before or since, till those made by the state in our own day.
The Church, as an institution, was from the first tainted by
the all-embracing claims of the Synagogue; and the more it
succeeded the more it underwent the fate of all institutions
when not saved from themselves by constant and remorseless
criticism. Institutions, no matter how well intentioned and
laudably initiated, no matter how admirable the ideas and
principles they wish to promote, can be put in practice
through individuals alone. These individuals will end by reducing the principles and ideals to their own comprehension,
their own convenience and profit.

It took centuries upon centuries for our small Western
world to attain a relative emancipation from a totalitarian
church, and from its successor, the almost totalitarian
Baroque monarchy. In the English-speaking world alone this

emancipation was valued and appreciated by a majority of the intelligent population. On the Continent it was little understood and perhaps never felt. After the last war the cry was raised for a return to authoritarian regimes. The economic crisis coming on top of offended and embittered nationalism led to the sacrifice of "hard-won liberties" and to the enthusiastic return to totalitarianism.

The present war may end by scotching it, showing up the weakness of these Central, Southern, and East European totalitarianisms, based as they are on absurd as well as inhuman "ideologies." But a totalitarianism is conceivable that would avoid the absurdity yet retain the inhumanity, a world-state run by biologists and economists like Platonic guardians, by whom no activity, no life, would be tolerated that did not contribute to a strictly biological and economic purpose. Vivisection on human beings would be practised, and those judged unhealthy or useless would be eliminated, including all whose age did not offer an adequate profit to the community.

It is such a world that I dread. Living as I have done physically if not spiritually on the Continent most of my life, I have become aware, as home-staying Anglo-Saxons find no occasion to be, of the fragility of both liberty and culture. We Americans were too apt to dwell on the seamy side of both, taking their invulnerability and their permanence for granted. We forget that even at home neither liberty nor culture is so secure that it can dispense with being fought for.

In such a world ruled by Oxford and Cambridge, Harvard and Yale, graduates of the highest standing, proud of their pitiless dutifulness, but dizzy with the fumes of power, incapable of listening to outsiders and reducing us to serfs of the tax-collector and to laboratory subjects for the government psychoanalyst, there might be room for physiological

relief in the shape of various entertainments, but surely none
for the humanistic arts and the building up of a House of
Life like the one advocated in this essay.

Art is not actual life, it is true, but it is ideated life and
perhaps as important. What distinguishes us from the other
higher mammalia is precisely the capacity for this ideated
life. This capacity leads higher and higher, and the longed-
for goal is far away. But the goal of totalitarianism is not
distant, and if it wins through it will shape man into a completely mechanized brute, guaranteed to remain a brute till
he becomes a domestic animal.

Every individual who feels the need of a human society
must learn to understand his responsibility towards art almost as towards life. He must avoid encouraging the undesir-
able let alone the bestializing forms, not only of life but of
art as well. This he can do only if he takes the trouble to
educate himself for the ideated as he does for the actual
world. For art can offer the surest escape from the tedium of
threatening totalitarianism. This art must not be reckless,
freakish, fantastic (as permitted in ages of freedom), but
must console and ennoble and transport us from the workaday world to realms of ideated happiness.

The epithet "German-minded," which I shall often use,
applies only to the last sixty years, during which there has
been among German-speaking people of no matter what race
or creed a rapid drift towards the cult of the sub-rational,
the cryptic, the hermetic. This has served to subvert the cultural as well as political values most dear to us, substituting
a state-worship inevitably ending in authoritarianism. It has
also produced a nihilistic attitude towards the guidance of
reason, and a contemptuous hostility towards everything that
reason has done for us. When it does take account of that
achievement, it is to treat it as a geological rather than a
human phenomenon, or, if human, then to discuss it in a

way that is so twisted, involved, and subtly obscure, besides being often so irrelevant, that persons like myself are left baffled and humiliated.

I am by no means the first to raise the cry against this now too prevailing German-mindedness. Long ago it was raised by William James and later by Paul Elmer More.

It may well be that I shall be charged with seeing all art from the point of view of a student of painting. But who can escape from the preoccupations and habits of a life-long devotion to a profession? Yet let me plead an attenuating circumstance. Painting is the most comprehensive, the most inclusive of the arts of visual representation, vying with sculpture in a way that leaves to it little advantage—except indeed its resistence to exposure and its consequent pre-eminence as an adjunct to architecture and other out-of-door needs of decoration or commemoration.

Architecture, like its sister in the world of sound, music, is not representational and therefore excluded from this essay. Yet I cannot refrain from a word about it.

The artifact architecture, more clearly than any other vis-ual creation, can be divided into two distinct parts: the craft of the builder, and the art of the architect. Building of sorts has existed from neolithic times at least, but it was as utilitarian as the styles of our recent years would wish to be. As an art, distinct from a craft, it may have dawned in the minds of early Egyptian and Babylonian builders, and their belated congeners in Central America. Solid mass in geomet-rical shapes is impressive; but these early piles must have been oppressive as well. One wonders what an Egyptian edifice such as Karnak was like in perfect state with roof on, and walls closed in. Temples in nearly untouched state, like Denderah and Edfu, give but small artistic delight, as com-pared with the remains of Komombo. That kind of building has to be reduced to the picturesqueness of a ruin to be felt

as art, as Riegl's *Alt-Schön*, and so should surely rank with
landscape rather than architecture.

> O time! the beautifier of the dead,
> Adorner of the ruin . . .[1]

Architecture as conscious art may have been a Greek invention. As form, as art, architecture is the twin sister of
lyric poetry; and, with the other un-utilitarian arts, it declined along with sculpture and painting. On the other hand,
the geometrical craft of engineering survived, although not
to the extent generally accepted. It is doubtful whether for
five centuries after St. Irene, St. Sophia, and S.S. Sergius and
Bacchus, all in Constantinople, and S. Vitale in Ravenna,
monumental structures went up in Christendom that even
as engineering manifested anything but decline. With the
exception of Charlemagne's imitation of S. Vitale, and its
modest sister St. Germigny-des-Prés, surviving structures of
those centuries seem to have been inspired by what remained
of Roman castles, towers, city walls, gates, and other utilitarian affairs. The builders grew so timid that they piled up
masonry of a ponderousness out of relation to what it was
expected to support. The result impresses us by its mass only,
seldom if ever as engineering, and never as the art of architecture.

As engineering, as structure, buildings begin to be interesting when they tackle and master the problem of vaulting. As
art they become enjoyable only when on the outside the
mass has composition and proportions, and the interior space
has relations that are both exalting and harmonious. Thus the
parallel between the fate of architecture and that of the other
visual arts in the pre-Romanesque centuries is not so remote
as is generally accepted by generations brought up, like mine,
to ignore in a building—especially in a mediaeval one—almost
everything that is not structural.

[1] Byron, *Childe Harold*, IV, 130.

Yet in architecture the decline never went so far as in the figure arts. The builders retained the necessary rudiments of their craft, while the sculptors lost them. As for the painters, they were reduced to daubing on walls or panels spectral puerilities of screaming colour and distorted shapes, which all over the Latin world stain churches that were too neglected, or too poverty-stricken, to be redecorated when art recovered.

If in places I may seem to contradict what I say elsewhere that is no wonder, for nothing we can say, except perhaps in the quantitative sciences, can be more than a half-truth. The other half will out occasionally, at least in one like myself, a casual thinker for whom systems and dogmas are like uprooted trees, lopped of their branches, denuded of their foliage, prepared and fit only to be hacked to pieces by the next system-builder.

I could wish indeed that I contradicted myself more often. It would prove that my way of thinking about art was not like a long dark tunnel, stretching from one point of light to another, but a road in the open with all sorts of attractive diversions that I could not help seeing, if only out of a corner of the eye—seeing, and at the same time regretting that the purpose in hand did not permit me to give them the attention they solicit.

Every attempt at a system is made at the expense of facts, fancies, suggestions, and ideas that clamour for notice like the denizens of Dante's Inferno. I can never get their cries out of my ears. Systematizing is instinctive and useful provided we do not take the product seriously and erect it into dogma that excludes experience, feeling, and thought. To every such construction one should say with Alice in Wonderland: "Off you go, you are nothing but a pack of cards."

"The day for art is over," thought Hegel; and unhappily he may be right—right, at all events, till another day dawns, following on the cataclysm and ensuing night in which we already may be plunging. The more reason why we should cherish, preserve, and try to understand what human genius has created down to our own so unhappy day.

It will be well to say something now about "Nature"— a term that will occur again and again in the course of this essay. Although I shall try in particular instances to state what I mean by this word, I will here attempt to define it at somewhat greater length.

The world outside ourselves, the non-ego, that stretches before and around us, is a script we have to learn to read, a script, moreover, not like the Chinese with its paltry forty thousand ideograms, but with an infinite number of them.

"Nature" is the material world that we accept as a matter of course, accept as existing outside ourselves, outside our egos at least; for nature may include our own bodies, and their functions; mental as well as physical. Thus the whole of us—body, soul, and mind—is and is not "nature"; and we compromise when we call it "human nature."

The average man, the naïve person accepts without question the reality as well as the actuality of this "nature." Few suspect that, although subjectively real, it is almost as much of an artifact as our towns, our gardens, our fields, our forests even. We know that towns are entirely man-made, gardens less so, fields less so still, and forests least of all. Our forests, however, are far from being as virgin as are Amazon jungles. Even the waters on our planet are subject to man's interference. As yet he has little hold on the open seas, although we Europeans try hard enough to prevent them from having their way with our shores, at which they are gnawing ceaselessly. Our lakes and streams we control with some success despite rebellions on their part. We have drained the land, so that, like Jehovah in Genesis, we have separated what is wet from what is dry, instead of abandoning it as a place of marsh and wild tangles where there is neither footing nor boating. Streams were silting up their mouths, extending the land into the sea so as to form the greater part of Mesopotamia and the whole of Lower Egypt. Only by perpetual watchfulness and continuous dredging do we keep our rivers to their beds, and give them a happy issue to the ocean.

If man, in the course of the ages, has been able to do so much to the world actually outside himself, it is no wonder that in the same lapse of time he has been able to gather and group, shape and fix into relatively stable, seemingly "objective" panoramas the infinity of visual images that it was so much easier for his mind to arrange in patterns. These patterns, accepted for thousands of years with little or no questioning (and that little during the last two millenniums only), constitute what counts for us as "nature" and likewise as "human nature."

This process must have been greatly assisted, as well as accelerated, by artifacts that attempted to represent objects. When these representations turned into painting, sculpture, and architecture, it was the artists who gave us our idea of "nature," as poets and musicians of "human nature."

They do so still, leaving painters to deal with the first and writers of fiction and musicians with the second. These artists are constantly widening and deepening our notion of both outside "nature" and "human nature." They present in their works shapes and colours, lights and distances that have not been seen before in visual art besides aspects and subtleties, depths and heights that have never before been clearly felt by even a cultivated public.

The critic for his part should reveal and interpret the work of art for others, as the work of art reveals and interprets "nature."

When, in self-conscious times like our own, the public ends by seeing and feeling what artists have taught it to see, the witty remark that nature imitates art is justified; and to this day it remains a lively sally connected with the names of Whistler and Wilde although it should be credited to Sainte-Beuve and Goethe, and their Greek forerunners.

Rightly interpreted, the phrase is nothing if not exact. It means simply that the public now sees and feels, in what it had previously regarded as nature, things that hitherto it had seen and felt only in recent works of art, paintings, narratives, music. As the public is inclined to believe the work of art to be a product of mere imitation or mere fancy, it is overcome with astonishment to discover correspondence between recent masterpieces and what these masterpieces have taught this public to see and feel for itself. After not too long an interval this accretion to the public knowledge is so integrated with the previous notions regarding "nature" as to form an indissoluble whole, and the public remains little more aware that it is by similar connections that our ideas of both "nature" and "human nature" have been framed. This process goes on and will go on while mankind flourishes on this planet.

The reader may become aware that the words "beauty" and "beautiful" rarely occur in this book. I have not avoided them deliberately, but art history is the history of art as an experience and is indifferent to questions of beauty. I tend to use either of them in connection with "natural" objects rather than with the representations of them. "Beautiful" is too comprehensive a word for our purpose. It is used to express satisfaction with any activity. Thus I recall phrases like a "beautiful surgical operation," a "beautiful solution" of a problem, a "beautiful trick," used with the same zest as a "beautiful woman," a "beautiful landscape," a "beautiful picture." For which reason among others I seldom allow myself to use the words "beauty" and "beautiful" when trying to appreciate as well as appraise a work of art.

I am one of those lovers of sounds and sights of whom

Plato in the Republic (476,B) speaks with pity, who "delight in beautiful tones and colours and shapes and in everything that art fashions out of these, but their thought is incapable of apprehending and taking delight in the nature of the beautiful in itself." He would call me a *philodoxos* and not a philosopher (*ibid.* 480,E) and I should not be angry, "for to be angry with truth is not lawful."

Settignano, November 1, 1941. Revised 1947.

CHAPTER I

VALUE

What is aught, but as 'tis valued?
SHAKESPEARE: *Troilus and Cressida*
Act II, Scene II, 50

A GREAT HISTORIAN, Leopold von Ranke, thought that the business of history was to find out what happened at a given time and place. Agreed! Yet for whom, and why, and to whose advantage? All sorts of things happen, an infinity of things, everywhere and all the time. Few attract attention, and fewer still are recorded. Our mind's eye is blinkered to everything except those rare events of the past that still smoulder with passions not wholly spent, or those that feed curiosity touching matters that the tendencies of the moment happen to stimulate. Let us take as an example the Crusades. We know what Villehardouin and Robert de Clary say about the conquest of Constantinople by the Latin Christians. Byzantine and Muslim chronicles supply a different picture. We expect a dramatically contrasted appreciation of the results, but are not prepared to find that the links of the chain leading up to the catastrophe, the events themselves, are neither the same, nor, when the same, are they given in the same order, and with the same emphasis.

Or take the various French epics about Antioch, Jerusalem, Reynaud de Châtillon and Saladin, St. Louis and his paladins. We read Arab accounts of the presumably identical happenings and personages. We admire and love St. Louis, but heretics and Jews had good reason for a less enthusiastic

41

appraisal of a charity from which they were cruelly excluded. What about such hallowed figures as St. Ambrose, St. John Chrysostom—very wolves to Jews! Not that the Jews were any better. And then the Emperor Titus to the rest of the world the delight of the human race; to the Jews the uniquely wicked. It is like diagrams that you can read off as concave or convex.

I cannot resist referring to the war that is going on between the East and the West—I say the East, because whether for good or for evil the East begins with the Rhine. I read dailies from Berlin, Paris, and London as well as from Switzerland and Italy. Not only are the evaluations of the events all but diametrically opposed; the accounts themselves are so coloured by passion that but for identity of place-names and dates, one might fail to recognize that they dealt with the same happenings.

In the course of war, emotions are deepened and passions heightened. They are always there, however, smouldering under the threshold of consciousness. They shape the story that at the moment they want to force others to believe. In the full sense of the words, then, Napoleon's definition of history as a fable agreed upon is correct—agreed upon by the winning side.

If we were able to attain accurate knowledge of what happened in the past, we could not cope with it. Time would not suffice, patience would not hold out. Long before either of them failed, curiosity would be satiated to the point of distaste. The most jejune chronicle has to be a selection, and is not so candid as may seem to the lovers of the quaint. It is a selection motivated by a definite interest with its smoke screen of ideals, even when made without malice. For in all probability the compiler, half aware perhaps that he was lying or inventing, remained imperturbably unaware of what was shaping his composition.

Were the historians of the nineteenth century so very dif-

ferent from those of the barbarous or Dark Ages? The best
of them undoubtedly avoided what they themselves recognized as untruths and fancies. They were nevertheless almost
as naïve in accepting with scarcely a question their Platonic
idea, their hastily conceived or preconceived notion of the
period or person they were portraying. More often than not
the documents they so painstakingly recovered and so eagerly
displayed could be used for a different distribution of light
and shade from the one in their picture. It has been done
since, but in that age of faith which the last century so
pre-eminently was, it would have been difficult, perhaps impossible. And what of all the documents that they more or
less deliberately put aside because they did not fit into the
desired pattern! And whence the pattern?

Until a few decades ago nobody questioned that events of
every nature had qualities attached to them as definite as to
things to eat or drink or smell. It was admitted that what
was one man's meat might be another man's poison, that
one man will prefer pork fat and another metaphysical poetry, that Pius V and his court will rejoice over the massacre
of St. Bartholomew and Milton cry for vengeance "on the
late massacre in Piedmont," that some would prefer the art
of the fifth century before Christ, and others be so exclusive as
to find perfection in one and only one particular Byzantine
coin; that there might be transvaluers who put Greco above
Velasquez and Luca Giordano above Titian, the Carracci
above Michelangelo, and Magnasco above Tintoretto; and so
on and so on in hundreds, and thousands, and tens of thousands of instances from every realm of being. But it is something new in the world that value, choice, preference, no
matter how freakish and how perverse, should be excluded
altogether. Not only is value to be tabooed in questions of
art but in questions of history and even of life itself. Thus I
have heard of an Italian nobleman in the best society, who

could not understand why there should be such an outcry over the treatment of Jews in Naziland and none over the forcible feeding of geese in Strassburg. And I once knew a lady who doubted our right to destroy noxious animals, including microbes, and regarded our clamours for help in the war against them as impertinent, and our claim for sympathy as impudent.

Behind this attitude there is, no doubt, the uncomfortable feeling that every entity has a right to exist on its own account, regardless of its effect upon other entities, and furthermore that there is good in things most evil, and beauty in shapes most ugly.

No doubt in a universe of everlasting ecstasy each entity would realize itself completely, without interfering with any other entity. Its intrinsic qualities would be allowed full play and never at the expense of others. No meanest being would be called upon to wither that others might flourish, to die that others might live.

But strict economy must be practised by us if we are to find shelter yet a while in the exquisitely contrived House of Life that we have been constructing in the course of millenniums.

No hawks from without, no vermin from within. "Hawks" are the hostile forces from the outside, "vermin" the destructive, disintegrating, cancerous energies within; from the microbes that still frustrate our most patient attempts to sterilize them, to the undesirables of our own species.

Nor are we unmindful of the fragility of our abode and the precariousness of our tenure. There probably has never been a moment when mankind was more ready to secure its position by casting out those of its own species who seemed parasitical or dangerous. In Germany it was the Jew, in Russia whoever is not a proletarian, in Spain the Reds, in Mexico the priest, in the United States the declared Communist, and in all countries militant rebels against the policy of the oligarchy in control.

Crushed under the weight of decrees piled high by police-minded bipeds, with their gross utilitarianism, and their zoological hopes and fears for a society in which they are to hold the highest places, some few succeed in wriggling out and, in unconscious reaction to values too brutalizingly narrow, take refuge in a realm of "unchartered freedom" where there are no values at all, no standards, no criticisms, no judgements. As if there could exist anything human, as distinct from the zoological, that was not a question of value.

In our domain, in the field of visual representation, those philologers known as "classical archaeologists" attempted to avoid this Polish anarchy, this *liberum veto*, by estimating a work of art according to the quantity of light it shed upon a text, a problem in ancient history, or on how much it served as an illustration to myth, fable, and history. A Winckelmann came to judgement in the middle of the eighteenth century. From materials already collected and even then being excavated not only in and near Rome but in recently rediscovered Herculaneum and Pompeii, Winckelmann tried to pick out certain shapes, profiles, and proportions, and to standardize them as canons of plastic beauty. We are all acquainted with his ideal embodied in the "Apollo Belvedere," the Ludovisi "Juno," Goethe's favourite, the "Laocoön," etc.

In Winckelmann these standards had much that was artistic. But for most archaeologists these shapes and patterns derived their authority rather from ancient writers, Pliny and Pausanias chiefly. The direct appeal of the object as an experience in art and taste was ignored. For example, an Apollo at Munich used to be admired because it was supposed to be a statue mentioned by Horace. When this identification was disproved philologers and archaeologists lost no time in deserting their former idol.

Happily, few writers to-day are such archaeologists, but their authority and dictatorship used to influence us all. Just as the most free and easy politician or journalist may talk Plato or Hegel without having read a word of either, so the most frivolous, irresponsible art critic may talk Winckelmann or Mengs, and remain as unaware of what he is doing as Monsieur Jourdain was that he was speaking prose.

With the triumph of the Romantic movement a certain tendency appeared among the most advanced French painters to emancipate themselves from the Winckelmannian and archaeological canons of art, but it made no great headway, even in France. Feebler still was the Pre-Raphaelite and Ruskinian movement. After 1870 "Philologia," goddess of the victorious Germans, inspired and domineered over archaeology wherever classical studies were pursued.

How the revolt against this tyranny started and how quickly it carried every position so long held by archaeologists, would make as interesting reading as the story of the recent disappearance of Orthodoxy from Holy Russia. Somewhere between 1900 and 1910 the classical archaeologist himself lost faith in his standards and systems. He discovered that he was being overwhelmed by wave upon wave of art objects which could not be appraised by reference to Winckelmannian shapes and proportions. These objects were brought from the Far East and the isles of the sea, from the hearts of inner and of nearer Asia, from darkest Africa and Central America, from regions, in short, hitherto without a place in art studies, also from periods absent in art books, the Aurignacian, the Capsian, the neolithic, the early dynasties of Egypt, the Byzantine, the Latin Middle Ages, not to speak of such revelations in the Greek world itself as the Minoan, the Mycenean. Finally in the holy of holies of more recent classical archaeology formerly restricted to the later fifth century, there came the rediscovery and revaluation of

3. Jacopo Tintoretto: Rediscovered bit of decorative border.
School of S. Rocco, Venice.

4. Lorenzo Ghiberti: Detail from gilded Bronze Doors.
Baptistery, Florence.

archaic marbles from Delphi, from the Acropolis, and from
the Attic plain.

The archaeologist dared not deny, as in my youth he still
used to, that these were works of art, but he could not find a
way to subsume them under a common denominator. The
only one he had was that of Winckelmann, and that did not
work. As we have seen, his whole training had been in philol-
ogy and not in art appreciation. There was nothing left for
him to do but to give up appraisal and join the merry rout
for whom there were no standards, who ignored or refused
to recognize the existence of means for judging the work of
art. All was reduced to the same level. Everything was
equally interesting intrinsically, or as a link in a chain of
events. There were to be no more invidious distinctions. A
bronze mass product—say, buckles from Minnusinsk—was
put on a level both historically and aesthetically with the
Theseus of the Parthenon, and scrawls at Dura-Europos with
the frescoes at the Villa dei Misteri or the Casa di Menandro
at Pompeii. And as the archaeologist, although he deserted
his own ship, still enjoys, or until the other day did enjoy,
the authority of a pilot, his negation of value chimed in only
too well with the absence of standards among the financially
and sartorially higher but intellectually lower society, for
whom the work of art is never more than mere news, and
trivial news at that. Thus I have seen and heard solemn pro-
fessors join fashionable museum directors and those incarna-
tions of conspicuous waste, smart society women, in exalting
the humble artifacts of Fuzzy-Wuzzyland.

The folk just referred to would be far from ridiculous if
they could feel and appreciate the positive qualities of these
outlandish products. For the up-to-daters I have in mind,
these products have a merely negative merit, the one of not
being objects raved about yesterday.

When Negro sculpture first came to Paris, some five and

thirty years ago, the dealer who launched it hoped to win us over by saying that no Greek masterpiece could hold up its head against it, and that it was in the round. This cry, that Negro sculpture was in the round, you heard for a season at all the Paris dealers', and collectors', and in all Paris social gatherings, and the next season everywhere in New York, and finally after a decent interval you read in luscious language in London dailies, weeklies, and monthlies, and heard at all London luncheon parties and tea-tables: "The great thing about Negro sculpture is that it is in the round." It occurred to nobody to ask the pioneer dealers and their disciples, the London critics and dilettanti: "What of it? What if they are in the round?" And "what has their round-ness to do with their being great works of art? Are not gazometers in the round, and the enormous pipes that dis-figure lovely subalpine valleys?" "Ah, but they are cylindri-cal," and no epithet could be more decisive, more majes-tically final.

These writers and amateurs would have been hard put to it to furnish a satisfactory answer, and so would the critics who ask us to admire a piece of sculpture because it is well carved, highly polished, or on the contrary far from finished; or a painting because it is minutely drawn, or, the exact op-posite, freely dashed in, daintily or boldly painted, because it is all cylinders, all pyramids, or all diagonals. What of that? What concern is it of mine? I am neither painter nor sculptor, and to one who is not a craftsman, displays of skill in the vis-ual arts are nothing like so exciting as similar displays in the circus, the boxing match, the cock-fight, or the bull ring. As for cylinders, cubes, and diagonals, what are they that I should be impressed and bow down and worship them? Are they perchance ultimates? If they are, prove that they are, and I too will adore them.

A relative indifference to value may be tolerated in or-dinary history. Its past events have been sifted by time, and if remembered it is for the interest they still can claim. They have ceased to be distinguishable as the energies they were in their time, and if in any measure operative, still it is only as merged in the ocean stream which is propelling us forward.

But works of art in general, and visual ones in particular, are still with us. Not only are they still with us, but they count as the only primary documents for art history. In that field written documents are ancillary and have no meaning except in connection with surviving works of art.

Nothing that survives, that is still alive, can be treated impassively. Willynilly, it affects us. One has to be either insensible, unconscious, or both to assume objectivity toward works of art. We cannot help being attracted or repelled by them, feeling them as forces to befriend or to avoid as with other living creatures. Whatever has life, and as long as it retains life, has a capacity for doing good or doing harm that we cannot and do not ignore.

Objects made by the hand of man are of two classes. Those that are without life, like most products of primitive mankind, we call artifacts. On the other hand, visual objects that are alive are works of art. An artifact is anything in any material done by human hands. A pot, a pan, a shovel, a spoon, a knife is seldom nowadays more than an artifact although it always could be, and in the past has been, a work of art as well. So a grocer's bill is not literature, nor, although on a higher plane, is the best expository prose *Dichtung*. A steam whistle is an auditory artifact, a bugle call is already music.

The chief reason for indifference to value has been that students, when historians, are busy exploring the archives for documents and as classical archaeologists intent on discovering what could throw light on antiquity. There would be no harm done if we, being human, were not apt to fall in love with the products of our activities and credit them with values, intellectual, spiritual, and artistic, which seldom pass current outside our private universe. The expert palaeographer and hunter of archives gets no training in the appreciation of quality, or in understanding what in a given style is creative and pioneering and what is imitative, stagnant, or even retrograde. In other words the palaeographer will not be able to judge whether to place the work of art in question at the beginning or at the end of a style. Furthermore archaeological interest threatens to wipe out the distinction between fine arts and industrial arts, between monumental and minor arts, between art objects and objects of curiosity.

By now archives have been ransacked and archaeological fields the world over ploughed and excavated. It is improbable that, within the range of our interests, discoveries are still awaiting us as mind-opening as those made in the last two hundred years. We need no longer seize upon an unpublished piece of script and show it off in triumph as even a real historian like the late Bishop Creighton did, at the end of his illuminating volumes on the Papacy during the humanistic period; or as some colleagues of mine will write up elaborately a rubber-stamped Bernardo Daddi or Andrea del Brescianino. There is no further reason for neglecting values in order that explorations may at all costs be encouraged. We can now afford to appraise objects and artifacts according to their significance, first as to the degree that they enable us to reconstruct the past in general; then to reconstruct the history of a given art; and finally to select and interpret the history of the past which can still vitalize and humanize us.

The past that history is called upon to reconstruct is not the past of the Andaman Islanders, of the Lolos, or of our own Redskins, nor even of such highly civilized people as the Chinese and their cultural dependents, Annamese, Japanese, Siamese, and Koreans. The past that concerns us Mediterranean-Atlantic folk, no matter what continent we

now inhabit, the past that is history for us is the succession
of events—fears, passions, illusions, and hopes—that have
made us what we think we now are. In a sense there are as
many histories to be written as there are individuals; and
every tribe, every association, every church, will have its own
private history. In other words history is the biography of a
community, large or small, as wide-flung as the white race,
as limited as the parish pump. It follows that past events
concern us in the measure that they contribute to our sense
of the past, as at the present moment we want to define it.

In ordinary human history, including the biographies of
artists, values whether political or ethical are connected with
formative events and creative personalities celebrated by Plutarch in antiquity, by the lives of worthies in the Middle
Ages, and in many books nearer our own day. In art history,
on the other hand, value is derived from qualities which
presently will be discussed at some length. In one overwhelmingly important respect it differs from other types of
history: its events—that is to say, its masterpieces—are to
some extent still with us and not merely known to us by
hearsay as is the case with kings, conquerors, statesmen,
preachers, founders in general, fiddlers, singers, play-actors,
in short spellbinders of every kind. Works of art speak to us,
appeal to us, act on us as living entities.

All the arts enjoy this advantage, but none so much as the
visual arts. How much easier it is to learn the language of
the Aeginetan marbles, the Acropolis Korae, or the Olympian
pediments, not to speak of more modern-seeming sculptures
like those of Paeonius, Lysippus, Praxiteles, and later Hellenistic sculptors, than it is to enjoy, in the original Greek, the
odes of Pindar, the tragedies of Aeschylus, Sophocles, and
Euripides, or the idylls of Theocritus. You can read them
in translation, but even the best version in another language
gives but a faint sense of their real quality, whereas a Greek
statue can be so well copied that, as in the case of the

Hermes of Praxiteles, it remains doubtful whether it is or is not that fascinating sculptor's own handiwork.

Materials

A little later than the Romantic revolt against cold-storage classicism, a movement was started to deduce standards from materials and techniques, as for example wood, stone, clay, gold, bronze, and textiles; or pigments and varnishes—in short, the raw materials and the technical devices that served in the production of the artifact or work of art.

Instead of considering the materials as we consider the rest of matter, as lifeless and inert until moved and given life by mind, the following doctrine, that still has its adherents, was preached: not that the artist must make the best possible use of materials in order to pursue his end, but that the end itself was inspired and directed by and not merely fashioned out of the materials. All the artist had to do, we were given to understand, was to let himself be guided by the nature as well as the caprices of the materials, to the exclusion of other interests. The means, that is to say the materials, not only justified the end; but by their own volition, as it were, by their own potential, created the end.

Thus in textiles, the degree of flexibility or slipperiness or brittleness of the fibres; in wood the grain, the knots, the pliableness, the splinteriness; in ivory and bone the same nearly; in metals their ductility, their malleability; in minerals and stones of all kinds, the crystallization, the density, the hardness, the resistance to fire and frost, to the hammer, to the chisel, to the saw, were qualities that decided the value of a work of art done in these materials. If art obeyed the exigencies of the same material, submitted to its resistances and caprices, the result was perfect, and if not it was a failure.

In a negative sense this is so. It is obvious that material will not yield its best to the artificer who does it violence, or ignores its caprices. He must not work against the grain of the wood or ivory or fail to take account of the knots. He will on the contrary take advantage of them and turn them to profit as Chinese and Japanese and Gothic carvers have done, as the Maoris with their canoes and their oars, and the Tlinkits with their grease dishes. If he insists on giving the same edge to porphyry or granite as he gets out of limestone or marble, he fritters away the specific qualities of concentrated density, hardness, and impenetrability that we enjoy in Egyptian statuary and late antique sculpture, with its fat contours and sagging shapes, or in the porphyry sarcophagi in the Vatican and in Constantinople.

Yet, except in unrepresentative *objets d'art*, the material has counted for so little that until the Renaissance and its discovery of an antiquity, whether in ruins of architecture or in fragments of statuary, that had been discoloured by time and weather, buildings were coated with paint, and sculpture was tinted when not fully coloured. When Praxiteles was asked which of his own marbles he preferred, he answered: "Those that Nicias coloured." As late as the fifteenth century painters as distinguished as Jean Malouel were employed to polychrome Sluter's calvary, now known as "Puits de Moïse" in the Chartreuse near Dijon. And let me quote Huizinga in the *Waning of the Middle Ages* (p. 235) on these same sculptures: "The pedestals were green, the mantles of the prophets were gilt, their tunics red and azure with golden stars. Isaiah wore a dress of gold cloth. The open spaces were filled with golden suns and initials. The pride of blazonry displayed itself not only round the columns below the figures, but on the cross itself, which was entirely gilt. . . . As a crowning *bizarrerie* a pair of spectacles of gilded brass . . . were placed on Jeremiah's nose." On the surviving figures no trace of all this coloured splendour remains.

Statues never exposed to the air nor painted by hand, like those of the twelfth century at Étampes, look raw as if wanting a skin. The same may be said of the architectural carvings lately dug up at Sarsina, inland from Cesena, which were overwhelmed by landslide some two thousand years ago before stucco and colour covered up the edginess of the raw stone.

Ivory and bone even of the finest grain were likewise painted. As for bronzes in the Greek world, they were burnished like brass, or gilded over, or so thickly varnished that their real substance was unrecognizable.[1] In all probability the Parthenon columns were polychromed with ultramarine and vermilion as in later times were Romanesque and Gothic porches. These various procedures made it impossible for the specific material to count in the effect. Moreover, in no visual representation do we perceive that design, shape, or even form is modified by difference of material more than is strictly required by their nature. A figure or group in Egyptian or Greek, Romanesque, Gothic, or Renaissance art, changes but slightly in obedience to the material in which it is produced, whether wood or ivory, bronze, marble, or baked clay, and does not change at all as it should if the materials decided the shapes and their grouping.

Or take the Greek vase of about 480 B.C. I can detect no connection between the humble clay out of which it is formed and its "Attic shape," adorned with figures of more functional line, of more subtle contour than later draughtmanship ever achieved.

In central Asia and the Far East it is the same; although the so-called "animal style" has even less regard for actual shapes than the most surrealist painters of to-day. The Koz-

---

[1] And now in 1946 while the "Gates of Paradise" and the other bronze doors of the Florentine Baptistery are being cleaned, it turns out that they were massively gilded. Ghiberti in his memoirs does not mention this, which proves that it was still common practice.

lev expedition of 1924 in Northern Mongolia unearthed objects in wood, in bone, in metals, and in wool as well. In all of them the same patterns, the same distortions prevail, regardless of the material.

Not only in the figure arts and the "fine arts," but in architecture itself, few Italian Renaissance churches or palaces depend for their quality on materials. Many a Florentine building, courtyard, cloister, and hall is stuccoed without, whitewashed within, with no more precious material showing than the grey stone of the columns and stone of finer grain for the capitals and jambs of doors and window frames. All else is a matter of space, of proportions, that is to say of tact, of taste—of trained mind, in short.

Material counts most where its nature is least liable to disguise and concealment. This could occur only in mosaic, in jewelry, in enamels, in glazed ceramics, in glass, and in small *objets d'art* of various kinds and climes. Even the tiniest fragments of Alexandrian glass afford feasts of translucent colour that nothing can surpass, not even Christian mosaics, let alone Hellenistic, Sassanian, and Persian textiles. The fascination of an *objet d'art* like the small round dish in dark hard stone, inlaid with little fishes in gold, from the treasury of St. Denis, now in the Louvre, cannot be described. It is as if in the palm of the hand you held night with its constellations. In the same Salle d'Apollon where this small dish is exhibited may be seen an equally small or even smaller thirteenth-century Limoges enamel the material beauty of which would be far more appreciated if the treatment of the subject did not absorb one's attention. Not even Giotto himself or any other artist painting the same subject, St. Francis preaching to the birds, has treated it more poetically.

And who shall say what was the effect of that paradoxically colossal *objet d'art*, the Great Pyramid! Even twenty-five hundred years after it was built, when Herodotus described its coating of highly polished monoliths each at least thirty feet long, daintily joined, with its tip of dazzling electrum, it must have shone under the Egyptian firmament like a mirror reflecting sunrises, sunsets, and rare clouds.

Abundance of a given material and the want of others may inspire artists to get the utmost effect out of its use. Thus Armenian architects surpassed their Byzantine models because they had at hand plentiful supplies of suitable stone, as did the designers of the gem-like yet noble palaces of the Grand Masters of Malta or the charmingly tasteful villas leading to the Ombla near Ragusa and those at Risan on the way to Cattaro. On the other hand, Lecce offers a sad example of the misuse of a too yielding material.

The wood carving of the Northmen, first on their ships and later on their church porches, is easily accounted for by the quality of the wood from forest trees appreciated and exploited by gifted artisans. This no doubt was the case also with the Maoris, who, however, must have valued their wood all the more since, unlike the Northmen's ships and porches, their carvings do not seem to have been completed by painting.

In picture painting there is much talk of materials, of resins and oils, of emulsions, and varnishes, and above all of tempera.

Van Eyck, Antonello, Titian, Rubens, Velasquez, Rembrandt all had an adequate technique. Masaccio was as great as any of them; but who talks of his technique? Antonello's technique was masterly, but what did he do with it before 1475? Little till that date. Then under the influence of Giovanni Bellini he became the artist who, in the three or four years of life left him, painted not only his arresting and convincing portraits but the sublime "Pietà" of the Correr Museum, and the nobly magnificent Dresden "St. Sebastian." As for Giovanni Bellini's technique, it consists of uniform little brush-strokes that solicit no attention.

I am not insensitive to the beauty of a well-preserved tempera or oil surface. In the company of two of the most passionate technicians that ever came my way, with the persuasive Roger Fry and the far more subtle, penetrating, and serious Denman Ross, I have been thrilled by the quality of a tempera like the Sassettesque panel in Berlin representing the youthful St. Francis hearing mass, or of an oil like Vermeer's "Painter and Model," of the Czernin collection in Vienna. Unfortunately few paintings preserve their original colour and surface long enough to be enjoyable in themselves or to give a correct idea of what they were like when they left the artist's hand. Not only is painted colour apt to undergo deterioration, notoriously so in the blues used by Italian masters, but the surface gets covered over with repeated varnishings that rot and darken—not to speak of deliberate repainting. By now, pictures that are centuries old seldom retain much likeness to their original state. Witness Tintoretto canvases at S. Rocco, most later Rembrandts, many Sir Joshuas, and paintings as recent as Sargent's, besides nearly all Dutch landscapes whose original vivid greens are now horn-coloured. Far from enjoying the material of a picture, the spectator gets only as it were a rouged and repainted skin concealing the corruption beneath. When attempts are made to get rid of this dirt and varnish and repaint, the amateur is outraged, and as in the recent case of a well-cleaned portrait in the Louvre, there rose an outcry of "on l'a ruiné, mon Rembrandt"; and no less indignation was expressed a little while ago over the restoration to its original character of a Velasquez in the London National Gallery. We have got as much inured to discoloured pictures as to colourless sculptures, and for the same reason, namely, that we almost never see a work in either art that still looks as it did when it was fresh. When by a miracle a painting has retained its freshness, as is the case with a Catena "Annunciation" at Carpi, it offends our present taste; and under the

Tintoretto "Crucifixion" at S. Rocco there is a piece of canvas folded back and never exposed to the light, which is much closer to a Renoir than to any sixteenth-century Venetian in its present state.

Material and technique—I often wonder what they are. Sculpture is carving a solid, we are told, and painting the application of a design to a surface. It follows from these definitions that Ghiberti's "Gates of Paradise" and Filarete's bronze doors of St. Peter's are sculpture. To my eye they are as much painting as any done by their Quattrocento contemporaries. Nor are Donatello's Santo reliefs in Padua sculptural in the sense that the Olympian metopes, the Parthenon marbles, and the Attic tomb-reliefs are sculptural. As for his last works, I cannot believe that their being in clay or bronze makes them so different from the last Rembrandts done with pigments. The Dutch "painter" has ever so much more in common with the Florentine "sculptor," of whose existence he may have never heard, than with any predecessor in his own craft, whether in the Netherlands or in Italy.

Or take the figures nielloed with silver on the bronze doors of San Michele al Gargano. They are drawn as sinuously, as functionally as an Antonio Pollaiuolo. Must we call them sculpture? And the contemporary eleventh-century enamels, the emperors and empresses, court ladies and gentlemen arrayed in their robes of splendour, fabricated with jewelled purity of colour by the craftsmen of Constantinople—what are they but pictures in miniature exactly like those in illuminated manuscripts of the same date and place, but done in materials and with a technique surpassing every possibility of gem-like refulgence that painting with pigments could produce.

Writing at the end of one of the most fruitful periods of art creation our world has known, Vasari, the Herodotus of art history, calls his book the story of the arts of design. By this he did not understand, as we do, design only in the sense of composition or pattern, but, as the Italian language permits, of drawing as well. To the Renaissance artist draughtsmanship was the basis of all the visual arts, and it was a matter of circumstance, command, or compulsion that led him to practise one art and not the other, as was notably the case with Verrocchio, Pollaiuolo, and Michelangelo.

At times I go further and ask whether the artist's materials do not consist of mind rather than matter? I mean mind in the sense of ideas and problems. The artist lives on these. The rest is a question of ways and means, whether it be as material or technique. The creator is he who like Masaccio starts a problem and speeds it towards a solution, or he who like Michelangelo finds the solution. Masaccio's technique, as I have already observed, excites no interest, nor does Michelangelo's. Although the latter confessed to having no practice in fresco, no achievements in this technique have equalled the ceiling of the Sistine chapel. Have any approached it? Perhaps not even Giotto, not even Masaccio. Michelangelo's hand is so indifferent to material and technique, that his chisel-stroke has the same calligraphy—as it were—as his pen-stroke, or whatever other medium he used in drawing. I contemplate therefore a less obvious and more significant classification of the arts than can be derived from the materials and techniques employed, a more psychological, more metaphysical, and less materialistic one. Let me in this connection add a note jotted down in March 1907, which reads as follows: "The material of each art is not its medium, but the life-enhancing ideated sensations of which it is compounded."

Earlier in this discussion it was allowed as something obvious, and indisputable, that the artist must never go against the nature of his materials or his technique, but on the contrary must take advantage of their idiosyncrasies and resistances. These present themselves as problems to be solved and thereby serve as a stimulus. As a matter of history, when the

artist becomes master of a material or a technique to the
degree that it can no longer oppose any resistance, it ceases
to inspire him. He is left without a problem and does not
know what to turn to, as has been the case again and again
in the course of history, and as it seems to be the case now.
For want of problems he yawns and gesticulates and boasts,
but does not create.

In other words, technique is an auxiliary stimulus, but
never a creator of art. Art can use a certain technique when
the problem of form requires it. Until then, art will ignore
it as the centuries preceding the Van Eycks ignored oils
although well acquainted with them. On the other hand,
when the problem is urgent, it invents the necessary technique.

Materials, technique, and colours also count more and
more as creative genius disappears, as draughtsmanship is
neglected and the figure arts decline. The men of mere craft
survive to adorn temples and habitations that depend for
their effect on the colour of semi-precious stones and mosaics. These constructions are reduced to *objets d'art* enjoyed
for the intrinsic beauty of the materials and for what the
artificer is allowed to extract from the materials with the least
mental effort. Other mere artificers fabricate jewellery consisting of childish settings of triangles and lozenges inlaid with
coral, with turquoises, with garnets, pastes, and coloured glass.
The preference for the last was destined to conquer our world
from Cádiz to Calcutta and to survive in the Near East till
our own day, in the shape particularly of windows and doors
filled with panes of screaming blue and ruby and yellow
glass.

Thus neither materials nor techniques offer standards for
the appreciation and evaluation of the figure arts, much as
they may interest students of crafts that never rise above
being minor arts, and easily decline to the products of gipsy
coppersmiths.

It is deplorable that we no longer make a sharp division between the fine arts and the minor arts. That is a distinction resting solely on the illustrative elements and on those elements chiefly which deal with the human figure. Indeed the fine arts may be best described as those whose principal concern is the human figure.

If you would understand what it is for materials and instruments to count, listen to music. There the sounds elicited by wood, or brass, or string tell in every note. In comparison, the effect produced in the visual arts by even the most favourable and undisguisable material is small indeed.

The enjoyment of materials and also the enjoyment of colour is perhaps more in the nature of actual than of ideated sensations. This may be the reason why indulgence in the virtues of materials leads to an indifference first to form and then to representation, ending with a preference for artifacts, while those finally are cherished most which sacrifice most to displaying the character of the material.

Hence no doubt the present cult of Byzantine coins and enamels as well as of barbarian jewellery, and of certain early Christian artifacts—a cult I cannot help practising myself although with a bad conscience.

Ultimates in Art Criticism

Ultimates in art criticism, if they exist, must be sought for in the life-enhancement that results from identifying oneself with the object enjoyed or putting oneself in its place. For the act of deciphering shapes in a given design, or pattern, or composition offers a satisfaction that is little more than mental, and scarcely at all life-enhancing. In order to be life-enhancing an object must appeal to the whole of one's being, to one's senses, nerves, muscles, viscera, and to one's feeling for direction, for support and weight, for balance, for stresses and counter-stresses, and for the minimum

of space required for one's indispensable bodily autonomy—
an autonomy so precious that to yield an iota of it is to be a
lover, to be compelled to surrender even an inch is to be a
de-individualized prisoner. How can you identify yourself or
put yourself in the place of a cube? It is easier no doubt to
imagine oneself a cylinder, but if that gave us joy, we should
love factory chimneys, and late Turkish minarets, like those
for instance of the Mohamet Ali Mosque on the Cairo cita-
del. I and most of my readers are too unsophisticated to
understand what bodily pleasure may be derived from the
diagonal. As for the pyramid, it has a suggestion of restful
compactness, and benefits by the ease with which memory
calls up Egypt and shapes that at Gizeh have overwhelmed
us with pride in the audacity of mere men, like ourselves,
who dared to build on the scale of the horizon, and to insert
into the pell-mell of nature rational geometrical shapes in
harmonious contrast with it.

An object to be life-enhancing must be one with which
we can not only identify ourselves, but identify ourselves
more easily, completely, and happily than we do in ordinary
conditions. In art the object must not arouse any of those
wakeful cannibal appetites that can never be satisfied, not
even by satiety. In the language of Keats, it must be

> All breathing human passion for above
> That leaves a heart high sorrowful and cloyed
> A burning forehead, and a parching tongue. . . .

It should not rouse us to action, although it cannot help
influencing conduct; it should not affect any of our pro-
ductive, reproductive, or transitive energies, but tune us like
instruments—instruments for ecstasy.

Natural objects, whether animate or inanimate, because
they stimulate activities that are greedy, predatory, or coldly
analytical, entailing excitement and exhaustion, with the resulting feeling of lowered vitality, cannot be life-enhancing.

5. Detail from Silver-inlaid Bronze Doors. Monte Sant'Angelo, Foggia.

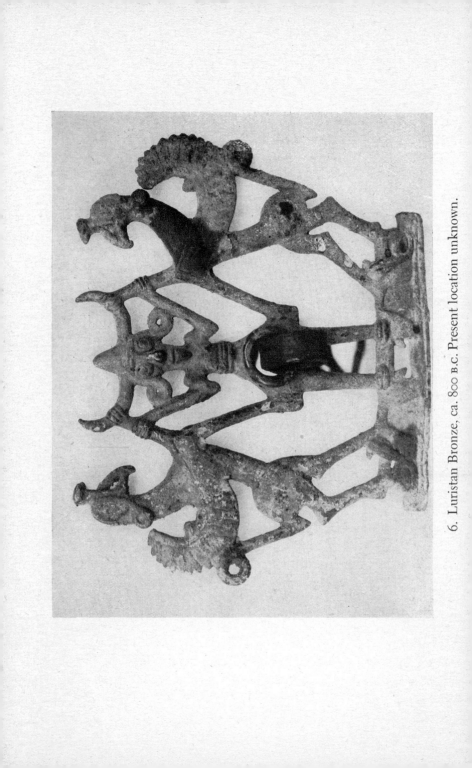

6. Luristan Bronze, ca. 800 B.C. Present location unknown.

To be life-enhancing, visible things—with which we are here concerned—must be presented in a way to make us feel that we are perceiving them more quickly, grasping them more deeply than we do ordinarily. The instantaneous result is an illusion of unwonted and unexpected ease of functioning, and its inseparable accompaniment the sense of heightened vitality, all of which we credit to the object so presented to us.

It follows that only works of art can be life-enhancing, for merely visible things by themselves are not—except where we have learnt to enjoy them as if they were already works of art, as is the case with landscape for many of us. We have been taught by assiduous if not always conscious looking at representations of landscape not only to enjoy *feeling* nature as some may instinctively, but to enjoy *seeing* it in terms of art.

Not all artifacts are life-enhancing. Some are and some are not. Why is this? What makes them so or not so?

When artifacts are not merely representations of shapes, whether in nature or in the mind, but have tactile values and movement, then only are they life-enhancing.

Tactile Values

Tactile values occur in representations of solid objects when communicated, not as mere reproductions (no matter how veracious), but in a way that stirs the imagination to feel their bulk, heft their weight, realize their potential resistance, span their distance from us, and encourage us, always imaginatively, to come into close touch with, to grasp, to embrace, or to walk around them.

Let me quote Bergson for the reason of this: "A body is essentially what it is to the touch. It has distinct shapes and dimensions that are independent of us. It occupies a given space and cannot change it without taking the time to occupy one by one the intermediate positions. The visual image that we have of it we judge to be a mere appearance whose different aspects must always be changed by reference to the tactile image. This image is the reality to which the other draws our attention." (*Les deux Sources de la Morale et de la Religion*, Paris, Alcan, 1932, p. 139.)

The struggle to keep alive in a universe where we have to defend ourselves incessantly against every kind of pressure and menace from without has made of us creatures who, with rare exceptions, perceive in a visible object those features only which may serve or disserve us, which we must avoid and which we must approach. The more successful we are, the more we lose sight of every other element in the same object. For most of us this object is reduced to a mere signal, attenuated to a cipher, or bleached to a blur. The only persons who naturally retain or laboriously acquire immunity from this disintegrating process are the scientists and the artists.

Both scientists and artists want to reverse this process by reintegrating the object. The scientist goes back to its constituent elements, to its dimensions, its mechanism, its potentialities. His reward lies not only in the satisfaction of curiosity and in justified pride of intellectual achievement, but in the possibilities that this reversal of the ordinary process furnishes him of exploiting the object for the material profit of himself and of the community at large. The artist, on the other hand, intuitively reanimates the utilitarian blur, the signal, the cipher that the object has become, to what he imagines to be the fullness of its own being. He sees the complete shape, perceives the organic necessity of every contour, of every spot and shadow, and every touch of colour. He not only sees and comprehends as does the scientist with his mind and understanding, but, unlike the scientist, he grasps the whole as a pattern, unique and irreplaceable because its particular individuality has never existed before, and never will exist again, and is therefore to be cherished as something at once sacred and intimate, remote and near, intangible yet caressing.

Moreover, the artist not only perceives the object but lives it and identifies himself with it. By communicating what he lives he surprises us with the joy of feeling lifted to a higher competence, clearer perception, completer grasp. The object that gives us this feeling is life-enhancing.

If this account of the artist as distinct from the scientist be allowed, it follows that the mere shapes of objects do not satisfy him. He himself must live them and be able to communicate them in terms that are life-enhancing; and these terms are first tactile values, and then movement.

This particular representation of shapes is furthermore what we mean by the word "form." Form must not be confused with shape. Form is never a shape—that is to say, a geometrical object looking the same to everybody. Form is a quality beyond common cognizance. And quality is that which one finds in an object when in one or more ways and on any ideated plane it is life-enhancing.

Form is that radiance from within, to which a shape attains when in a given situation it realizes itself completely. It is like a robe thrown around shapes, not a consuming one like the mantle of Nessus but a vivifying one like the robe of Isis, provided you do not lift it; for in art appearance is the only reality.

Form is the life-enhancing aspect of visible things. It is a monosyllable so universally used in writing about art, and almost as universally misused, that I beg the reader to keep in mind that in this book (and in every other book I have published) the word "form" means tactile values first and foremost, and that these two denominations occur often as synonyms. The "significant form" of which some of us speak means just that.

Against tactile values one cannot turn and ask, "What of

them?" as we have done when told to admire works of art because they were well painted or carved, or because they were full of cylinders, or cubes, or diagonals. Tactile values are life-enhancing and do not excite mere admiration, but give gratification and joy. They therefore furnish a basis upon which, as critics, we may erect our standards of judgement. Through all the ages, and in every place, whenever a visual representation is recognized as a work of art and not as a mere artifact, no matter how elaborate, smart, and startling, it has tactile values. It may have much besides, which is of more or less importance or none at all, but to be accepted as a work of art these other attractions must rest on a basis of tactile values, or be in close connection with them.

Thus in certain phases of primitive Mesopotamian art and in archaic Greek sculpture as well as in early Romanesque and all Central American stone carvings, whether in the round or in relief, and especially in the so-called "animal art," there is scarcely anything but tactile values to excuse their ugliness, their awkwardness, their lack of proportion, and their grotesqueness of expression. Or to come down to our own days, what is it but tactile values combined with movement that make us pass over and almost forget in so many of Degas' paintings the vulgarity of his washerwomen, his far from appetizing ballet girls, and his shapeless females tubbing and sponging? One could cite hundreds of other instances from recent or contemporary art, in particular Cézanne as a figure painter. We pass over their shortcomings because they vitalize us with a transmission of energy that would be overpowering but for the important fact that they belong to the realm of ideated sensations and not of actuality. On the other hand, most Italian Seicento art, for all its illustrative content, its command of every trick of the trade, its magnificence, its ornamental ingenuity, remains what indeed it had sunk to be, an ancillary art, an art that gives splendour to gorgeous temples, as well as to recondite cabinets of dilettanti.

Ideated Sensations

I must now explain what I mean by the phrase which I have just used, "realm of ideated sensations."

To begin with, ideated sensations are not the sensations psycho-physically experienced at the moment of perceiving and contemplating the representation of an object or event (whether the object is of the world without or of the mind within). Ideated sensations, in our field, are the images of sensations that the same representations offer when they are works of art and not mere artifacts.

Thus in the presence of a painting we may have all sorts of actual bodily sensations, as of good or bad air, heat or cold, nervous visceral and muscular comfort or discomfort, that have nothing to do with the painting, although they may dispose or indispose us towards enjoying it. We also receive retinal sensations of contrasted spots of light and dark with or without colour, and these, as I shall try to explain later, may be used as instruments in the orchestra of art.

Ideated sensations, on the contrary, are those that exist only in imagination, and are produced by the capacity of the object to make us realize its entity and live its life. In the visual arts this capacity is manifested primarily and fundamentally through varieties of imagined sensations of contact and their multiple implications; and through the equally imagined sensations of barometric, thermometric, visceral, and above all muscular alterations, supposed to be taking place in the objects represented. Needless to say, these chiefly concern animate, and most of all human, figures, although they also may include the entire vegetable kingdom, plants of every kind, flowers, shrubs, and trees, and inanimate shapes as well, such as streams and other liquid expanses, rocks, cliffs, and all landscape features which we animate to such a degree that we instinctively speak of rivers running, trees waving, bending, drooping, or reaching out their branches, and of mountains rising. We go so far as to use a phrase like the "lie of the land," thereby taking advantage of the utmost elasticity of the idea.

Ordinarily we have no occasion for admitting these imagined sensations, images of sensations, "ideated sensations" as I prefer to call them, within the threshold of consciousness. They are perhaps of no immediate use, and besides they are not insistent, and still less clamorous. People who are not self-conscious, not awake to what goes on under their skin, will seldom become aware of their shy presence, and even those who do study their own clockwork will encounter them only when properly introduced. That task is left to the artist: a task which he accomplishes not (as he himself is apt to think, and as the culture-snobs who listen to him think they think) by the technical proceedings of the draughtsman, the painter, the sculptor, the engraver, or whatever the particular craft may be. The artist does not use his craft, and exploit his particular technique, to reproduce an object as through a reflecting mirror. If he did he would only *duplicate* the outer aspect of the object, without getting nearer to creating a work of art. No, he imagines all the sensations felt or supposed to be felt by an object which the limitations and advantages of his craft permit him to organize and harmonize into an equivalent of what he feels the object to be intrinsically, and what at the same time it says and means to us. The man of letters will do it with words, the sculptor with his plastic materials, the painter or engraver or etcher with light, and shade, and pigments. Leaving the man of letters out of the inquiry, as being not a visual but a verbal craftsman, we may say that what the artist has to do is to oblige the spectator to feel as if he were the object represented, and to imagine its functional processes to the extent required by the representation. To what extent must be decided by the artist, if indeed one may speak of deciding in the case of an activity probably so unconscious and certainly so undeliberate as is that of the artist behind the ever conscious and highly purposeful craftsman. I am speaking of real artists and real craftsmen, and not of their imitators, and I am thinking of the relation between the artist and craftsman in the case of a Leonardo, the most self-conscious artist excepting perhaps Delacroix, who has left a record of himself. And yet how little Leonardo seems to have thought seriously about art and how earnestly about matters of technique!

The artist has only one way of making the spectator put himself into the place of the object he wishes to represent. It is by drawing attention to the muscular changes, the tensions and relaxations that accompany every action no matter how slight. He succeeds in fact by accentuating these alterations where it is easiest to feel them and where they are most marked, namely at the joints and other articulations. He will also somewhat exaggerate the manifestations of anatomical structure so as to make us more aware than we usually are of the stresses and counter-stresses, of the resistances and yieldings, and above all of the relaxations. For it is obvious that any failure of tissue and muscle to reach repose, after exercising their functions, would be life-diminishing, and to that extent anti-artistic. Even when the object represented is inanimate, like a mountain range or a building, it has to be dealt with as if organic and alive.

These manifestations must never be exaggerated, as is done by mannerists to facilitate their task. Even the best of them, say the Florentine Pontormo, attempt to interest us in acrobatic displays rather than in the normal actions of normal people; while the cubists of yesterday went so far as to reduce shapes to their geometrical hypothenuses, human beings to skeletons (as the Florentines Rosso and Salviati had already done in the sixteenth century), and any combination of figures to a dance of death.

On the other hand, vital primitive arts tend to concentrate on communicating energy. This is manifested in representations of man and beast in violent action that adorn capitals of Romanesque buildings; for most Romanesque sculpture and many products of barbarian art the world over, the so-called "animal style" in particular, are exasperated expressions of vitality and animal energy.

Not all ideated sensations are artistic, but only those that are life-enhancing. Thus representations that communicate feelings of dejection or nausea would be the less artistic, the more skillfully and successfully they were done. On the other hand, they must not incite to action, not immediately at least, although in the long run they cannot help influencing conduct. They must remain intransitive, inspiring no definable desire, stimulating no appetite, rousing no lust for sensual enjoyment. We must not glide or slip, or still less leap from ideated to real sensations, from art to actuality. The verses that stir to battle like a trumpet or a drum are not poetry. The visual representations that produce excitement in the normal adult may be exquisite artifacts but they are not works of art. For the ideated sensations that constitute the work of art belong to a realm apart, a realm beyond actuality where the ideal is the only reality, a realm of contemplation, of "emotion remembered in tranquillity," a realm where nothing can happen except to the soul of the spectator, and nothing that is not tempering and refining.

Possibly such a realm of ideated sensations is the one where our first parents lived, before the itch for action took hold of them and threw them out of the Paradise where Deity meant them to exist in everlasting ecstasy. Conceivably it may anticipate a heaven in which (with the sensations and experiences of earthly life employed as late antique architects used marbles and hard and precious stones) we shall ideate the ideal Athens, the City of Man.

Movement

Movement—which, after tactile values, is the most essential element in the work of art—has nothing to do with change of place, or even with change of attitude or pose, and still less with transitive activity of any kind. Movement is the manifest indwelling energy that vitalizes the delimiting outlines of an artifact and the delineations of all the parts within these outlines. Outline or delineation thus energized is a contour. In sculpture in the round these contours are infinite and their number can be diminished only by placing the sculptures so that they act as high or low reliefs. The lower the relief, the less the quantity of possible contours, while in two-dimensional representations they are reduced to the number that the artificer himself determines.

To describe this vital energy that turns a mere line or curve into a contour, that is to say into a line or curve with movement, is a task I cannot undertake. It is most like what we see in swift-flowing but smooth streams, where the eddies, swirls, and vortices produced by the current remain constant for the duration of the same conditions, although no drop of water that goes to shaping these aquatic patterns is the same for two consecutive seconds. No doubt like every other visible entity it is mathematically measurable and definable. That would offer no greater help to our perception than the formula for mathematical infinity brings one nearer to the Divine Infinitude for which we yearn. What I can say is that in my own case it is accompanied by an ideated tingling on and in my own skin corresponding to eye movement, both retinal and muscular, but that the feeling as a whole is one of aesthetic identification, as if there were nothing in me that was not living the life of the contour as it glides, turns, is swept on, smooth or rough, always animate and sentient, eager and zestful.

This direct contact with an otherness, but for the circumstance that it need have no touch of "uplift," is in essence a mystical experience, no more common perhaps than other mystical experiences. I recall when it first came to me. I had already published two books. For years I had been inquiring, excavating, dredging my inner self, and searching in my conscious experience for a satisfying test. I needed a test to apply to the artifacts that I thought I admired but could not hypnotize or habituate myself to enjoy with complete abandon, while the worm of doubt kept gnawing at the felicity of the ideal paradise. Then one morning as I was gazing at the leafy scrolls carved on the door jambs of S. Pietro outside Spoleto, suddenly stem, tendril, and foliage became alive and, in becoming alive, made me feel as if I had emerged into the light after long groping in the darkness of an initiation. I felt as one illumined, and beheld a world where every outline, every edge, and every surface was in a living relation to me and not, as hitherto, in a merely cognitive one. Since that morning, nothing visible has been indifferent or even dull. Everywhere I feel the ideated pulsation of vitality, I mean energy and radiance, as if it all served to enhance my own functioning. In nature nothing is dead for me, although some things are more alive than others. Nor can the hand of man produce complete lifelessness; at least it could not until a little while ago. Now it can perhaps, for to-day when the hand is permitted to do certain things generally left to machines it is on condition that it become machine-like. The machine alone can turn out artifacts guaranteed to be nonconductors of a vitalizing spark.

The revelation that came to me while looking at the façade of a church at Spoleto fifty years ago did various things for me.

In the first place, it emancipated me from the need of art, for I had become my own artist, as it were, and saw in terms of art. To illustrate what I mean, let me tell what happened

years later one frosty afternoon at Detroit, Michigan, while
I was visiting the famous Freer collection. I had been looking for hours at Chinese pictures of trees in snowy landscapes. The light of day was failing, and as no lamps or
candles were permitted, there was nothing to do but to start
going away. As I was getting up from the table I turned
round, and without realizing that I was looking through a
window at the out of doors, at natural objects and not artifacts, I cried out, "Look, look, these trees are the finest yet!"
So they were, for how can man compete with "nature"?
I had been enabled to feel this without the aid of an artist
to reveal it.

I am not competent to deal with the problem, and having
read little philosophy I do not know whether it has been
dealt with—I mean the question as to what it is that I, having become my own artist, see in any given object, say a
flower, a tree, an animal—a quality of art that no work of
art representing the same object rivals.

Being, as we are, practically identical vessels for scooping
up so much of chaos, and equally identical instruments for
shaping it into objects which presumably we all recognize as
identical, what happens to the objects when the subject perceives in them, besides what everybody else sees and feels
with regard to them, an art quality that only few of us can
see and that no artifact can rival? Is it there and has it always
been there, remaining hidden from perception till some of us
with certain gifts attempt to unveil it and succeed in making
it more and more perceivable? The veils, to be sure, seem
innumerable, so that we never penetrate to the full manifestation, and the revealer, the artist, may never come in
sight of the end of his task. Or is it in the subject, who happens to be an unusually contrived instrument for shaping
and forming, who, as he shapes and forms, acquires ever
keener powers and greater capacities for emitting from himself the qualities he communicates to those who are most

like him in perceiving and appreciating, although not in creating? I ask these questions but can conceive of no answer that I could understand or argue about.

But to return to the revelation I had at Spoleto: this revelation increased my enjoyment of the work of art, and the greater the confidence I felt in my own sensations and perceptions, or, to speak more accurately, in the genuineness of the successive ecstasies I was experiencing, the more I was relieved of uncertainty about their subjective reality and reliability. In other words, as is the case in all mystical experience, I acquired faith in my vision and its revelation of values. This faith has never abandoned me, although often enough one has moments of dryness when, as to the religious mystic, God is out of reach.

Finally this same revelation led me to perceive that while the feeling for movement is perhaps not quite the same as the feeling for quality, the two are nearly the same, in fact quite identical when on the same path, the path, namely, of lines and curves and linear figures. Only where it is an attribute of light and shade, that is to say of modelling with transitions from dark to light, or light to dark, instead of with contours, only then is movement not identical with quality.

If the feeling for movement or the feeling for "functional line"—as I have called it in my *Drawings of Florentine Painters* (1903)—is almost identical with the feeling for quality, and if it is psychologically a condition of ecstasy, it may be as rare as the mystically religious experience and as unintelligible to those who have not had it. In the realm of art, as in the realm of faith, the spirit bloweth where it listeth, and anyone with a taste for dress, and even his valet or maid, or anyone with a sense of furnishing may have this feeling while the painter or sculptor who creates works that have movement will often enough not be consciously aware of it in his own work and fail to recognize it in the works of others and indeed in nature itself.

So it has happened to me not rarely to find quicker, deeper feeling, more conviction and confidence in the presence of works of art, among tailors, dressmakers, haberdashers, and upholsterers, in smart young men, and in dashing young women than in most of us historians, critics, and aestheticians.

I cannot forget that one of the most admired authorities of my time, himself a painter, a stylist in prose, and a pioneer in discovering ever new genius, asked me what I could mean by movement in a line. I succeeded in making him feel it at the moment. He was, however, already too famous, too generous in giving out, to have energy or leisure left for taking in. As for the pundits who approach art through texts, inscriptions, archives, and the written word only, I cannot recall many whose publications betray that they have experienced the movement, quality, or style of line.

I said just now that I equate movement with quality. I go further and equate both with style. I am well aware that much explanation may be required to make my meaning clear, and much discussion before it can be accepted by others. Let me here take occasion to remark that "good drawing" is another synonym for movement. A correct drawing may be a valuable artifact, full of desired information about the object reproduced, but it remains a mere diagram unless it has movement as well. When it has movement we can also affirm it has quality and style.

Before leaving the subject of movement in the sense proposed, let me recall the anecdote of Apelles and Protogenes and ask whether it does not betray an identical appreciation of line in movement: Apelles called on Protogenes and, not finding him at home, left as a visiting card a line drawn on a panel prepared for painting. "Giotto's O," recounted by

Vasari, may also be brought into connection. I am tempted at this point to ask whether Plato in the Philebus could possibly have thought of line in movement when he says that by beauty of form he means straight lines and circles and the plain and solid figures which are shaped by turning lathes and rulers and measures of angles. He affirms that these are not only relatively beautiful like ordinary things but eternally and absolutely beautiful. It is to be feared that Plato had in mind exactly what "abstract" and "non-objective" painters are producing now. But if he returned to us at present he would find his wish fulfilled not so much by the "abstract" and "non-objective" paintings that are momentarily the fashion, as by our machinery and our weapons. Their dialectic, their realization, their geometrical perfection would surpass anything he could have imagined or conceived.

Essentials in Figure Arts

Having proposed definitions of "tactile values" and "movement," mere working definitions, yet sufficient for the present, I return to the statement made earlier, namely, that the essentials in a work of art are first "tactile values" and then "movement."

Not remotely would one suggest that they suffice to make complete and perfect works of art. There is much besides tactile values and movement in all great painting and sculpture. There are the proportions of the single figures and the arrangement of the design; there is space composition; there is the matter of illustration, the question of spiritual significance, over and above the core supplied by tactile values and movement. It is my intention as this book proceeds to touch these elements of the problem, and emphasize their importance. But I here repeat, that an artifact will remain a work of art no matter what it looks like, if it possesses tactile values or movement, or better still both.

With this conviction as a touchstone, we may roam the world over, and from the earliest Aurignacian and Magdalenian remains scratched and carved on rocks, daubed and painted in caves, or modelled in clay, down to the achievements of to-day, nothing need escape our appreciation, our delight, our love. Altamira and the caves of the Dordogne as well as the more recent bushman have left mural designs that have adequate movement and tactile values. So have Negro and Maya sculptures and Indonesian and South Pacific and Scandinavian wood carvings; Irish illuminations, Scythian bronzes, Shang and Chou vases, and the frescoes of Ajanta; Wei sculptures, and Sung paintings, and ever so many artifacts that would not have seemed art at all to my own educators some sixty years ago.

These educators still breathed in a world of shapes which alone seemed worthy of regard as works of art; shapes confined for the most part to a couple of centuries of Greek achievement and its imitators, a generation or two of Gothic, the "High Renaissance," and a few individual artists since then, Guido, Rembrandt perhaps, and still doubtfully Velasquez. All else was ethnology or bad art. I recall as a boy having my first glimpse of Chinese and Japanese carvings in natural history museums; and are not the finest specimens of African, Pacific, and even Central American wood and stone objects still to be seen only in ethnological collections? As for Romanesque sculpture, who at that time knew of Moissac or Souillac or Saint-Gilles, or of the wealth of twelfth-century statuary and reliefs all over Latin Europe, from Atlantic Galicia to Danubian Hungary, from Bergen to Bari?

Yet those who (like the compiler of a recent picture book on Greek art, who deliberately ignored all the masterpieces created between the archaic and the Byzantine) dislike antique sculpture and dote on everything exotic have no cause to sneer. They also see the shapes only, and it is enough that these are not classical but distortions of our traditional way of seeing, to give them the satisfaction of being up to date as lovers of art. Yet all they are doing is to curse the shapes that their elders blessed. Those shapes went far towards constructing a desirable House of Life, whereas the Fuzzy-Wuzzy ones, as mere shapes, can at best initiate us into the civilization of a savage kraal.

Tactile Values and Movement in Sculpture

Tactile values and all that we mean by them: How, it may be asked, can we apply them to sculpture? It is a question I hope to discuss in a book to follow where that art will claim more attention than painting. Here it may be enough to observe that sculpture, while using materials that have their own mass, shape, and weight, transcends them when it does not ignore them. Who, when he looked at the chryselephantine Athena of Phidias, thought of the original mass, weight, and shape of the gold and ivory that went to produce it? If mass and heft retain meaning in sculpture, it is as in painting through the represented figures and not through their original bulk. This would be more manifest if sculpture retained the colouring—more often than not startlingly life-like—that it nearly always had till well after the Renaissance, when it fell out of use. Pediments with figures in the round and friezes in low relief seen at a certain distance must have looked more like pictures than we now can believe. The same was the case with statuary in the portals of mediaeval churches, as we still can see in actuality at Saint-Germain-des-Prés in the heart of Paris and in reproductions in numberless paintings and illuminated manuscripts.

How little the feeling of bulk and weight in stone or marble as such means in sculpture is beautifully illustrated by late Gothic statuary all over Europe. It is every bit as

7. Detail from Façade of S. Pietro, Spoleto.

8. Antonio Pollaiuolo: Altarpiece. S. Miniato, Florence.

flimsy and as little able to evoke anything solid as is the painting of the same period, whose faults it shares so abundantly, while partaking so little of its qualities.

Colour

I have now enumerated various elements, besides tactile values and movement, that go to make up the complete work of art, but I have as yet made no mention of what may seem of the first importance, the element of colour.

According to the method of thinking that has been roughly sketched here, where the work of art is envisaged as existing in a realm of ideated sensations and not of sensations like those experienced in the workaday world, colour is a difficult subject to treat. For colour belongs to the world of immediately present and not merely imagined sensations, and is only less material than tasting, smelling, or touching, because it is perceived by one of the two signalling, reporting, informing senses, and not by the three more cannibal ones. Coloured artifacts have much in common with pastries or cocktails. Like these, they can be delicate or delicious and the product of high skill on the part of the cook or the barman. Only in textiles produced by un-Westernized nomads does colour play the sovereign rôle, design consisting merely in the contrasted surfaces of a geometrical pattern. The princes of Ormuz and of Ind who pass their fingers through sackfuls of precious stones, not only for the pride of power which great possessions give, but also for the touch, and perhaps chiefly for the gaiety and sparkle of colour, will scarcely be credited with enjoying them as works of art.

One may well ask how much art, as distinct from mere craft, there is in our best twelfth- and thirteenth-century stained-glass windows. Their pattern is not easy to decipher, so much is it melted into the colour; and when deciphered how inferior it is in appeal! I have seen windows, not mere fragments, but entire windows, from St. Denis removed from the interior they were intended to transfigure, and I confess that one's enjoyment of them thus isolated was not so different from the Rajahs' gloating over handfuls of emeralds, rubies, and other precious stones. The Turks, guided by their creed, understood this and made no attempt at figures in the jewelled windows of their mosques, in the Suleimanieh at Constantinople for example.

In precious and hard stones, and their imitations in paste and glass, as well as in ceramics and textiles, the sensuous enjoyment of colour so outweighs any ideation evoked by design, that they can be classed as works of art in a limited sense only. As already hinted when speaking of materials, they play a subordinate part in epochs of great creation, and take a commanding position in times of decadence. Probably Greek colonnades were painted with ultramarine and vermilion. Many if perhaps not all marble sculptures of the Greek centuries before Christ were tinted. Plato speaks as if in his day all statuary was coated with pigments (Republic, 420 c.). It was only under the Romans that Greek architecture and sculpture took to using first multi-coloured marbles, then hard and semi-precious stones, basalts, granites, porphyry, and finally glass mosaic. This last, by the way, may have been suggested by the coating of gold applied to the inside walls of temples, as was done by Antiochus IV at Antioch. It would seem as if form and colour could not exist together, and that as the first declined the other waxed and flourished. It appears, moreover, as if form was the expression of a society where vitality and energy were severely controlled by mind, and as if colour was indulged in by communities where brain was subordinated to muscle. If these suppositions are true, we may cherish the hope that a marvellous outburst of colour is ahead of us.

In all the varieties of visual representation and reproduction of objects that are assumed to be outside ourselves, and of images flitting through our minds, colour must necessarily be the servant, first of shape and pattern, and then of tactile values and movement. Colour cannot range free but must serve rapid recognition and identification, facilitate the interpretation of shapes and the articulation of masses, and accelerate the perception of form, or tactile values, and movement. In the figure arts you cannot sacrifice any of these in order to attain the unadulterated enjoyment of colour that is offered by textiles, jewels, precious stones, and glass, as well as by certain metals and enamels.

Colour then must be subordinated, in painting at least, where our sense of veracity and of what is "true to nature" is most easily offended; and colour can play the part only of tinted light and shade, of a polychrome chiaroscuro. "The most beautiful colours laid on confusedly," says Aristotle, "will not give as much pleasure as the chalk outline of a portrait" (Poetics, VI, 15). Pink and green horses may be tolerated in an *incunabulous* experimenter like Paolo Uccello, but I remember wincing at the sight of Impressionist portraits with faces and bosoms and hands blotched with vivid vegetable green reflected from the surrounding foliage, orange and scarlet from the sunshades held by the subjects. If the clearly expressed intention of Uccello, or Besnard, or Rolle, or Zorn had been to study the effect of reflections on horses' hides or women's skins, we should have adjusted ourselves accordingly. That was not the case. The portraits referred to will scarcely find now the admirers they had when their mere newness excited and, for an instant, fascinated the spectator.

So as they grew to be the complete masters of their art, the aged Titian, the aged Hals, the aged Rembrandt, and Tintoret and Veronese in their maturity, tended to paint in a sort of monochrome, of a low tone in the case of the first three, and of a high one in that of the others; but in all of them far removed from the childish display of gold, scarlet, ultramarine, and other dazzling pigments: and this accounts for the response the Trecento or the Catalan and German Quattrocento find in all of us, who have not outgrown the hankering for fairyland, or the longing for a new Jerusalem visualized as a Christmas card.

The problem of colour in the figure arts as well as in the other arts of visual representation is complicated. Far be it from me to fancy that the preceding paragraphs offer as much as a synopsis of the questions to be discussed. All I wish here to suggest is that colour is subordinated to form and movement; as for instance hair on the head, so ornamental and transfiguring, is subordinated to the skull and face. The justice of the comparison is strengthened by the fact that, like human hair, colour may continue for a while a sepulchral animation of its own, after spiritual and physical life has deserted the body. Colour may survive most other features of a decaying art.

Before leaving the matter for the present, I venture on two further remarks. In the first place colour is a poor imitator. Form and movement can seem to render the objects in a way that corresponds closely to my own vision; colour never. Where in the whole range of painting is there an adequate, let alone a perfect, reproduction of flesh? We accept pictures of the nude without expecting them to match the colours of the skin. Neither Botticelli, nor Giorgione, nor Correggio, nor Titian, nor Rubens, nor Rembrandt, nor Boucher, nor Ingres, nor Manet, nor Gauguin, nor Degas, nor Renoir offer more than conventional substitutes for flesh colour.

Then I must further observe that we are apt to confuse the problem of colour with the problem of paint or pigment; for paint is not merely colour, or colour only. The real painter, a Veronese or Tintoret, a Rembrandt or Velasquez, a Renoir or Cézanne, does not, like Botticelli or Michelangelo, use colour to tint his cartoons with, but uses it as a material, like clay, or marble, or bronze in which he works, mastering or circumventing its resistances and profiting by the advantages it affords. A great painter is one who makes the best use of pigments in the way just indicated. He may be a great colourist as well, for the most gorgeous effects of colour can be produced only by the craftsman who elicits out of pigments the visual equivalent of what the composer gets out of his musical instruments. In that sense what painter is a supreme colourist? Surely not a Renoir.

I mention Renoir precisely because he is so colourful, and I wish to make the point that to be colourful is not the same as to be a colourist. A Florentine mosaic is colourful. So are the reproductions in coloured or tinted marbles of pictures made for the altars of St. Peter's. So are the poorer Rubens, and the best Jordaens. So are Holman Hunt and most English "Pre-Raphaelites," and so are all the German "Nazarenes." Nor would I place among the great colourists an artist like Greco—the Greco admired by culture-snobs—who uses pigments to startle and strike like so much stage thunder. Melodrama is no more great art in the visual field than it is in the world of words. Art is too mighty a monarch to have need to shout and scream in order to attract attention. The Lord came to Elijah not in the storm and uproar, but in a still small voice.

So much for colour as decoration. Later in connection with Illustration we shall come upon it again. But let me insert a note jotted down April 29, 1931: Visceral values are to colour what tactile values are to form and respirational values to space composition. Tactile values refer to our corporeal contacts with the outside world; visceral values refer to the feelings of comfort or discomfort inside our bodies; respirational values (which I equivalate with spatial ones) refer to our feeling of liberation, of freedom from heaviness, and to the illusion of soaring into harmonious relations with sky and horizon. Visceral values, which I equivalate with colour values, are closely related to thermal or temperature values. Indeed we constantly speak of colours as "hot" or "cold," "warm" or "icy" or "tepid." For this among other reasons, in painting tone must count above local or variegated colour. Bits of different colour spread over a surface can yield but pin-pricks of warm and cold, icy and hot, whereas tone produces one dominant continuous effect.

There may be no absolute in dialectical aesthetics but visual art enjoys a relative absolute, for it depends on such constants as ideated bodily functions. Visual art becomes freakish, flighty, and at best merely amusing when it gets clean away from those functions; and it ceases to be art when reduced to geometric shapes and abstract diagrams.

Finally, if a picture appeals through tactile values to ideated outside contacts, through visceral values to ideated inner sensations of every sort, and through ideated respirational values to our harmonious relations to space, then painting is, as Leonardo maintained, the most comprehensive and the completest of the visual arts.

The Aesthetic Moment

Some paragraphs back I used the phrase "aesthetic moment." A word of explanation may not be out of place here.

In visual art the aesthetic moment is that flitting instant, so brief as to be almost timeless, when the spectator is at one with the work of art he is looking at, or with actuality of any kind that the spectator himself sees in terms of art, as form and colour. He ceases to be his ordinary self, and the picture or building, statue, landscape, or aesthetic actuality is no longer outside himself. The two become one entity; time and space are abolished and the spectator is possessed by one awareness. When he recovers workaday consciousness it is as if he had been initiated into illuminating, exalting, formative mysteries. In short, the aesthetic moment is a moment of mystic vision.

Decoration and Illustration

Terms that will constantly reappear in this book are "decoration" and "illustration." A sharp distinction was first made in my *Florentine Painters*, written in the spring of 1895. It did not fail to be taken up, but not as it should have been, no doubt because it was put too briefly and too abruptly. This must be remedied before we go further. Without a keen sense of the difference we shall continue to confuse issues, to misunderstand one another, and to quarrel.

Decoration comprises all the elements in a work of art that distinguish it from a mere reproduction of the shape of things: tactile values and movement of course, proportion, arrangement, space composition, in short everything in the field of visual representation that is made life-enhancing by means of ideated sensations. In other terms, decoration is presentative and not representative. The representative part is illustration.

Tactile values and movement have, I trust, been sufficiently defined for the purpose in hand, although far from adequately in any metaphysical sense. A word may be in place about proportion, arrangement, and space composition.

Proportions

Proportions are the relations of the various parts of the human figure to each other which best lend themselves to rendering tactile values and to offering the illusion that we are one with a body that stands so well, breathes so well, is so well adapted for competent action that we get the utmost life-enhancement out of it. For the full effect of this imagined self-substitution, the nude is preferable. It is through the nude only that the identification is complete and instantaneous, as in fifth-century Greek statues, those particularly of the so-called "severe style."

The Nude

The nude is not the naked. It is a conventional product, the result of thousands of years of conscious and unconscious effort and much hard thinking. It began perhaps with predynastic Egyptians, and engaged the minds of ancient Greek and Italian Renaissance artists. The nude in art is a canon handed down by these creators, and now so firmly established that every Jack and Jill visualizes in its terms as naïvely as he uses his native idiom, which by the way has taken fewer centuries to fashion. It forms his standard as well. He will ascribe beauty to naked human bodies in the measure that they approach this shape or pattern.

The nude then is already an art creation, begotten and gestated by the need of providing the shapes with which we can most easily identify ourselves: shapes like our own, but freed from blemishes, flatteringly proportioned and moving freely.

Therefore the nude, and best of all the nude erect and frontal, has through all the ages in our world—the world descended from Egypt and Hellas—been the chief concern of the art of visual representation.

Composition

When the figure is not seen only by itself but along with others, arrangement becomes necessary, and the more necessary the more the figures are in action. Standing vertically, they do not get in each other's way, and can be read off and enjoyed as if each was alone. If, on the other hand, they act, and act together, care has to be taken that the tactile values and movement of one figure are not confused with, or even hidden behind, those of another. If the entire figure cannot be shown it must be so placed that one does not miss what is not represented. Crowding therefore must be avoided, unless indeed the artist deliberately aims (as Michelangelo in certain drawings for his Sistine frescoes, or Leonardo for his Epiphany, or Rubens in his numerous oil sketches in Munich and elsewhere) at an effect of compact mass with the same common energy throbbing and heaving within it.

Space Composition

The art of getting the utmost tactile values and movement out of figures and masses in action is known as composition or design. From the beginning of history the tendency has been to compose in two dimensions as if there was no space behind single figures or groups. Rostovtzeff has established that Pompeian painting systematically avoided depth of landscape. When Florentine science finally enabled painters to arrange objects in perspective, they went on placing the figures as if standing on the fore-edge of a map in relief. For examples we need but look at Pollaiuolo's altarpiece at S. Miniato, or his Hercules diptych in the Uffizi. It was Perugino who initiated and Raphael who perfected what I have called "space composition," composition that (as practised by the Van Eycks two generations earlier) is not only in three dimensions but suggests the amplitude and the compassed freedom of cosmic dimensions. So little appreciated was this last acquisition that it remains doubtful whether it was ever felt again as creatively as Raphael felt it. Claude and Turner often, and Rembrandt, Seghers, Constable, and

Cézanne at times only, seem to have understood and tried it with a certain success. Merely scenic imitation sufficed most artists. Even the problem of relating a solid to a given space is far from solved in the painting of to-day, and it is conceivable that despair and exasperation over the difficulties involved have led to cubism, futurism, dadaism, surrealism, etc., all of them characterized by jeering at or bluffing over the third dimension, and ignoring space relations.

But what about Chinese landscape? The oblong or square or vertical Chinese landscape has space composition as often as do European landscapes. The answer is more difficult with regard to the continuous landscapes of the famous Sung Masters. It is curiously easy as we unroll them to display bits that by themselves make good space compositions, so easy that we do it instinctively. How this comes about is a problem I must leave to others to solve. Perhaps it is because, having become our own artists, we unroll what suffices for one act of vision, just as in nature itself we take in with one look what makes a space composition?

That would be enough for the present about space. Unfortunately yet another German professor with a Slav name, August Schmarsow, some sixty years ago initiated an interest in space, not as the negligible void for which it had been taken hitherto but as the one and only existence. Objects, no matter how large or how small, exist only to make us realize mere extension, and exist for that alone, although even they are but impertinent interruptions of the mystic void. So the art writing of the German-minded has been more and more dedicated to discussing space determination, space filling, space distortion, space this, space that—but to my recollection never to space composition. Objects are interesting to the degree that they occupy space. A much admired writer on Giotto went so far as to declare that tactile values were only questions of space.

This preoccupation has led to a cult of space in the ab-

stract, and to fanciful interpretations of the treatment of
space in so-called "early Christian" painting. As a matter of
fact this painting, falling more and more into senility, returned to the primitive infantile way of ignoring space altogether as the early Egyptians and Sumerians did. Indeed,
until Empedocles no one seems to have taken sufficient
interest in space to notice that it was not an utter void, but
was filled with air.

The trouble with the German-minded is that they never
seem to take art as an experience. If any of them did, it
might have occurred to him how he, as a child, tried to
represent objects on a slate or a paper, say dogs, horses, and
bipeds of all sorts. I recall clearly that the question of representing space extending between solids and masses never
troubled me. Space as an entity did not exist. I marshalled
objects to right or left, up or down with no thought of their
relation to each other. Early dynasty Egyptians had barely got
beyond this way of visualizing space exemplified in prehistoric Nilotic civilization—the Badrian, for instance. They
represented it by placing solids in rows one above the other
with emptiness between them. A subtle German Egyptolo-
gist recommended that we should look at such a representation not on a vertical plane as we usually do, but on a
horizontal one when these rows of figures, biped or quad-
ruped, and other objects will rise up and take their place
one behind the other like battalions on parade.

And thus it was with most attempts at representing various solids on the same plane, more or less as on Chinese
vases, almost down to our own time. It was the Assyrians
who awoke to a notion of space as we now feel it, and in
stone and bronze relief first succeeded in giving a sense of
what existed, and what took place in the intermediate positions between solids, and thus invented landscape. It was
taken up by Greeks in Lycia, and through the Mesopotamian
high road got down to India. Across the Aegean it had scanty

success. The Greek world as a whole seems to have had faint interest in space beyond one's back door, so to speak. Perhaps it was never strong enough to penetrate to mere artisan painters and sculptors; which may account for its absence in work they did for fellow proletarians, the overwhelming majority of early Christians.

Landscape

Landscape, as until lately and for several centuries we have enjoyed it, is the art of representing an out-of-doors where "nature" (as defined in the Introduction) dominates and permits no artifacts, no matter how near to each other, how massed or how important, to monopolize the spectator's attention. When they do, as in Pannini, in Canale, in Bellotto and a thousand like them, they are town views or pictures of architecture and not landscape. Cézanne on the contrary, even when he masses or terraces a number of buildings, never leaves you in doubt that he is not interested in the structures alone but much more in the intermediate positions, the perceived distances between them.

Painting, as it acts only through the eye, can make us enjoy nature as we seldom do while experiencing it, and thus fulfills its highest aim, which is to give us the illusion of better than ordinary workaday functioning.

It is not the purpose of these few paragraphs to discuss how this is to be brought about. We can afford only to glance at what landscape can do and has done.

The crudely pictographic or symbolic representations of latest antiquity gave place in Byzantine art to the sort of token landscape which we find in the Menologia of the Macedonian period. This was taken up by painters of the Latin world, whether of manuscripts, panels, or frescoes, and was in vogue till the fifteenth century. It was followed by two divergent treatments: on the one hand, the Van Eycks,

Rogier van der Weyden, Van der Goes, Dierick Bouts, and the Rhenish followers who, like "the Master of the Life of Mary," vitalize us with the illusion of increased and illumined eyesight; and on the other, artists like Gentile da Fabriano and Sassetta who naïvely, with the appropriate use of gold, ultramarine, and silver, appeal directly to the heart, using the eyes as a mere spring-board for reaching it.

Followed topographical landscape, almost cartographic, as practised for instance by Baldovinetti and Pollaiuolo in Florence and in a less crude way by the emergent Giovanni Bellini in Venice. By the beginning of the sixteenth century landscape painting was becoming more and more evocative, romantic, scenic, not only in Italy with Giorgione and Titian but in the North with Patinier and his fellows.

Despite individual attempts at mere description, the most successful of which was made by Constable more than a hundred years ago, landscape has been evocative rather than literal. I venture to question whether even Constable with his marvellous sky-dramas does not fascinate us more as a poet than as a student. Landscape like music liberates feelings and dreams rather than stimulates observation, and that is as true of Cézanne and his nineteenth-century French precursors as of the Dutch in the seventeenth century and the Chinese of the Sung period.

CHAPTER II

ILLUSTRATION

A NEGATIVE DEFINITION of illustration as that which in a
work of art is not decoration, will not do. Such a definition would reduce illustration to something indifferent,
negligible, or even opposed to what is most specific in the
work of art. Illustration as practised by all but the great
masters does lay itself open to such accusation, but it need
not do so. It is not merely because they draw and paint
better that we prefer a Giotto to a Gaddi, a Raphael to a
Giulio Romano, a Dürer to a Kulmbach, a Rubens to a Jordaens, a Goya to a Lucas, and so on. It is because they
created greater visual myths.

A myth is the precipitate of a mind that has been ferment-
ing with the sensations, emotions, and impulses it has received from contact with a vitalizing object or event. In verbal art, that is to say in literature, the object has to be a hero
and always life-enhancing. If he fall or even perish it must
be because of an excess of vitality, of an overabundance of
energy that brings him in conflict with overwhelming forces
massed against him.

If on the other hand the events, in the Aristotelian sense,
are more exciting than any individual engaged in them, as is
the case in the Iliad, the Eddas and other Icelandic sagas, or
in our ballads, the French epics, and, of course, the German
Nibelungen and Gudrun, these events must lend themselves
to the applause of a society indifferent to consequences, so
long as it is provided with orgies of communal self-importance.

ILLUSTRATION 93

What Visual Art Can Do

Visual art is more innocent. It cannot soothe, cajole, and flatter, and still less can it juggle us into entertaining an even momentary illusion that our defeats were victorious, or would have been but for treachery and meanness! Visual art cannot lie, and should not be accused of doing so, when it happens that ignorance or fraud attempts to persuade us that a given portrait is not of Lenin but of Peter the Great, or that a daub by Sinibaldo Ibi is by Raphael. In such cases it is not the representation that is mendacious, but the people who try to pass it off for what it never pretended to be. Nor indeed can they deceive any but the gullible.

What visual art can do and what it had better leave to literature has been fought over too often and too decisively to demand further discussion. The problem lies entirely within the realm of illustration, and outside the bounds of decoration. There is no room for the ugly in art as decoration, but only in art as illustration. Decoration gives its own value to objects regardless of what they are in actuality. It is indifferent to subject matter and may be used to vitalize any representation. But if a representation causes disgust or stirs up adversion, or is merely incongruous, the "aesthetic moment," as we have called the instant of life-enhancing ecstasy, is not attained and the intended effect is not produced.

Incongruity and the Grotesque

I have just mentioned incongruity. We take its opposite, congruity, so much for granted that we seldom stop to think, and rarely realize, what a part is played by it. We take certain shapes for granted, especially all familiar animal ones. If we enjoy the incongruity of monstrosities like the Kuban finds, it is because they never deal seriously with the human figure, but with fishes, horned quadrupeds, etc., having only the remotest relation with human shapes. The human body in and by itself is no more than any other "natural" object endowed with the life-enhancing qualities of a work of art. It is pleasing for various biological reasons, with which are associated many ethical ones. Its authority is derived from the fact that it decides without appeal as to what is and what is not coherent and congruous in all other living bodies, and how much room it leaves for play. Certain deviations made by deliberate caricaturists in all times, as well as by distortionist painters of to-day, amuse so long as they remain well within the sheltering walls of the permissible grotesque. The distortion must avoid humiliating approximations or even parallels. I recall the loathing I felt as an infant when I first noticed the likeness of a swimming frog to a human creature. It is curious, by the way, that we have less repugnance to facial resemblances with other animals, frogs, fishes, bears, cats, elephants, birds, than to those of the entire figure; perhaps because our faces are so mobile that we are accustomed to startling changes of expression. As a matter of fact, our bodies as wholes are seldom caricatured. The intention would not be recognized. The canine-headed Anubis, the feline-headed Khesmet, and the cow-like Hathor have normal human trunks and limbs. The grotesque is not the incongruous, and must indeed avoid it. The grotesque may pull animal and human figures out of shape, exaggerating this or that feature, elongating or thickening and reducing proportions, but must never change the anatomical relations or multiply them. Thus, besides other reasons that make later Indian art distasteful, none are more valid than the many arms and legs of its disporting and dancing deities. Eyes must not wink from the belly, a hand grow out of the skull, a foot out of the groin. Moreover, features like the mouth and ears,

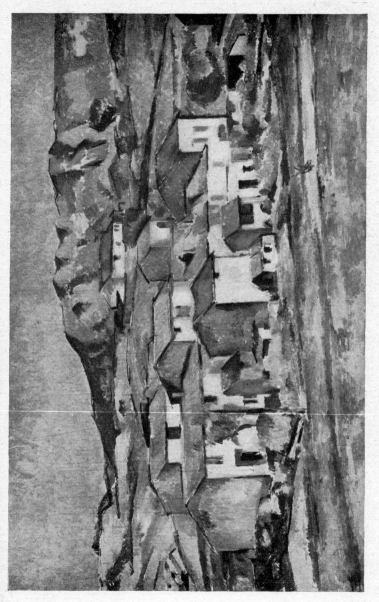

9. Paul Cézanne: Landscape. Loeser Collection, Florence.

10. Guido Reni: Massacre of the Innocents. Art Gallery, Urbino.

ILLUSTRATION 95

eyes and nose, have no attractiveness of their own. The early nineteenth-century taste for the likeness on ivory of a mouth alone, or an eye alone, is repugnant now; and even the marble or wax portrait of a vanished hand is more quaint than moving.

The veto power that distaste, loathing, or obstinate indifference can exert is considerable. Even the mild nastiness of a Bosch, a Breughel, or a Brouwer tends to divert the current of sympathy set going by merits won in the field of decoration. If we tolerate certain pages of Rabelais or Joyce it is perhaps owing to the fact that verbal evocations are so much feebler than visual ones. The danger lies the other way. An attractive face, lovely limbs, graceful action may be used almost unconsciously to create a yearning for Eros, or may be misused deliberately to excite lust. They may also be employed for sentimental appeals, and they may easily be turned from the intransitive, the aesthetic plane, the realms of ideated sensations, to the transitive and active one.

Facial Expression

Facial expression as a specific art and likewise gesture belong first and foremost to the mime and the stage. The painter or sculptor who exploits them competes at his peril with the actor. The actor looks and behaves the way he does for the minutes only that his impersonation would have in life, whereas the painter and sculptor perpetuates indefinitely what should be a flitting moment. Of course there are good and bad ways of doing what pure art had better let alone. Thus certain Spanish wood-carvers and picture-makers supremely, and certain Germans to a high degree, can express grief and even despair in a way that rouses sympathetic admiration, while the French do it indifferently and the Italians nearly always badly, at times abominably.

The Italian was too much the artist to succeed in what art should not attempt. For in visual art, isolated suffering only can be represented, the grimace of pain, the emaciation of anguish; unlike literature, which can simultaneously represent and reconcile us to the reason, heroic or perhaps retributive, that led to this suffering.

Autonomous Illustration

Illustration as an independent, an autonomous art expresses in terms of visual form the longings and ecstasies as well as the idyllic dreams of the heart which, when conveyed in words, are poetry and in wordless harmonies of rhythmic sound are music. It is much narrower in range, and far less poignant in appeal than poetry or music. Just because it is so much less evocative and exciting, it lends itself better to contemplation, to the enjoyment of "emotion remembered in tranquillity." It cannot express the *cri du cœur*, or the rapture of delight, or the indignation, or the pity or tears that poetry and music can express. If it attempts any of these it is doomed to fail because violent gestures and distorted features, upturned eyes, and convulsive movements are as likely to beget repulsion as sympathy, and are, at best, informative rather than kindling. Sounds that are music and words that are poetry go straight to the heart. If illustration persists in such attempts it falls into the puerilities of the mediaeval Psalter illuminators who represent David in full regalia sending forth his soul in the image of a swaddled babe, or else it displays distortions of the features through explosive self-satisfaction, as in Franz Hals; or gross merriment, as in the Breughels, Jordaens and Co.; or grief, as in Carlo Dolci or Morales; or the vapid ecstasies of Guido, Greuze, and their kind.

Yet even Guido is at times an illustrator in the best sense

ILLUSTRATION 97

of the word, as in "Atalanta's Race," the "Samson," and the "Massacre of the Innocents," for the reason that in these masterpieces of the Naples and Bologna galleries and better still in that radiant composition, his Rospigliosi "Aurora," Guido does not get his effects through facial changes only, which describe rather than communicate what the subject may be feeling, but through life-enhancing elements as well; through tactile values and action of the bodies, as the arrangement of the figures and their relation to the space they dominate.

What a secondary artist like Guido could achieve with his relatively feeble tactile values and bloodless flesh colour could easily be surpassed by better designers, the Attic vase-painters for instance, and other antique masters whose greatness we descry dimly in copies on the walls of Pompeii and Herculaneum; or the late Hellenistic creators of the sublime iconography of the Church Triumphant; by the Romanesque interpreters of Christian story culminating in Giotto; the Tuscans, from Masaccio, with his solemn frescoes, to the majesty of Michelangelo in the Sistine chapel. Then there is Raphael, who gave the humanistic world the visual equivalent of what it could accept of the narratives and characters of the Bible, Giorgione and Titian, the Keats and Shakespeare of painting, and the magicians of light, such as Claude and Rembrandt, ending with the galaxy of illustrators of the Napoleonic period from Flaxman to Géricault and Delacroix. I can be uplifted, transported, and enraptured, I can sing and dance within myself as I look at their works; and I feel no more need of words than when listening to music. I do not ask to be told what they represent; I do not want to have every figure labelled. It is true that I get a certain merely mental satisfaction if the information allays my curiosity; but it is fatal if it be far-fetched or excessive. Nor should a work of art arouse, in the well-tempered instrument that the spectator ought to be, the kind of curiosity that demands elaborate verbal explanation. The simplest descriptions sufficed a connoisseur of the High Renaissance like Marcantonio Michiel, while no explanation is elaborate enough for the insatiable commentator of to-day.

I cannot refrain here from quoting Shelley:

> "Like a poet hidden
> In the light of thought
> Singing hymns unbidden
> Till the world is wrought
> To sympathy with hopes and fears it heeded not"

> "Made sweeter by distance"

> "Dearer for its mystery"

> "Unsculptured image"

And Gérard de Nerval said of his own sonnets *"qu'ils perdraient de leur charme à être expliqués, si la chose était possible."*

Nothing should be read into the illustration that is not manifestly there, in terms of visual representation. After exhausting all possible themes that pictures by Botticelli, Giorgione, or Titian were intended to illustrate, texts from obscure poets or lines from forgotten versifiers; after admitting the scholar's industry and acumen, and acknowledging that the episode was dinned into the head of the painter before he began to work, what have we achieved? When we are told that the three men in the Vienna "Giorgione" really and truly represent Aeneas, Evander, and Pallas, and that in the Borghese Titian the naked female represents Sacred and the draped one Profane Love, or Venus and Medea—as Wickhoff after painstaking research and elaborate argument tried to prove—what is there that remains? Nothing would be left over if the mere matching of verbal subjects and personages and incidents with visual representations were all

· ILLUSTRATION 99

that the artist could supply. To the real artist the subject is little more than a spring-board from which he dives into a world of his own. In that world we take no account of inspiration and orders, no matter from what exalted or far-fetched source. In that world we listen only to what the figures sing and what their surroundings orchestrate. Where is the poet who could explain the meaning of Giorgione's "Fête Champêtre"! Who could have whispered in words what Watteau meant by his "Embarquement pour Cythère"! What elucidation, what gloss could deepen or enhance the fascinating and mysterious presence in Piero della Francesca's Urbino "Flagellation" of the three bystanders who seem so unaffected by what is going on? No! Illustration as an independent art is as autonomous as music or architecture, and as infinite. If not, it would be a diagram, a pictograph, or merely informative, as is the case with reproductions in most illustrated papers and books. These, I grant, are invaluable in their way. It would be a privation to have to do without the *Illustrated London News* and its competitors; but while they reproduce works of art in generous abundance they themselves are not works of art. On the other hand, their descriptions and comments on what they reproduce can be recommended to all those critics who would "tell the clock by algebra." These same pundits might learn even more from the labels which a great interpreter like Rostovtzeff puts under reproductions, and might discover that labelling is in itself an art.

We must resist the impulse to translate every other art into verbal terms. We should feel the work of art and let it exhale suggestions, notions, dreams. We do not want to know some story, or some doctrine, which may have excited the artist but which his art could not express. What he could bring off is all that interests us.

So many effects in nature and in visual and musical art

say much through overtones, all sorts of vague symbolical allegorical suggestions which cannot be put into words, not even by the greatest poets.

Explanations can satisfy only in a world of objects that have no attribute but measurableness. In the world of art, where quality is paramount, explanations are no more than vehicles. They cannot touch the work of real art, but only of sham art: I mean the informative artifact, self-assertive display, or conspicuous waste. History has to reckon with these products, to record and interpret them, but the less artistic they are the easier they are to write about. Their historian should not mislead readers into the belief that he is writing about art. Every work of art has to be first and foremost a permanent joy and inspiration, and cannot be degraded to serve as document in the history of technique and taste or of civilization in general.

Illustration Presents Patterns

Illustration as an autonomous art has, to begin with, a mission in presenting patterns of how people should hold themselves: how they should stand and sit, use their limbs, compose their faces, dress and walk. The patterns themselves have their origin in by-products of the search for figures whose proportions, whose tactile values, whose action will be most life-enhancing singly or in combination with other figures. In highly creative moments, art imposes these patterns so successfully as to make it impossible to enjoy other shapes, or to believe that they have the right to exist.

For six full centuries Greek art imposed its way of seeing not only on its own people in their wide-flung migrations, but on barbarians, Etruscans, Romans, Scythians, Iranians, Africans, Iberians, Gauls, Britons, and at long last Teutons. The troubled outposts of civilization, like Dura-Europos, or

ILLUSTRATION 101

the settlements bordering on the Garamantes, the Picts or the Ceruscans, did their best to obey the canons of Greek art. If you got sick of its products you would have had to join tribes which had no representational arts at all, like the nomads of Arabia and their kindred who were shoving and pushing each other from the Amur and the sources of the Yangtze to the Rhine and Danube; or indeed you would have had to force your way through these and to take refuge in China. The same is true of Gothic, which imposed its patterns upon every object from a cathedral to a breast pin not only in Northern France, the land of its origin, but all the way to Trondhjem, all the way to the Carpathians, to Cyprus and Syria, and all the way to Belém. For three centuries no one within these boundaries could make an object that was not Gothic. Since the fifteenth century, we of the Western world, despite the fact that the various styles derived from the Renaissance never attained the calm uniformity of the ancient and mediaeval styles, have in four hundred years failed to get away from its version of the antique. We tried it with the Baroque, we tried it with Rococo, only to fall back on the Neo-Classical and *Empire* and even Louis-Philippe—a fall indeed!—progressively impoverished styles, precursors of the *art nouveau*, with which the story ends. For since 1900, except for survivals, we have been stumbling and wallowing and strutting and, at every change of position, boasting like Jack Horner what good boys we were; but not one of the new geniuses has dared to remain in any one position, and the most notorious have ended not by denying representation altogether but by reducing it to the proto-hieroglyphic rebuses of primitive secret societies with the same relation to the art of painting that cowrie-shells and wampum have to the Sicilian and Attic coins of the fifth century B.C.

To return to illustration, something must be said about the interpreters. For most objections that students like myself have to illustration are not to be put to the account of illustration as an autonomous art, as autonomous in its own way as decoration itself, but to the misuse and abuse made of it by these interpreters. Let me explain.

The Interpreters and the Artist

These interpreters have the right to deal with the work of art as with any other entity. Every entity can be discussed from the points of view of an endless variety of interests, curiosities, aspirations, prepossessions, and obsessions. Thus you are free to ignore in the Parthenon everything except the mineralogical aspect of its marbles, or the cost of carrying the columns from Pentelicon to the Acropolis. You are at liberty to see in the thermae of ancient cities, the Baths of Caracalla and Diocletian for instance, only the problem of the entire forests it must have taken to bake the quantities of bricks required for their construction. No one should discourage you from devoting laborious days to the investigation of the diseases that attack ancient bronzes.

Chemists, foresters, experts on hemp and linen, on tempera and oil and plaster of every kind, may be allowed to investigate paintings on wall, panel, or canvas. These are not only legitimate occupations, as indeed are all occupations not immediately and manifestly harmful, but may in a remote contingency turn out to be helpful to the lover of art.

More doubtful is the effort to discover what was the intention of a painter or sculptor while creating a masterpiece; or what precisely was going on in his mind at the moment; what poems and books he had been reading, what obscure verses, or even obscurer prose passages of a Church Father, or mediaeval theologian, or teller of old wives' tales kindled his creative imagination. Samuel Butler somewhere in his notebooks says that commentators on great poems are useful

ILLUSTRATION   103

if you wish to learn the mind of the commentator. I doubt whether one can know the mind of the artist even through the confession of the artist himself.

Goethe, when asked by Eckermann just what he meant to convey when he wrote his *Faust*, burst out with "How can I tell you! How do I know! My head was in a buzz"—or words to that effect. Socrates in Plato's *Apology* says that almost any man in the street would talk better sense about poetry than a poet. There is the story of Delacroix's utter bewilderment at all that Baudelaire could suppose was going on in his mind while he was composing one of his pictures.

Many years ago in the studio of the one artist of the first rank still alive, I expressed regret that the types in the canvases he then was painting were so Cambodian. He assured me it could not be so. "But you have been imitating these," I said, pointing to scores of plaster casts cluttering up the room. He had not been aware of it.

The real artist, if at the moment of creation he thinks at all, thinks of little but his craft, the action and arrangement chiefly, and of all the skill and mastery he has acquired previously—I mean how to draw, how to paint, what proportions, what types to give his figures. These are now his style, that is to say his habitual way of visualizing and executing, his habitual handiwork. The real artist may be humble like the Japanese illustrators of their country's war with Russia. I remember the Battle of Tsushima designed by one of them, as it might have been done by his predecessors who had never seen European pictures. Every single shape, their ships and the Russian ships, their uniforms and those of the enemy, were *Occidental*. Yet the spacing, the horizon, the perspective, the outlines marked them as of the Far East. Or he may be like the early Soviet illustrators who appealed to the people through the Byzantine terms of the icons to which they and their public were accustomed, whose shapes were intelligible to them both. The real artist, if great, imposes his vision upon his contemporaries, and if small he goes with the stream, without a program and without saying, "Go to, now let us take thought and start a new way of seeing and feeling." Real artists do not bother about feeling and vision, but only about learning how to draw and carve and paint in a more satisfactory way. They do not have to think of the shapes, the spacing, the compositions, for these they draw unconsciously from the common fund pooled by all the art activities of the moment. Even in the Italian Renaissance it was not the humanistic craving for the splendours, glories, and majesties of the ancients that absorbed the artist, but the technical methods and achievements of the antique.

Illustration, I repeat, is an independent art and not a visual gloss upon a poem or the visual accompaniment of a narrative. It should be complete in itself, and in no way dependent for its artistic merits on outside support whether by way of information or interpretation. Much of what is objectionable in the German-minded way of studying art is that it is pursued either by philologers, with methods forged in the study of texts, inscriptions, and documents, or by historians who use the work of art only as a help to reconstruct the past.

These methods are out of place in the study of works of art created in times about which we have abundant information, and that still exist in the original. Like all things in a wrong place, these methods are a nuisance. They succeed only in burying the work of art under heaps of rubbish, and before long it will need rescue parties to bring it to light again, so that it may serve the primary purpose of any work of art, which is to give life-enhancement.

Antecedent preparation helps one to appreciate a work of art, and there have been writers who helped in the only way that anyone can help a spectator, by putting him into a state of eager and zestful anticipation. There is the risk of dis-

ILLUSTRATION 105

appointment; and authors of the Romantic period, imbued
with all they had read about the keepsake Middle Ages, or a
coloured vignette Renaissance, or a brazen Baroque, authors
like Mrs. Jameson, Rio, Lindsay, and Ruskin, do not always
(not even Ruskin) furnish the vintage for which they make
our mouths water. Yet I cannot sufficiently acknowledge my
debt to Pater for what he wrote about Botticelli and Giorgione, to Burckhardt for his unforgettable and irreplaceable
"Cicerone," to Wölfflin for his masterpiece on classical art,
to Bode for his handbook on Italian sculpture, to Fromentin
for his famous *Maîtres d'Autrefois*, to Baudelaire for all he
said about his Parisian contemporaries, to Jacques Blanche
for articles on nineteenth-century French painters, worthy of
Vasari at his best, to Foucher for his clarifying and constructive work on Greco-Buddhistic art, to Blochet for his essays
on Near and Far Eastern art, and to von Falke for his invaluable history of silk weaving. Nor have I anything but the
highest praise for philologers like Matsulevich and Kalgren,
who in recent years have been able to prove: the first, how
late most surviving Byzantine silverware is, and the second,
how early are many of the Chinese bronzes, thus contributing by their researches not only to the history of art but to
the history of civilization in general.

Before leaving these masters of humanistic appreciation
and scholarship, let me mention Emile Mâle, whose studies
on the iconography of Christian art from the twelfth to the
eighteenth century offer the information and interpretation
best calculated to give one a keen appetite for the enjoyment
of the works of art he is discussing.

Art and Philosophy

Now a word about the philosophers. I use the word because the one I should like to use, the word "sophist," has

taken on a sense well enough justified in most but not in all cases, a sense of deliberate mental trickery, of intellectual dishonesty, or rhetorical meretriciousness. A sophist may be a man who, when called upon to talk on a given theme, frankly confesses his unpreparedness, honestly faces the unsolved problems, and sincerely sums up and concludes. There have been such sophists. The greatest was Socrates. Until the other day we could be proud of Paul Valéry, and we still have George Santayana. Unfortunately, few are like these. In our field, most of them write in German, even when the words are English, French, or Italian. For them the work of art is not an object to be enjoyed, loved, and consumed, an enrichment for ever, but an occasion offered to professional thinkers for delighting in their own acumen, their own subtlety and dialectical skill. They are generous, and would like to share with us the pleasure they get out of exercising their own functions over the work of art. Unluckily, that is not what we should demand of the critic. He should make us hunger and thirst for the work of art, should make us taste it and think of it and not of the critic.

I would not deprive an author of the right to get what he can out of a work of art or literature or of any other thing in the universe. If he is a poet, he will tell us that the heavens declare the glory of the Lord, or that they display "huge cloudy symbols of a high romance." As an interpreter he will give us Pater's famous tirade about Monna Lisa, or Gundolf's penetrating analysis of Shakespeare, or Romano Guardini's of Dostoevski. All is well so long as we do not take the author literally and provided that he sticks to what he sees and feels, and does not foist upon the work of art what exists only in his philosophical imagination or his psychoanalytical dream.

Yet we are far from wishing to throw over illustration, much as we may deplore its being misused and abused not only by the artist but by the historian, the aesthetician, the

ILLUSTRATION 107

metaphysician, the chauvinist, and the cynical popularizer. These exploiters may exasperate us to a degree. The more reason for not wreaking vengeance on the victim of their predatory activities, the art of autonomous illustration.

Illustration as Representation

At bottom, illustration is representation. Memory stores concrete shapes and patterns as images but retains qualities as abstractions only. It is natural therefore that, when we call to mind a work of art, it should appear as a complete design or composition including shapes, attitudes, expressions, and qualities as well; but all as an undivided unity, based on shapes and patterns created by tactile values, movement, and composition. You cannot detach illustration from representation except by reducing the graphic arts to mere geometry; and this has never happened successfully among people who once have practised representation. Even during the most geometrical periods of Helladic art, anthropomorphic and zoomorphic shapes persisted no matter how elongated, angular, and attenuated, as for instance on the Dypilon vases of about 1000 B.C. and indeed in the paintings of the geometrizers of to-day. These last, realizing that no flight from resemblance will get them further than misrepresentation and misshapen distortions, have attempted to imbricate segments of circles and squares over other segments of squares and circles, behind which you are expected to descry the projection of a shape, that is to say of a representation; yet not fixed on the plane before us but coquettishly hidden in the mazes of the artist's brain. Even thus, they seem to find that it is not easy to get away from ordinary shapes; for scrawls, unless reduced to rhythmic order, will tend to assume the aspect of objects as articulate sounds will suggest meanings, although not perhaps those which in the moment of utterance were in the mind of glossolalists like Miss Stein and the latest Joyce. Did not Richepin in his day proclaim that *"Le sens n'est qu'un parasite qui pousse quand même sur le trombone de la sonorité"*?

After nearly sixty years of almost daily wrestling with the question I must confess that the subject, the illustration, is so necessary to the arts of visual representation, that without it these arts cannot exist, and that it is consequently as essential as quality and touch. For art is great only when the decorative and illustrative elements work together. Without spiritual significance the work of art may sink to the level of an object engaging the interest of the wine-taster or the curiosity of the antiquarian, and may rise at highest to the life-enhancing qualities of a spirited sketch, a Japanese *netsuke*, or a *danseuse* by Degas—mere playthings for grown-ups. The complete artist endows his creation with an aura of value and sets it up to be worshipped in the aloofness of a sanctuary. To be thus complete the artist need not confine himself, as was thought until the other day, to subjects whose importance lies in the fields of history, mythology, or romance. Chardin and Cézanne can give this kind of mana to a still life, Velasquez to his weavers, beggars, and blacksmiths, Hals to his old women, Rembrandt to whatever he touched in his last years, Dürer to almost any drawing, Watteau to his wistful idylls. In the presence of these works of art we become the Ion of Euripides, the Joas of Racine, Abraham at Melchizedek's sacrifice, a communicant at the high altar of a cathedral.

Let us ask what we carry away and remember of a painting. The answer will not be the same for all. It must vary from individual to individual, who can be divided roughly into three classes.

Craftsmen, who take in everything touching their craft, and appreciate the problems solved, and the difficulties overcome.

ILLUSTRATION 109

Collectors, whether of public or private galleries, dealers and connoisseurs, intent on possessing the right article, and taking pride in the material and mental means enabling them to acquire it.

Then there are those who love a picture, as they love a friend, a child, a landscape, a noble action, the heroic dead, as they love magnificence, simplicity, dreaming and musing and talking, as they love all these things, but each in a distinct way, not to be confused one with the other. It may be argued that they alone fully and wholly appreciate the work of art, even if they are more interested in the content than in the form, without their thinking of either. It may be asserted even that to the extent that the two other classes also enjoy the work of art, they cease for the moment to be collectors and producers, and become lovers and consumers.

The craftsman, the artist, the producer in short will give praise or blame for the technical proficiency or incompetence of a work of art and will learn practical hints about his craft. The collector-dealer-connoisseur will evaluate it, display it, catalogue it, and quite likely never look at it again. The lover alone is disinterested. He has no desire to own nor even to frame it in time and space with the exquisite precision of philological scholarship. He only wishes to love and enjoy it for ever—seeing that masterpieces are inexhaustible, and by human measurement eternal. *Vie de rose pas de jardinier mort.*

What does this lover, this amateur, carry away from the ecstatic commerce with the work of art if it be not the image, the representation, in short the illustrative part? It is the picture he recalls and cherishes, if it has convinced him of its ideated existence, and he remembers its shapes in their balanced and rhythmic arrangement; not for their own sakes alone but as integral parts of a whole, of a universe where, for a moment no matter how brief, he has touched perfection.

I who am writing this, and have made a certain reputation as a connoisseur and taster and "expert"—what do I carry away from enjoying a picture? I bring away an image of the whole as definite and clear and complete, but as unanalyzed and undetailed, as if it had been a person, and not a representation, with which I had made acquaintance. I classify, identify, and name it exactly as I should any other shape encountered. Its art qualities are as inherent in the shape of the object as character is in the shape of an individual. As I identify a man by something in his silhouette, bulk, carriage, and gait, and above all in his look, so in painting I catch at first sight something which reminds me of a certain artist. Here too it is a look, a turn, a flash, something that he alone puts into his paintings. Nine times out of ten an attribution so made is the right one, and the specific question of art, as distinct from representation, has contributed nothing to the result.

As a matter of fact, with most of us, when off guard, the picture or statue or bas-relief appears in consciousness not as decoration, certainly not as pure decoration, but as illustration or representation, that is to say, as a composition consisting of so many shapes; and I suspect it is through these shapes only that the work of art fufills its mission. It is not the artist's intention, or purpose, that counts in the long run, but the effect of his creation when so weaned and severed from the artist who created it that it has passed utterly from his control. For in art as in life man proposes and events dispose.

The work of art serves not only as a joy for all time, seeing that it offers permanent possibilities of life-enhancement, but from the moment of its completion, for generations to come, it serves as a model, after which the society in whose midst it has appeared tends through its most sensitive members to shape itself. One may venture to say that while the business of the artist is to create the work of art, the business of the

11. Piero della Francesca: Flagellation. Art Gallery, Urbino.

12. Byzantine Cameo: Stylicho and Serena. Cabinet des
Médailles, Paris.

ILLUSTRATION 111

work of art, when created, is to humanize that monstrous polyp "man in the lump." By unconscious imitation of shapes and attitudes, look and gesture; through the ennobling and refining effects of space in architecture and landscape; through the appeal of music and poetry and fiction, and above all through the sublime transports of the art which resumes most of the other arts, ritual as we know it in the Orthodox and Roman Churches, man no matter how slowly, and with what discouraging relapses, is little by little ceasing to be a foul cave-man, a self-glorifying cannibal, a hybristic barbarian, and is growing to be human. Exploiters as well as teachers of their fellow bipeds, from Lycurgus and Plato to Stoics and Jesuits of every myth and creed, have all acted as if well aware of this moulding effect of art, and none more so than the neo-neanderthalers who are now having their day.

The arts of visual representation have had their full share in the task, almost as hopeless as that of the Danaides carrying water in sieves, the task of trying to humanize mankind; and they have had an even more obvious share in recording the steps of this progress. The visual arts furnish the only obtainable record of man's past as it unrolls over early millenniums. Without them we should know nothing of palaeolithic or neolithic man. When written documents and poetry begin, what can hieroglyphs, and cuneiforms, and syllabaries waiting to be deciphered, tell of Egypt, of Mesopotamia, of Crete and Mycenean Greece, that brings their civilization home to us as do their paintings, their seals, their statues, and their bas-reliefs? But for these, we should merely hear boasts of conquerors, penitential groans of primitive psalmists, and obtain glimpses of legal systems anticipating the dreariness of the Biblical Leviticus. For literature is a late comer, and before "Homer" and his Hebrew contemporaries, writing was not used to express and record the sheer joy of living that we find depicted in the Early Empire reliefs of

Egypt, and the pride of life radiating from the body of a Kephren or a Naramsin. When the written word finally triumphs, leaving other instruments of expression behind, we should not only fail to supply it with the right imagery but we would have to visualize this imagery as absurdly as did our forebears of 1700, who staged the heroes and heroines of antiquity in wigs and furbelows, and crinolines and small clothes. Early Greek vases tell how Homer pictures his Achaeans and Trojans; paintings at Pompeii and marbles in Rome how Virgil visualized Aeneas and Dido; ivories and mosaics how Claudian saw Stilicho and Serena, and how Procopius saw Justinian and Theodora; while Giotto and Simone Martini reveal how Dante pictured to himself his Beatrice, how Petrarch his Laura. We have learned the lesson so well that except as a sensation of the day no experiment succeeds which attempts to depict or stage events of the past in the costumes and surroundings of the present. Our very fictions must, like Shakespeare's *Hamlet* or Goethe's *Faust*, be put in their historical perspective of time and circumstance.

CHAPTER III

DEFINITIONS AND CLARIFICATIONS
The Significant

S O MUCH for illustration, and it is a great deal. "If illustration and representation are so important," you may well ask, "why all this fuss over decoration, over form? You made them all but sovereign, and now you do the same for the others." Not quite. Decoration is sovereign only in objects of art, as I have observed more than once. It is a minor kingdom but a kingdom of its own. Illustration is not so autonomous, at least not in the same way. Unless it is reduced to mere pictography, as still practised by little children and people of arrested development, illustration is based on the products of decoration, I mean the striving for tactile values, for movement, for space, for arrangement, for harmony—on form, in short. Form creates the types and proportions, the action and the spacing, the pattern in fact that intervenes between the artist and things visible, and dictates his particular way of seeing, his individual communication. This, however, cannot come about after the manner of a game of draughts or chess. Behind it there must be a sense of the significant.

What do we mean by "the significant," a term that has considerable currency in the art writing of the last few decades, although, as so often in this species of writing, nobody seems to have been at the trouble of defining it? I have myself used it generally in two senses, and have written of "material" and "spiritual" significance, as if they were en-

tirely different. Perhaps I was too sure fifty years ago that the
border line between the two could be clearly drawn. The distinction I must have meant to make then, and that I still
should insist upon, may be stated in some such way as this:
Material significance refers to the tactile values, the movement, the arrangement of figures tending singly or in combination to the impressive, the monumental, the heroic. I
discover little that is imposing or majestic in the bronze
colossus of Barletta, or in the even huger marble statue of
Constantine whose fragments stand and sprawl in one of the
courtyards of the Capitol, nor yet in the "Farnese Hercules."
Neither bulk, nor mass, nor muscle bestows material significance. Pindar speaks of his townsman Hercules as a little
fellow, and it took a Macedonianized and, worse still, a
Romanized Hellas to represent him as a giant. It is not the
physical but the ethical, the moral weight that overawes us
in the presence of certain Giottos, Masaccios, and Piero della
Francescas, in a way that Michelangelo himself seldom
equals, and Giulio Romano, Salviati, Vasari, and Allori with
their prize-fighters never so much as suggest. The Giottos
and Masaccios and Pieros are convincingly present, every bit
as present as the diorite statues of early dynastic Egypt, as
the finest Sumerian basalts, the marble fragments of the
Parthenon pediments, or the overpowering seated figures
from Branchidae. No work of the quality of these in sculpture or painting has in the course of fifty years failed to comfort and tune me. "Tune" is the word that expresses what
works of art with material significance do for us. They do
not say anything that could not be said better in words
(Velasquez is never eloquent and Veronese is almost dumb),
but they tune us to feel as noble and serene as they are. And
what would one not give to have that feeling even for a
minute!

By "spiritual significance," on the other hand, I mean to
designate whatever affords us the prospects of easing the

dead weight of matter; whatever gives us the hope that our lives will amount to something more than the unwinding of the coil of energy which we brought with us at birth; but promises that our activities will be progressively directed toward the building of a social structure where it will be safe and praiseworthy to live free from care, and greed, and cunning; where being will count more than doing, the intransitive more than the transitive; where man may dwell once more in an earthly paradise, but this time feeding as sinlessly from the tree of knowledge as from the tree of life, and blessed by the gods revealed by his own consciousness and conscience.

How is all this to be rendered in the terms of sculpture and painting?

The arts of graphic, pictorial, and plastic representation take place in space. They consist of separate visual units even if their contents, when narrative, comprise successive episodes, as happens in the so-called "continuous" manner, which is common occurrence in times of emerging and declining art, but is rare at other times. Such is the marvellous scroll that twines about Trajan's column and which came at the end of a period that was still creative although approaching a precipitous decline. The visual arts cannot compete in expressing spiritual significance with arts like music and poetry, the drama, the opera, and ritual. This for a double reason. They cannot deal with the passage from one state to another, nor with transition from pleasure to pain, joy to sorrow, or the reverse. They can convey only one action and one mood at a time; but, as said before, they have the advantage and suffer from the disadvantage of permanency, while what takes place in time vanishes and can only be approximately reproduced.

It follows that selection plays a more decisive part in visual representation than in the other parts. Homer may nod, Beethoven seesaw, and Wagner moo, but the switch-back railway over which they hurry will swing us on to a new excellence before the effects of the inferior minute have found time to annoy; so that in the end the creator's purpose is manifest, and inadvertencies and blemishes are forgotten. The painter and sculptor, on the other hand, must think out clearly what design, what pattern of lines and colours, of projections and retreats, light and shade, will make the spectator perceive what he, the artist, sees in a given subject. What he achieves lies open for permanent inspection. He must bear in mind that faces which always grin, looks always agonized or ecstatic, bodies contorted with suffering, will bore or distress and are not life-enhancing but life-diminishing.

The problem then is how to convey, in terms that are life-enhancing, a full sense of this spiritual significance and not merely information about it. I speak deliberately of "information," for many if not most people discover spiritual significance only where it overawes or even terrifies. But are the Ottonian miniatures, the Beatus manuscripts of Spain and Aquitaine, and the gables and portals of Languedoc, of Vézelay and Chartres, representing apocalyptic images of dread and woe, or their stupendous culmination in Michelangelo's "Last Judgement," are these life-enhancing or merely overwhelming? Are the two qualities usually known as the sublime and the beautiful, so much as compatible? Are they not mutually exclusive?

Defenders of this type of art, that occasionally occurs in France, and rather more frequently in Spain, that is rare in Italy, but pervades Germany, where it attains to Ottonian genius, and which in Dürer reaches universal and not merely national eminence—the advocates for these fierce illustrators call them Expressionists, and we may accept the term, seeing that they give expression to their own feeling, and forget the event or object itself, screaming out their own reactions towards it, with the purpose of frightening us away from what makes life worth living, and directing our energies and our concentrated effort to preparing for the day of judgement.

This kind of message, I repeat, is no more art than the bugle or trumpet that incites to war, or the pornographic story or picture that excites to lust. Its undoubted claim to superiority rests not upon artistic, but on ethical and metaphysical grounds. No matter how distorted, how bogey-faced, how grotesque the apocalyptic message, it serves to remind us of the fundamental truth that lies at the bottom of spiritual values—the truth, namely, that human life, consciously lived, rests on tragic foundations. For whether you mythicize the universe or refuse to give it an anthropomorphic Deity, this universe seems indifferent to humanity. The religions that still require such a god make him so abstract that we cannot conceive him. As for his purposes and behests, we know too well that they are not his, but are imposed by the social order to which we belong. If our highest destiny were to glorify him for ever, as we used to be told, even when he submits us to worse tortures than the material universe ever does, what comfort can that bring (to any except word-intoxicated, incandescent mystics) that cannot be obtained by ecstatic admiration of astronomical clock-work! The universe may not even be accused of as much as indifference to man. Nothing should be attributed to the universe that implies consciousness or any kind of awareness.

It is more than doubtful whether anywhere outside our own species there is an awareness of the distinction between subject and object, so that we can risk entertaining and acting upon the conceit that in the entire universe it is only we human beings who are endowed with that miracle of miracles, consciousness of self, and who are aware of the universe as an object of contemplation, of study and research.

The universe we ordinarily have to deal with, we who are not physicists or astronomers, the universe within the range of our almost unassisted senses, we designate as Nature. It is not by submitting to it completely, or by wallowing in the satisfactions with which it rewards every other animal, even those of the most rudimentary type, that we have evolved into the humane as well as human intelligences that we now are. It is rather by facing nature and getting the better of her, and making her work for us and, if need be, fight for us. Not only in the world without but within ourselves must we face and fight nature and try to tame the tiger, the snake, or the louse lurking in the innermost recesses of the most civilized heart. We must get as far as we can away from the jungle, where, as wild beasts, we struggle with other wild beasts for food, for sex, for power, and for display. As far away as we ourselves can go without losing any advantage of being the instruments that we are: instruments not only of intelligence and precision, but of feeling, of sympathy, understanding, enjoyment, meditation, and dreaming. At all costs we must avoid perfecting one side of the instrument at the expense of the others. We must not, like the Japanese military caste of the last decades, turn our energies to becoming mere mechanisms of destruction, "human bullets" as one of their own writers called them, nor like Nordic barbarians must we sacrifice everything to berserker orgies of furious living, nor again, like animals in rut, become mere agents of the reproductive instinct.

On the other hand, we must beware of refining and thinning down the instrument till it breaks. Man must keep a firm control of his senses and his impulses, but not destroy them as would the ascetics. Plato would have man a charioteer commanding and directing his passions and appetites like well-trained steeds, but we must not be like the driver who, unable to make them obey, chooses in his despair and spite to destroy them.

If the universe becomes self-conscious in man alone, he is justified in using it for his own purposes, than which, for us, there are no higher. Living according to nature did not to the ancient Greek, and does not to us, mean living according to nature as we have just defined it, that is to say the universe of our ken, but according to our own nature, as the instrument whereby we grasp and use the world outside us. Living according to nature means therefore not, as Rousseau would have it, living in a state of nature, but according to what we can get out of nature for the perfecting of ourselves as instruments, and for the continuous improvement of our House of Life, founded on nature but distinct from, and in a sense beyond, and above it.

The effort of man, ever since he began to be human, has been to build for himself a nest in which he can find shelter first from hostile inorganic and organic matter, then from his own kind, and later from the figments of his imagination. Although he could not eliminate death, he almost learned to deny it, and was fast eliminating disease. "The heir of all the ages in the foremost files of time," the average man of let us say 1910, what with Christian Science, what with "twilight sleep," and other cults of the "somehow good," was feeling so safe, so cosy and cheerily confident, so buoyed up with hope, so happy in a nest enlarged and transformed into an ideal cowshed, that when the *Titanic* sank with the loss of thousands of highly respectable lives, there was a cry not of woe and contrition, as over the loss of the "White Ship" eight centuries earlier, but of indignation as over a contract that had not been properly carried out, a disaster not different in kind from a failure of the New York and New Haven railway. A tragic note was scarcely heard, and the feeling of awe, the sense of the tragic seemed lost. It has taken the man-quake started in 1914, and still troubling us, to bring back some sense of the tragic. The full return of that sense to Euramericans may not be too dearly paid for by the dreadful happenings of the last thirty-five years, and the loathsome vapours of brutal doctrine which they discharge.

Spiritual Significance in Visual Representation

We should now be ready to give a rough definition of the term "spiritual significance" as appertaining to the arts of visual representation. It is what inspires and pervades the compositions which offer the noblest models for mankind to attain, models of realizable and never impossible states of being and ways of living. It permeates with tragic feeling pictures which seem to be images of the pride and the joy of life. It excludes tragic events, because they are fit subjects for literature and music and not for the visual arts, but it can suggest the fragility and the precariousness of our condition in a universe that knows nothing of our needs, our pretensions, our claims.

To make my meaning clear let me adduce examples dealing with or illustrating ideals: Raphael's "Disputa," "School of Athens," and "Parnassus" seem now, as they did fifty years ago, the clearest and most convincing visions of the perfect existence for which we yearn, and which we hope to attain. The Elgin Marbles and kindred creations of Greek and Hellenistic art, a few of Giovanni Bellini's maturer works, a number of Giorgionesque portraits, single figures and compositions, as many by the mature Titian, by Veronese and Tintoret, Velasquez, Rembrandt and Van Dyck, as many again by Reynolds and Raeburn, David, Ingres, and Watts, each and all and many of other works of art, not least in the field of eighteenth-century French sculpture, have all contributed toward peopling the House of Humanity which art was gradually constructing. The space composers like Bramante, Raphael, and Bernini, and the designers of the Place de la Concorde and of the stretch from the Champs Élysées to the Arc de l'Étoile have offered appropriate urban surroundings for a humanized population, and Perugino and

Domenichino, the Carracci and Poussin, Claude and Turner, Corot and Rousseau have furnished the landscape backgrounds.

Let me turn to some instances of visual art that bring home our precarious position in the universe. I am not sure whether to mention here the early marble in the Roman Thermae Museum of a young woman (perhaps a daughter of Niobe) falling on one knee and starting back as if shot down by envious gods. Her pain is almost too physical. The same objection certainly excludes the far inferior Laocoön group, and the Slaves of the Louvre, not so much better than the Laocoön, despite the fact that they were done by Michelangelo. The funeral reliefs of the fifth and fourth centuries B.C., generally although not always Attic, communicate the regret for life with a poignancy that touches but does not wound. The precariousness and fragility of existence are brought home to us with almost the same stab in Botticelli's "Spring" as in his "Birth of Venus," in Signorelli's "Pan," in Giorgione's "Soldier and Gipsy" as well as in his "Fête Champêtre," in Watteau's "Embarquement pour Cythère," but with a sharpness that has no sting, a reminder that in painting, as in music and poetry, "our sweetest songs are those that tell of saddest thought." Sadder than these but yet soothing and inviting to serene resignation are the landscapes of Ruysdael, Rembrandt, Seghers, Koninck, Constable, and of many a Sung painter, as for example the master of the "Tartar Horseman" or Hsia Kwei with his noble synopses.

In actual life, few experiences give us this shudder over the evanescence of human achievement, the futility of endeavour and the frivolity of glory. There is no more ironical and yet more soothing comment on human fate than the sight of ruins, not to be sure like those now of Rome and presently of Athens, faked up like bad teeth by dentists, grazed by hurrying and thundering traffic, elbowed by the denizens of a vast rabbit warren, but ruins still unruined like Karnak and Palmyra, Leptis and Lambesis, Ephesus and Miletus, Priene and Hierapolis, as lonely as Shelley's Ozymandias, and as deserted as "the courts where Jamshyd gloried and drank deep." There you behold fortresses, palaces and towers, basilicas, quays, vast colonnades and colossal entablatures gnawed by the tooth of time and falling under their own weight; while gigantic statues and obelisks evaporate like ether, although in thousands of years instead of in so many seconds.

This actual experience cannot be communicated in the visual arts by the mere representation of ruins. The painters who have indulged in it, like Pannini, and Piranesi, and Guardi, seldom give me a sense of the gnawing of time. Their interest is either too pictorial or too expressionistic, or merely scenic, as were their early precursors Mantegna, and Cossa, and Bramantino. On the other hand, I find it in Verrocchio's design for a Nativity now at Sheffield, in more than one late Titian, his Bridgewater Diana canvases for instance, in his Escorial "Martyrdom of Saint Lawrence," or again in his sublime last work, the Venice Academy "Pietà." Most frequently and most convincingly it is brought home to me in the paintings of Hubert Robert. It is not the arrogant crushing pilons of the Sesostrises, Sargons, and other oppressors that Hubert Robert displays as crumbling, breaking, and falling, but the noble structures of civilized man, splendid dwellings with their pleasant terraces and gardens, their statuary and vases neglected, in disrepair, peopled by waifs and strays, and falling into dust under the pitiless touch of time. You would not dare to tread these stairs, lean on these parapets, or rest under these arches.

A feeling not remote from this, yet more ironical, and at the same time more tragic, overcomes one before a portrait like Titian's Philip II of Spain, the dapper little man, offering an infant son to Victory. The contrast between what we see and what we know is too great, between this homunculus and the vast burthens weighing down this cropped and bearded head, so commonplace yet lying on its starched golilla like the Baptist's head on Herodias's platter. Or look at a small full length of Charles I of England painted by an inferior Dutch artist who portrays him as he saw him; a pretty silhouette, daintily placed against magnificent edifices which he does not dominate or even possess. It is so different from the "man of blood with his long essenced hair" of Roundhead imagination, and still more unlike the gracious figure in surroundings as much his own as the garments he wears, which Van Dyck offers us. Plastered against the events in which he was involved, this small figure produces scarcely more effect than a postage stamp on a wall.

Illustration in the hand of a master of visual representation can do this and more besides without violating the rules of the game. It can make one shiver as with a wind blown from beyond "the flaming walls of the world." Certain skies and horizons of Van Eyck, Giambellino, and Savoldo, Titian and Tintoret, to confine myself to artists with whom I am best acquainted, produce that effect, yet not so cosmic nor so sublime as the heavens in early Christian mosaics, no matter how much made over—those, for instance, of Santa Pudenziana, or SS. Cosmas and Damian in Rome. The gold background is responsible for much of the impression, and the rest is due to the orchestral effect of juxtaposed colours in the individual glass cubes, each with its own refulgence, surpassing what could be obtained by a kindred process with wools or silks in textiles, or with oil paints as practised by our late Impressionists. With these means, and with such a background, the artist needed but to use the vocabulary, the accepted shapes of his period, to produce a majestic design like the "Vision of Ezekiel" in the Apse of Hosios David at Salonika, or the "Virgin" at San Donato in Murano, sublime and interstellar. But the walls of Hagia Sophia, corruscating with the splendour and glow of their gold tesserae alone, with small crosses only to intensify by slightly breaking the monotony of the sensation, inspired perhaps more yearning for a heaven which they somehow suggest and almost reveal, than any figure compositions. And indeed many a panel picture of the fourteenth and fifteenth centuries, whether Italian or German, French or Catalan, owes half its appeal to its gold background.

Here let me say parenthetically that mosaic makes us stumble over a curious paradox. It is that in the arts of visual representation colour in the widest sense of the word, including black and white as well as gold and silver and lapis lazuli, is far more effective in illustration than in decoration. It affects moods almost as quickly as music does, and like music liberates memories and inspires dreams. With the help of line it can suggest, as by themselves figures seldom do, the Beyond, the Sublime, that is to say the horror of the outer universe that knows us not, the starting back as from an alluring abyss, and the joy of the ensuing relief.

This and much else could be said about illustration if, instead of offering brief and perhaps inconsistent jottings, one were to write about it exhaustively. And partly for that reason they may sound as if in flat contradiction to what I wrote earlier about decoration. There it may have seemed as if decoration were all that mattered in art, and now as if illustration alone counted.

Decoration and Illustration Are Critical Fictions

The truth is that no thinking can be done without fictions. Not even the law, where exactness is so imperative, can get on without the notorious "legal fictions." Yet there is nothing more dangerous than to mistake these unavoidable verbalisms, these verbal myths, for entities of experience.

Unless we keep well in mind that they are mere aids, mere nets for seizing and retaining the little of chaos that we can grasp and fix, unless we are constantly aware that they are no more than tools, no more than makeshifts in the struggle for expression, they will turn into those principles and dogmas philosophical, theological, ethical, political, which are the chief source, except for "acts of God," of most of the disasters that mankind has to endure.

"Decoration" and "illustration" are myths, abstractions of the kind just described. In experience they are one. Only for purposes of discourse do we separate them as I have done, seeming to assign primacy to the one I happened to be discussing. In the conscious enjoyment of the work of art the contradiction does not have to disappear. It never existed.

Art is great when technical and spiritual advances, progressing independently, synchronize and give each other the hand, as in Greece from the sixth century B.C. to the Antonine period and even later, in Byzantium during the Macedonian period, in France during the late Romanesque and the early Gothic period. Otherwise it is apt to degenerate into genre and Kleinkunst if technical alone, and into illustration if only spiritual.

It has been a commonplace of the ages to say that form and content are inseparable and even indistinguishable. Yet few are those who perceive them so. The craftsman and the dilettante who dabbles in a craft and tries to babble its cant are scarcely aware of the contents, while the mere spectator seldom gives a thought to anything but the illustration. My experience is that there is more hope for the second than for the first. If the spectator has the culture to feel the representation intensely, one can often succeed in leading him to an appreciation of the form. I cannot recall instances of the opposite. "If he has the culture"—but what do we mean by culture? I, for my part, mean the state of mind, the attitude toward life, the ever present, ever tormenting problem of human destiny brought home to us by the awareness of man's place in the universe, the conduct dictated by this awareness, and the effort to build a House of Life where man will be able to attain the highest development that his animal nature will permit, taking him ever further away from the jungle and the cave, and bringing him nearer and nearer to that humanistic society which under the name of Paradise, Elysium, Heaven, City of God, Millennium has been the craving of all good men these last four thousand years and more.

Art, in the fullest and most inclusive sense of the term, plans, builds, and furnishes this House of Life, and it is natural that this should be best understood by those who have been brought up on the classics, that is to say the works of art which manifest that purpose. To my knowledge it is none of us professional critics or historians who have written most comprehendingly about the painter's art, still less the painters themselves, but novelists like Balzac in his *Chef d'Oeuvre Inconnu*, Gogol in his *Portrait*, and Ljeskow in his *Sealed Angel*. Among my own acquaintances it has nearly always been those brought up on the Bible, the Greek and Latin literature, on Dante and Chaucer, Shakespeare and Milton, Tasso and Racine, Wordsworth, Keats and Shelley, Matthew Arnold, Goethe, Schiller and Hölderlin, on Pergolesi and Bach, Gluck and Mozart, Beethoven and Berlioz, Brahms and Bruckner, who have most enjoyed and best appreciated the architecture and sculpture of the centuries and the painting of the last eight hundred years. I venture to say that not only the architecture of the Italian Renaissance was humanistic, as Geoffrey Scott wrote, but that all art which *is* art and not mere curiosity, or dexterity, or technique, or a mere plaything, is humanistic.

Humanism, as I would wish to interpret it, is the will to shape, to adorn a world which we as instruments can function in, to the ever greater advantage of ourselves and of the

13. Page from Ottonian MS. Staatsbibliothek, Munich.

14. Fifth-century Greek: Funerary relief from Dipylon, Athens.

universal House of Life we are busy constructing and establishing.

By "humanism" I do not mean what it perhaps originally meant, when cultural advance seemed impossible without the recovery of the classics, namely devotion to the grammatical studies of the Greek and Roman authors, so well pictured in Browning's "Grammarian's Funeral," but what I attempted above to define as "culture," and what I will now try to explain in greater detail.

Humanism consists in the belief that something worth while can be made of life on this planet; that mankind can be humanized, that it is happiness to work toward that goal. A humanized mankind is the supreme creation, the greatest conceivable work of art, the work of art which the philosophers of antiquity from Plato to Plotinus tell us that God was creating. We are his helpers, whether aware of it or not, each contributing what he can, rubble, ashlar, or foundation stone; ornament, decoration, or humble utility according to his capacities. Humanism would make us conscious of our task, and not only would give us faith in its ultimate, if ever so distant, achievement, but teach us to delight in the pursuit; and as it developed, our understanding would reveal more and more of the vision and fortify the determination to realize it. Our world may be nothing but the order that we, as instruments created for a peculiar way of selecting and ordering, are shaping into a cosmos. The more we refine and perfect ourselves as instruments, the better the cosmos that we are winning out of chaos will be.

Humanism stands in no contradiction and still less in conflict with the hope of a Kingdom of Heaven, whether within us or Beyond. It is opposed to no life-affirming religion. It quarrels with those beliefs only that condemn the enjoyment of life upon this earth by proclaiming it a hell, or at best a vale of tears. Humanism believes that if there is a

Beyond—which it neither affirms nor denies—it will be a state for which terrestrial experience has prepared, trained, and educated us. There it is at one with St. Basil the Great, who taught that the world was an educational institution for the rational soul. And the great humanist Wilhelm von Humboldt says: "We are here to live, and only what we have achieved through living can we carry away with us."

The earth, then, is the school where alone we can learn what our minds and souls are capable of receiving. Religions that command us to shun this training ground, this playing-field, this gymnasium, this university, we must abandon to their suicidal impulses. We must, however, be on guard against their contagion as well as against their deliberate attacks on our House of Life. Yet those who turn their backs on the earth, on the body, on the world are not the most dangerous suicides. Despite their zealous and tireless preaching, they have few genuine followers. Their doctrines are too repellent for half-humanized men and women.

The worst enemies of humanism are not these, but those who commit suicide with regard to the effort that, for thousands of years, mankind has been making to tame the brute within us, and to strive toward a society based on goodwill, mutual understanding, and mutual respect, in which we must work eagerly and rationally to realize the utmost humanization of which we are capable.

· For the average man and woman, that is to say for the incompletely humanized man and woman, this is an ideal hard to entertain, an effort too strenuous to undertake. They are ready to be persuaded that these ideals are lies and that it is vain to strive after them. On the contrary! They are determined to cast off what humanization has already been imposed upon them, and give vent to animal impulses. Being, however, animals with minds, they must use their minds, as the Japanese have done in the last three quarters of a century, for mechanical organization only, for mass production, for frenzied living, ever ready to fall upon their neighbours, to kill as many as convenient and exploit the rest at their pleasure. Doctrines, so opposed to what churches, philosophies, and the arts have tried to inculcate with uncertain results, are accepted by the half- or quarter-humanized person as corresponding to conclusions about life which they of themselves have subconsciously reached. Moreover, the preachers of these doctrines offer a certainty of animal satisfactions that appeals irresistibly to this average or sub-average person in all grades of society from the highest to the lowest. He is promised freedom as well, the only freedom he can appreciate, freedom from responsibility, from having to take thought. Everything will be done for him from cradle to grave, everything directed: his training, his labour, his leisure, his mating, and all with communal marching to step and hypnotizing music. Nor is religion left out. He will be taught to have faith in the increase of his tribe, in its right to occupy the earth, and in the infallibility, invincibility, and omnipotence of its god, its leader.

The apostles of these doctrines may compromise with the churches, those particularly whose policies tend toward a Jesuit Paraguay. To us humanists they can offer no terms: our ideals are irreconcilably opposed. Between them and us there can be no peace nor truce. Our opposed policies cannot be neighbours on this small planet.

They have every apparent advantage. The crowd-minded—still the overwhelming majority—are with them. Force, fraud, conclusions drawn with unswerving logic—the logic of the mad—from inhuman axioms and perverted premises, magnificent and persistent organization, are theirs. (It is sad how easy it is to keep up continuous efforts for evil, and how hard for good! [1])

Nevertheless history teaches that mankind is tending toward our ideal. Slowly, it is true! After an advance of a hun-

[1] Written in 1940.

dred feet it slips back ninety-nine feet and nine inches. Yet given time, three inches gained in each hundred years means progress. The effort avails and, sure of our goal, we can labour zestfully to reach it. We are not discouraged by setbacks. Like the artists that we are, we enjoy each day's work, grateful for the day's gift of happiness in the gratifying exercise of our highest functions. We can, moreover, cherish the same faith in the destiny of mankind as one has intuitively in the future of one's great-grandchildren, a faith which makes us glad to work for them although we do not expect to see the results of our efforts.

At the far distant end we descry a perfected Humanity. No Philistines, no Ishmaelites, no Goths, no Scythians shall prevent us from realizing our ideal of a completely humanized Mankind. All the arts contribute their share, and not least those arts of visual representation which engage our activities as students of art history.

Realism

In terms of art history, I venture at this point to say a few words about recent tendencies in art and their relation to events in politics. We may be sure that what has happened and is happening is typical of what has occurred again and again, although not on such a scale; and if the worst has not yet occurred, as it did in our fourth to eighth centuries, it is because the decline has not gone far enough. Indeed, the worst may be avoided.

Realistic literature and art were bound to serve as a prelude to "realistic" politics. What is realistic art? As at present practised, it exists to celebrate those cravings of our nature for what is most animal, physiological, and zoological which idealism tried to ignore when it could not suppress them. "Behold your gods, O Israel." Not the invisible and unapproachable Presence of Deity but a pig, a hyaena, a snake.

Realism would tear the mask off the happy hypocrite and reveal, not as in Max Beerbohm's apologue, a face grown as beautiful and as kindly as what he wished to appear, but as gross and cruel as enraged pessimists expect to find it.

Modern realism has had forerunners: in antiquity the Cynics; in the Middle Ages monkish preachers like St. Bernard. The Cynic, the late revivalistic Cynic, was not contented with recognizing the obvious facts about human nature. He insisted on tracking the basest and foulest motives to the lair where they lurk and hide from consciousness; he delighted in smoking them out, as it were, and making men fully aware of them. In doing this, the Cynic compelled men to measure the abyss yawning between their ideals and their animal nature, he forced them to face facts humbly and to try to get the better of the beast within them, thus preparing the way for Christianity. The mediaeval ranter wanted to turn us away from the abominations of this life to a beatitude to be attained in the future. Our contemporary realists would impose their view of society as the eternal and only reality, presenting it as the cowboy waiter handed his unsavoury dish with one hand, a pistol in the other, and the snarl: "There's hash."

For realism is not disinterested. It has a dogma to proclaim, a theology to defend. It teaches that man is born a beast, that civilization does not make him less but more of a beast; that life is hell and that the only satisfaction to be got out of it is to recognize the fact and to dance over it a witch's sabbath of sneering glee.

The earliest modern realists, Zola for instance, were still romantic enough to admit animal joys which were social as well as physiological, as even Petronius did in Nero's Rome. But now nothing is considered real that does not present to our lips the vilest dregs from the sinks of human nature; all the rest is bunkum, fairy tales, dope, drugs, administered by capitalists to keep us enslaved.

Art offers a vision and prophecy of coming events. It deals with easily shaped subject matter, not with hard facts. Art is imagination, and it takes less time to imagine than to perform. Yet soon enough what art has manifested turns out to have served as a model that life tends to copy.

If art has persuaded us that we are beasts and that life is a hell (it is not hard to believe both, seeing how readily we discover them in our own breasts) then away with lies, with hypocrisies, with "humanity" so-called, away with ideals and aspirations. Let us live as the brute beasts, and, not being human, let us feed on bread alone, material bread, and give up longing for spiritual food; let us indulge in sex like worshippers of Priapus and multiply the power of our rulers, the archfiends for whom possession of this power procures the supreme satisfaction a devil-man can enjoy.

On this foundation totalitarian New Orders are erected, and meet with the consent and approval of the many who believe nothing to be real but the satisfaction of the animal appetites, and of lust for power.

Unfortunately, all institutions have to act more or less on the same assumptions, and seem hypocritical and false to the puerile and half-educated mind which cannot believe that some institutions mean to be not only administrative but educative. As administrators they must act on a low view of human nature. Yet they do not always rejoice in iniquity while profiting by it. On the contrary, the best of them try to lead toward a goal that will be divinely human, where the individual will be a full partaker in an endless but glorious and zestful adventure.

Until not long ago art helped to construct and light the way to this divinely human goal. Society followed, and with some success. So-called realism, sneering at everything that is abysmal in human nature, can do nothing but debase it into droves and herds or, at best, into hives.

After a visit to an exhibition of Negro sculpture held more

than thirty years ago at the Petit Palais in Paris, I recall saying that its success presaged a return to savagery, no difficult journey compared with the one undertaken by the Italian Renaissance when, on the discovery of so many Greek and Latin authors and of a few ancient marbles, bronzes, gems, and coins, it aspired to return to "the glory that was Greece and the grandeur that was Rome." For it is only too easy to believe what is said against mankind, while education of a high order is needed to inspire confidence in the possibilities of spiritual improvement.

Classical education has been an attempt in this direction. If it could be given to every member in a community, success would follow, however slowly. Unfortunately, even the best intentioned governments of to-day must waste their wealth on war and preparation for war, and cannot afford to educate the masses, who therefore fall victims to policies that promise and to some extent fulfill the promise of bread and circuses.

Function of Art

Art in the full sense of the word (which includes ritual and myth no less than the twin sister of both, the opera), art does not humanize by precept but by example. No matter how little the artist means to influence character and conduct, he yet does influence them; and the less he preaches the more he creates. Sermons may edify, frighten, or stir, but their effect is as momentary as immediate. The artistic creation, beyond the ideated sensations it may convey, penetrates into the depths of our organism through the proneness to identify ourselves with objects, and to imitate them. As observed again and again, we cannot help assuming the scale, proportions, and attitudes, imitating the actions of the figures as well as feeling the mood of a work of art. If both are heroic and serene we tend to become heroic and serene; if both are mean and tormented, we tend to become mean and tormented. From Plato's day at latest, states, societies, synagogues, churches, and conventicles have deliberately tried to harness art for their particular advantage and, failing that, to suppress it altogether. Ethical considerations and questions of conduct are nevertheless not excluded in one's appreciation of the work of art; nor indeed can aesthetical values, resting as they ultimately do on instinct and will, be separated from ethical. We must, however, allow no sophistries to weaken our conviction that value exists only for valuers. As we ourselves are the sole valuers we know of, and as we can never get beyond ourselves, values must remain human and, if civilized as well as human, they must be humanistic.

Great art is the exponent as well as builder of this ideal, and has the advantage over the other so-called religious ideals that it excludes dogmas and the sanctions resting upon them. The only drawback to the humanistic ideal is that it offers no make-believe consolations, and no inconceivable immortality. It is an ideal, as Walter Lippmann would say, for the ethically and mentally grown up, and therefore faces death serenely as inevitable, provided it comes, as come it will when we are more advanced, not merely in the course of nature but as an ecstasy of realization. Considering that, in the ever changing universe, it is unthinkable that climatic conditions will always remain favourable to a humanized society upon this planet, is it not a more desirable consummation to "end in beauty," too refined to live under unceasing adverse circumstances, than to submit to the worse and worst, and sink into conditions more and more brutish, before perishing like the pterodactyl, ichthyosaurus, and others of our geological forebears. Better cultivate the state of mind of Homer's Alcinoüs, who knew that Scheria and his Phaeacians would incur the wrath of Poseidon if he treated Odysseus humanely, and perish if he sent him home to Ithaca. He preferred humane conduct to survival. "Man's story," said Arthur Balfour, "is a brief and transitory episode in the life of one of the meanest of the planets." True. The more reason for making it unique. For us it is the only reason for the existence of the universe.

Removal of Misunderstandings

I must say no more in this place about illustration, and should not have ventured to say so much but for the likelihood that I may not have another chance to correct the impression made by my books of fifty years ago. One cannot write anything, certainly nothing critical, philosophical, or historical, without conscious or unconscious reference to current ideas. I was then addressing a public accustomed, under the influence of Rio, Ruskin, Lindsay, and the Pre-Raphaelites, to see little in a painting but the illustration. I felt the need of emphasizing the importance of decoration, at that time so seldom mentioned except among craftsmen, and by them from the merely technical side. It never occurred to me that in consequence I should be accused of ignoring or despising illustration—I who never failed to insist on the spiritual significance of a Michelangelo or a Raphael, a Leonardo or a Piero della Francesca, a Fra Angelico or a Giotto. But the public takes no notice of reservations, or attenuations, and recalls that passage only which brings them something startling. It is less easy to understand that serious students should have written of me as if I were an apostle of "mere visibility" in the work of art. I never have been that, if they mean that the work of art for me stops at the purely retinal sensation. To begin with I have never believed in such a sensation in relation with the work of art, and besides I have always maintained that the same work of art had a prodigious number of things to tell us, and have been no more disposed to sacrifice them for "mere visibility" than was Goethe for instance in that ideal piece of criticism, his essay on the Laocoön. I simply insisted that the work of art itself should tell it, and not have it told by some poet of the past or the present, or by a sentimental or subtle commentator who, perhaps without being aware of it himself, makes the work of art the vehicle of his own moods and tenses, joys and sorrows, and aspirations. I have pleaded that the work should be left to speak its own language. It is unfortunate that in human discourse we can speak with words only, and it is inevitable that we should try to find verbal equivalents for everything we see and hear; yet this should not lead us to attribute these verbalisms to the mind of the artist and to claim that they influenced him. They are only our humble efforts to make others, who have not yet learned his language, feel what he is saying.

To resume and conclude: Illustration should be autonomous and say all it has to say just as much as poetry, and with no greater need of being translated into any other medium of expression. Indeed, if an illustration does not succeed in creating a world of its own complete in itself with convincing shapes and a spiritual atmosphere, it is not illustration in the sense which I have attempted to render current, but in the commonly understood sense of book or newspaper illustration.

Life-Enhancement

In my previous publications I never questioned that what life-enhancement meant in connection with illustration was self-evident. Much, however, is self-evident in youth that ceases to be so as, with age, one recedes further and further from the naïve certainties of early years. Let me say then that by "life-enhancement" I mean the ideated identification of ourselves with a person, the ideated participation in an action, the ideated plunging into a state of being, or state of mind, that makes one feel more hopefully, more zestfully alive; living more intense, more radiant a life not only physically but morally and spiritually as well; reaching out to the topmost peak of our capacities, contented with no satisfaction lower than the highest. The impulse to this ideated identification possesses everyone. On the lower level we live ideated moments with athletes and prize fighters, with stunt aviators, with sensational criminals, with cinema stars; on a somewhat higher level with successful businessmen, triumphant politicians, and victorious generals; on the highest with pioneers, civilizers, heroes, saints, gods. Many of us read incessantly about Napoleon and his epic, and would read as much about Alexander if we could know more than is told in the pages of Curtius, Arrian, and Plutarch. Although one may question the value of Napoleon in the progress of humanity, there can be no doubt as to his importance as a subject for literature. Indeed, one wonders whether there is any other reason so good for not deploring the existence of Napoleon as that it furnishes matter for song and story.

"Though He slay me yet will I trust in Him." What better instance of how irresistible is life-enhancement, that is to say the increased sense of power and vitality felt when identifying oneself with a greater and more easily functioning, more effective energy! The idea of God is so life-enhancing that some Christians regard it as the highest privilege to dedicate life on earth to praising and magnifying Him, while yearning for a Heaven where this occupation will comprise all existence. So to come down to the conqueror, the victorious usurper, or even the successful go-getter of to-day: he dominates not by fraud and violence alone, but by a tendency on the side of his victims to voluptuous identification and submission.

Needless to add that fiction whether in verse or prose provides similar life-enhancement, but enjoys the advantage of being free to treat its heroes and heroines more plastically, more flexibly. Fiction that aspires to immediate favour has to be life-enhancing on some level. If on a low or mediocre one it is soon forgotten. Likewise with the drama, the opera, and all the other arts which stir the emotions. The visual arts, as repeatedly observed, have this advantage: that even when reproducing the sensational events that increasingly disfigure the daily and weekly press, their power of exciting is limited. The only visual representations likely to stir to action and thereby to step out of the realm of art into the world of actuality, are pornographic ones. The visual arts, moreover, have beyond this negative advantage the positive one that they can portray the heroes, the gods, the saints in their ecstasy, in their transfiguration. This has been the highest achievement of sculpture and painting from Phidias with his Olympian Zeus and Parthenon pediments, to the Sung painters with their rakans, to Sassetta with his St. Francis, and Raphael with his Plato and Aristotle, his Apollo and the Muses, to Signorelli and Michelangelo with their prophets and sibyls. When after a thousand years of decline and recovery art can again portray the individual, we encounter innumerable interpreters of character who are at the same time masters of form and design, from Van Eyck and Fouquet down to Ingres, Watts, and Degas.

There are various kinds of life-enhancement. The one we are most concerned with in this place is derived from the feeling of higher potency, fuller capacity, greater competence, due to the sense of unexpected ease in the exercise of our functions, induced by the arts of visual representation.

We must, however, distinguish between such exercise when it is purely or almost purely intellectual and when it is systemic, that is to say concerned with all the senses as well as with the mind. If it be concerned with the mind alone, or as nearly so as is possible with creatures like ourselves in whom nothing is completely separated from everything else, then the ensuing state is one of intellectual triumph, pride, and exultation, but is only to a minimal degree an artistic one, even if the object over which the mind has been exercising itself be an artifact.

Of the life-enhancement derived from experiencing and living the work of art, enough has been said earlier. We now must give a moment's attention to that almost purely mental life-enhancement which accompanies the act of cognition, the quick assimilation of the newly presented, and the joy of calling it by name—which joy, by the way, is the chief if not the only delight of the connoisseur, of the so-called "expert."

The mental effort required for this purpose should be easy but not too easy; for with our extravert instinct of objectivating our pleasures and of focussing them on an object instead of on ourselves, we tend to enjoy and admire only what, after sufficient effort, we end by recognizing.

When we have taken cognizance of the constituting elements of an object, so that for us with our training, our profession, and our prepared expectations there is nothing more to discover for the time being, that object begins to bore us. We sidle away from it, avoid it, and succeed in forgetting it; unless indeed, as happens to many when young or perpetuated in adolescence, we insult over the corpse of our dead but not yet buried admiration. We thereupon begin to hanker for a fresh object upon which to exercise our cognitive faculties, a state of mind which can best be described as a lust for novelty, for otherness. It is a lust that has greater power in art than in life itself, art being so much more plastic, more ductile, more fluid than life.

Novelty, Otherness

Novelty, otherness, then consists in the easy, but not too easy, satisfaction given to the cognitive faculties when these throw themselves upon an object after exhausting a prior one. It is so full of craving, so lustful that it is no better judge of the artistic qualities of the object procuring this satisfaction than the physiological or chemical affection known as being-in-love is a judge of the moral character of its object. And just as love cannot assert itself, and make sure of its reality, until being-in-love is over, so artistic qualities can be descried only when the excitement and fever of newness has cooled. Few are gifted by nature, and not all of these have the education and training to extricate themselves from the metaphysics, philosophies, misinformations, and prejudices (sucked up in their preconscious, earliest years) that beset the approach to the work of art, if it is to be enjoyed for its intrinsic qualities and not for its newness. Moreover, it requires intelligent co-operation. We cannot remain passive. We must be not only receptive, but responsive.

They who can enjoy and feel in the artifact little more than its otherness, its novelty, are like nomads who quickly use up a territory and dash on in search of new game, in quest of fresh pasturage, or, if they are already consumers of cereals, in the hope of soil still untouched, to skim in passing. The nomads in the realm of art would leave no more trace of their excitement and exhilaration than have the migrants of old.

If it were fashion alone of which people wearied—fashion begotten by the love of novelty or the lust for showing off— the loss would be small. They, however, who enjoy little in the artifact except its novelty will get as weary of what in the work of art is of more than passing interest and is of enduring value. They will laugh and jeer at masterpieces that they have done with, as they will run down last year's extravagances. Thus generations and centuries may pass before a Botticelli is rediscovered or, still later and more tumultuously, a Piero della Francesca. Brought to notice again, along with the glorious company of their contemporaries, they do their stunt as at a variety show, are applauded, called back again and again, and then forgotten in favour of some other exhumation of the past, more poignantly novel because more and more remote from our traditional standards. So we Atlantic peoples have reduced the Quattrocento to a single artist, Piero della Francesca, as the Central Europeans have narrowed down the Cinquecento to Michelangelo, while the most advanced of us turn up our noses at all of these and find no satisfaction for our exquisite cravings except in the frescoes of Mount Athos, in pre-Cimabue Madonnas, in the incunabulae of Romanesque sculpture, in Negro wood-carvings, South Sea idols, and Tlinkit totem-poles.

The lust for otherness, for newness, which seems the most natural and matter-of-course thing in the world, is neither ancient nor universal. Prehistoric races are credited with having had so little of it that a change in artifacts is assumed to be a change in populations, one following another. The same holds for the more or less unhistorical peoples of relatively recent or quite recent date like the Peruvians and the Mayas and Aztecs as well as the African and Oceanic tribes. Even people so civilized as the Egyptians changed so little in three thousand years that it takes training to distinguish a Saitic sculpture from one of the early dynasties. In Mesopotamia also change was slow. But for Alexander's conquest there might have been almost no newness in India, and but for the Buddhist missionaries as little in China. Why was there so little craving for novelty everywhere on the earth? It could scarcely have been due to the possibility that the sources of visual pleasure, stored up in extant artifacts, were so inexhaustible that no demand for new ones could arise. Likely enough people were too inert, too indolent to use their cognitive faculties, and crave for change. It would seem as if the Greeks were responsible for the introduction of this hankering for otherness, for newness, with a spirit so opposed to the ancient Egyptians and Persians that the priests of the one and the satraps of the other could compare them to unruly children. The Greeks carried this spirit with them wherever they went, but without permanent effects upon Asiatics and Africans, who tended to stay where they were to mummify and ossify like Copts or Mesopotamians, Arabs or Hindus, with almost no conscious need of newness, with no liability to change, excepting of course under such destructive or creative impact from the outside as came to India with the Greeks after Alexander, with the Arabs after Mohammed, and with Turkish tribes in late mediaeval Persia. The West, on the other hand, was entirely won over to the spirit of change. Our most stagnant moments have been of a relatively short duration, and not devoid of stirrings; while from the beginning of the present millennium change has been continuous and ever quicker. Finally in this twentieth century it is conquering the entire earth. Before long we shall have to voyage to the shores of western Kamchatka in search of the last unchanging folk-ways and artifacts, to be disappointed perhaps when we got there.

In proto-historic times, then, change occurred only when there was a displacement of population, tribes succeeding tribes, bringing their own artifacts. In pre-history such clean sweeps must have been even rarer. Occupation of the land had become too complete and too dense for massacre or pestilence to leave it empty for newcomers. If these arrived as conquerors they killed some of the best artificers with as little awareness or conscience as had the Roman legionary who cut down Archimedes at Syracuse. Others they enslaved and compelled to cater to their own nomadic and infantile tastes. As a rule the ancient occupants ended by getting the upper hand of the invaders, and were perhaps the better for the enrichment received from the fresh blood the newcomers poured into the veins of their common descendants.

15. Giorgione: Gipsy and Soldier. Academy of Fine Arts, Venice.

16. Chaô-Ming-Fû: Tartar Rider. Stoclet Collection, Brussels.

Conquests of the Mind — Florence

I come now to the conquests of the mind and spirit which may follow in the train of military advance, but may equally well accompany peaceful penetration or trade, or the migration of individuals finding no satisfactory employment at home.

Classical examples of civilizations accompanying conquering armies are furnished by the Macedonian invasion of the East, and the successful wars of the Romans in the West. Shining instances of the other are the Hellenization, except in language, of the entire world of antiquity, the oecumene, the subsequent Judaization of the same world known as Christianity, and later the submission of this world again to French culture in the West, to Byzantine in the East, both dominating until the other day, yet from 1400 to 1800 sharing their empire with Italy in general and Florence and Tuscany in particular.

The Florentine and Italian penetration into the rest of Europe must rank as one of the most heartening triumphs of mind. To write its history will some day, and let us hope soon, engage the energies of Italian scholarship. Its study has one advantage over that of the peaceful penetration of the Greek spirit into nearly the same regions some two thousand years earlier. The course of the latter remains almost as unchronicled and as anonymous as pre-history, and like prehistory is known by its fruits alone; whereas the Italian penetration is vivified by the possibility of tracing it in detail through individuals, and of identifying their personal achievements.

Confining ourselves to what concerns the arts of visual representation, the effect is well known of the sojourn of the Sienese Simone Martini and of Matteino da Viterbo in

Avignon on the painters of the regions stretching from Flemish Bruges to Spanish Valencia.

Florentine art was perhaps as pervasive and probably as early or even earlier in spreading its influence. Portable pictures like the triptychs turned out by Bernardo Daddi were sold at the most frequented fairs of Champagne, and Trecento frescoes still remain at Toledo, pictorial embroideries at Manresa, and tournament shields in the Alhambra of Granada. Antonio Florentin was court painter to John I of Portugal while the gorgeous illuminations limned for the magnificent Duc de Berry were done by Franco-Flemish craftsmen well aware of what was going on in Tuscany.

By the beginning of the fifteenth century Siena had exhausted her influence while Florence was only preparing for her widest expansion. She sent Donatello and Castagno, Fra Filippo and Piero della Francesca, Michelozzo and Leonardo to spread her light over the Lombard plain, from Milan to Padua, to Ferrara, and even to still Byzantine Venice. Some of her less known sons, or sons according to the spirit only, established themselves on both shores of the Adriatic. At Rimini and Ancona, at Traù and Sebenico may still be seen more playful, more lovely creations than the severe mother city would condescend to cherish. She dominated Umbria as well as the Marches, and Rome was her suburb. Florentine architects were reaching out to Cracow, to distant Moscow, and to remote Delhi, while Florentine painters or their works penetrated into Hungary. By the sixteenth century, Florentine art had infused or transformed the art of the entire Italian peninsula. It is scarcely an exaggeration to say that henceforth Italian art is Florentine, with incompetence, bad habits, and obstinacy producing regional variations, some, it is true, as well justified as Venetian painting. Before the sixteenth century had run half its course Florentine art by the agency of Andrea del Sarto, Rosso, Cellini, Primaticcio, and Niccolò dell'Abbate had planted a colony in France which until the other day flourished generously, never denying its parentage. It had sent out Andrea Sansovino, Leone Leoni, and the Venetianized Byzantine, El Greco, to convert Spain, and had sent Torrigiano first to Portugal and then to far-away England, whither he was followed by Zuccari. If we do not hear of famous Italians going to the Netherlands and to Germany, we know that some of the most gifted painters and sculptors of those countries, Dürer and Pacher, Sustris, and Scorel and Heemskerk, Adrian de Vries and Giambologna, Rubens and Van Dyck came to Italy, and some of them spent years there, returning eventually to their homes laden with all the Michelangelo, Titian, and Cellini that they could carry. Nor did Italian influence stop in the seventeenth century. Velasquez came twice to Rome for long periods and left it each time clarified and advanced; Rembrandt and Vermeer—the mysteriously Caravaggiesque and so Italianate Vermeer—pored over Italian masterpieces. By the beginning of the eighteenth century no artist or man of taste believed he would have his chance if he could not go to Italy for what nowadays would count as a long sojourn. France had already under Richelieu founded its famous school, later known as the "Villa Medici." Other nations followed, and as recently as this century was started the "palatial plant" of an American Academy. Throughout the eighteenth century Italy was sending its geniuses in every direction: architects who built or decorated the playfully sumptuous churches of Austria and Catholic Germany, and grand cities like St. Petersburg; painters who like Tiepolo not only adorned Madrid but prepared the way for Goya.

That is what Florence did, a smallish town of money-mongers, not to say usurers, wool-combers, and cloth-weavers with little military force and next to no political authority. Florentinized Italy exerted this diluvial influence upon the entire white man's world, and beyond it, at a time when Italy was a "mere geographical expression." Armies may or may not prepare the way. In the long run influence is spread through craftsmen, artisans, architects, wood- and stone-carvers, men of letters, school teachers, singers, dancers, tumblers, clowns, pedlars, medicine men, hairdressers, fiddlers, as it was spread in late antiquity by Greeks and then more and more by Syrians, Jews, and Copts, the same people who at first contributed so much towards the disintegration of the Hellenic world, and then towards saving Europe from sinking to a dunghill economy and berserker barbarianism.

Style

Style is another term frequently recurring in art writing which must be touched upon and defined. Like many abstract words in common use, this one has more than one meaning. Those who succeed first in liquefying our nebulous notions on the subject and then in crystallizing them, are likely to end by realizing that the word "style" is used descriptively as well as critically. Thus we can describe certain artifacts like buildings, pieces of furniture, utensils, dresses as being "Louis Quinze" or "Georgian." We can also speak of persons, of whole societies, as well as of artifacts as being good or bad style or as having or not having style. What is it that makes style in the descriptive sense? How do we recognize style? And of what elements is it composed?

In the case of Gothic, it is the pointed arch, the undulating male or female figure, and the smile that are the more obvious traits of the style. The connoisseur knows of much else—the voids, for instance, in the spacing, the relation of verticals to diagonals, the swing of draperies, the various facial types, the proportions of the figures, and so on. The student will have in mind that, in our Mediterranean world (except in ancient Egypt and Mesopotamia), no style in historical times remained the same for long, and the more alive were the practitioners, the farther flung the outposts of their activities, the more oscillating, the more vibrating were the styles, the swifter to change and the more subject to local variants. But through all changes the most obvious characteristic of Gothic for the three centuries of its prevalence remained the same pointed arch, as previously the round arch had been characteristic of Romanesque. The public no less than the artists, while those modes and fashions reigned, found it difficult if not altogether impossible to conceive of any piece of furniture, any scheme of decoration, any bit of ornament, let alone any building, that did not display the round or the pointed arch, or was not derived from it.

Nothing is so tyrannically exclusive and levelling as a firmly established reigning style! No faith is more intolerant. While it is being constituted or when recline sets in, it may suffer disturbing attraction from the outside. In its full strength it crushes and grinds every shape that comes its way, and suffers them only if it can force them through its own moulds in accordance with its own pattern. Nowadays it is hard to understand what authority and prestige a given style had in the past. To get some idea of it one must see what happens in the arts that are still alive: dressmaking, tailoring, haberdashery, and all that has to do with foot-gear, with hats and caps for men, but most of all with head-coverings for women. Even in these last surviving arts there prevails in our times an indulgence to individual caprice that would not have been admitted when a style imposed its patterns not on a town, or a country, or a broad kingdom, but on the participants in a civilization that extended beyond its political frontiers.

Yet even to-day, despite the caprice and licence accorded to the smart individual, it occurs to no man or woman to ask whether, except for a costume ball, he or she will dress in a "Louis XV" or "Louis XIV," or "François I" or "Henri II" style. The moment, however, that they think of building or furnishing a house, they feel at liberty to select any style of architecture, decoration, and furniture; or rather they are tossed about by this "unchartered freedom" and know not what to choose, filled with *"le sentiment de la multiplicité des compossibles,"* as Jacques Rivière calls it. A perplexity like that would not have been thinkable before the French Revolution and the successive reactions that followed in its train, the Gothic Revival, for instance, and all the other revivals that followed fast and ever faster down to the other day. Your outermost garments—I mean your buildings and squares and gardens—were in those days as little subject to discussion as your clothes, like these only in so far as it was a matter of expense, and appropriateness to your private situation. Otherwise you built as you dressed according to the prevailing style, Romanesque from about 1000 to after 1200, Gothic from that date to beyond 1500, then François I followed by Henri II and succeeded by classicizing styles, taken over from Italy. There followed the exhaustion of all acceptable variants upon the rectilinear, and the consequent adoption of shapes swerving in undulations not only up and down but outwards and inwards, along with their playful mouldings and gay scrolls and swags known as Louis XV.

These styles from Romanesque to Empire grew out of each other as blossom out of bud, flower out of blossom, and fruit out of flower. There occurred, to be sure, a turning back to antiquity which took place after every change that could be wrung out of the Gothic formula had been tried, when people were tending by automatic reaction towards the rectilinear, and thus getting ready for the column, the entablature, and more symmetrical design in architecture, as well as for the vertical in the figure arts.

Antiquity helped them to accelerate this process, lighting the way and cheering with examples of successful effort. It is possible that in Italy architects would have reconquered the Hellenistic positions, as indeed Bramante and Sanmichele,

Sangallo and Palladio eventually did, without the models of antiquity. It would have taken longer, but the tropism of pattern would probably have taken them there. It may be argued that without the example of Hellenistic antiquity, no matter how mannered and inferior it may seem, neither Michelangelo nor Jacopo Sansovino would have so closely rivalled the ancients. I should hesitate to overestimate in Michelangelo's case, at least, his debt to what marbles were then accessible, the "Apollo Belvedere," the "Laocoön," and the famous "Vatican torso." But Titian, the mature Titian of the Borghese "Education of Cupid," what could he have known of paintings which recall him so vividly, like those of the Villa dei Misteri at Pompeii, discovered only the other day? He, surely, by himself and unaided, recaptured the heights reached by the originator of those frescoes.

Finally, what characterizes style when fully formed and before serious disintegration sets in, and what gives it value from every point of view, is its imperviousness to outside influence. "Influence" we shall discuss presently. I take this opportunity to say that the Chinese no more modified anything essential in Italian painting than the Persians modified the art of antiquity. The "Miltiades Kalos" of the Acropolis Museum is unmistakable early fifth-century Athenian, although he has put on Persian trousers. The shepherd of Mount Ida known as Paris is not less Greek for wearing a Phrygian cap. Nor did Amazons decked out in full Iranian costume prevent the vase paintings and sarcophagi on which they occur from being a whit less Greek. Likewise the presence of an Eastern rug wafted to Siena and used as a studio property by the Lorenzetti and their successors down to Giovanni di Paolo, or of Chinese silks in the later Florentine Trecento, or of Ming bowls in Giovanni Bellini's famous "Bacchanal" (now in the National Gallery, Washington) in no way affected the respective styles of Siena, Florence, and Venice in the fourteenth and fifteenth centuries. No number of shapes from a foreign repertory disturbs the integrity of a style, so long as this style can assimilate them. The interest of these borrowings lies not in the realm of art history but in that of commerce, and cultural interchanges; and it is the same with the out-and-out Mongol types in Lorenzetti's Martyrdom of Franciscan friars at Tana, or the Mongol pigtails in the frescoes of the Spanish Chapel. In the same way the Italian artists of the sixteenth century did not hesitate to take what they wanted from Dürer, Lucas van Leyden, or other Northern masters. But the moment one of them, Pontormo, was not contented, so to speak, to melt down the stolen goods, remoulding them according to Italian taste, but attempted instead to use them unchanged with all the crinkles and edges of Teutonic contour, a howl of indignation went up which prevented the repetition of the Certosa experiment.

Protest against Restoration

Interesting in this connection is the treatment of the antique by mediaeval and later artists. All translated it into their own terms, although as, little by little, styles from the fifteenth century onwards approached the antique more closely, the divergence grew less wide and absurd. Thus from the beginning of the Renaissance till the nineteenth century Greek and Roman statues, if without legs and arms, and even lacking heads, were completed in the style of the restorer's period. Antique sculpture, the one field where, despite pedantry and irrelevance, art has been taken seriously, no longer is subjected to this indignity. Paintings still suffer restoration to a greater extent than laymen will readily believe. Canvases are no longer cut down to the shape and size required for use as mere furniture-figures. Yet more is still done than should be. Quite recently cases have occurred of heads in pictures being erased that dealers fancied might put off a client. We do not yet think of letting an "Old Master" go stripped of additions and restorations, so as to appear as time has left it, a rag faded and discoloured, but the authentic ruin of the original. We insist on having it patched and faked up in accordance with our guesses as to what it must have been like when it left the painter's hand. These guesses are inspired by the taste, good or bad, that is to say by the *style*, of our day. Often a trained eye can identify not only the time but even the place where a picture was restored.

This holds good not for the visual arts alone but for music and literature as well. How little we are allowed to hear what has not been "arranged by So-and-so." This is true of nearly all music before Mozart, so little is the work of those periods agreeable in its original pitch and harmonies to the contemporary ear. Even later creations are liable to be manipulated by composers with more popular taste, as was notoriously the case with Rimski-Korsakov's arrangement of Mussorgsky's *Boris Godunov*. In the many kingdoms and provinces of literature, the layman reads a translation or even a darned, patched, ironed-out original page of a Hebrew, Greek, or Latin classic with no idea of the condition in which the text reaches us; often how unintelligible, how much emended in accordance with successive tastes; heroically classicizing in the seventeenth and eighteenth centuries, increasingly anthropological and "realistic" in our own times. Nearer home, to us English-speaking people, is the sad case of Shakespeare's text, as distressing as any handed down by antiquity and as subject to variations of artistic belief, as is abundantly testified by the emendations registered in Furnival's "Variorum" edition.

CHAPTER IV

HISTORY

Influence

THE PLEA FOR standards of value in the history of visual art has been made and I assume that we consent to base these standards on tactile values and movement. We have offered definitions of both these terms and of decoration, illustration, and style as well. These discussions of fundamentals enable us to turn with greater ease to the more specific problems of our task.

We begin with the more abstract, and turn first to one already touched in the last few paragraphs, the problem of influence. Strictly speaking, the question of influence has nothing to do with the enjoyment and appreciation of the work of art, and little with understanding it. Scarcely more than for an Englishman to know whence come the various ingredients of his meals, whether the wheat comes from Canada, or Danubia, or Russia; the butcher's meat from Australia or the Argentine; the eggs and poultry from Denmark or New Zealand, the spices from Ceylon or Java, the fruits from South Africa or California. Knowing the origins does no doubt enrich enjoyment. To trace the history of shapes, as of the Doric or Ionic column, or of the vegetable scroll, or even of facial types, may partake of a pleasure not wholly unlike what must have been enjoyed by the discoverers of the sources of the Nile, or Niger, or Mississippi. The search for influences is, however, seldom free from nationalistic prejudices, rash inferences, and ill-founded conclusions. Jealousy of Greece is at the bottom of recent attempts to belittle the Hellenic achievement and to exalt Etruscan and Roman art. Distaste for the creations of the "hothouse civilization" of antiquity leads so-called Nordics of to-day to turn against classical art of every kind, that of visual representation particularly, and to find satisfaction in scratchings, chippings, and interlacings executed by the early occupants of marsh and forest, fell and tundra from whom these presumptive Nordics fancy they are descended. The labourer is worthy of his hire, and if his hire is paid in flash-lighting his discoveries we may not begrudge it. Only we must not take the distortions produced by the ensuing contrasts of fierce light and blackest shade for normal shapes. Thus it is good to know that art reached the farthest outposts of pre-Renaissance Christendom and beyond. Yet had one ardent student not been cut off in the midst of his efforts, he might have attempted to prove not only that there were in Ireland some few artifacts worthy no doubt of high mention in the realm of pure ornament, but that monumental sculpture revived there and started the French on a course that led straight to Chartres and Rheims. Another and far more advertised professor, whom we have already referred to, has excluded the human figure from art history, and admits other animals or even vegetables (whether carved in stone or wood, or cast and chiselled in bronze or iron or more costly material) only when pulled out of ordinary semblance and reduced to ribbons or cordage in an entangled pattern.

With Professor Strzygowski [1] in this, his last phase, one would have no quarrel, for every student has the right to narrow his field of research as he pleases, and to define his terms. But before attaining this cosy exclusiveness, he and his following reached the certainty that European architecture of the earlier Middle Ages was almost entirely Armenian, and all ornament Coptic or Sassanian, and the figure arts

[1] Written while he was still alive.

Parthian and Mesopotamian. If there was art in Europe at all during the years from 400 to 1200 it was thanks to practitioners who came from the East, and to their direct pupils and followers. We are even expected to believe that Tuscan painting of the fourteenth century was indebted for its essential constituents to remote China.

One of the startling facts of history, a fact undeniable but not easily accounted for, is the irresistible attraction of a superior culture. It makes its very conquerors submit to it in the way the Romans did to the Greeks, Arabs and Turks to Byzantines and Persians, Tartars and Manchus to Chinese, and thousands of years earlier Semites and Gutians to those Sumerians who supplied art, and perhaps religion, to the more western and northern parts of Asia.

In defining "style" we declared that one of its qualities was impenetrability and even impermeability, from the moment the style was fully formed. In that fully formed phase a style would not suffer any kind of influence. Italy for instance was strewn thick with the remains of Roman building and carving. Yet we discover but faint trace of acquaintance with either among its mediaeval artists. These few traces had to be translated into their own visual language by architects, sculptors, and painters of the fourteenth and even of the fifteenth century before they would use them. Only in its tentative stages, or when it is already disintegrating, can a style be seriously affected from the outside. We must inquire to what extent a style in dissolution or reconstruction is, so to speak, liable to be deflected and pulled out of its orbit by the approach of an alien planet.

Art has to do with two kinds of shapes:

1). Those furnished by nature.
2). Those furnished by form.

Natural shapes we shall not return to, but refer the reader to what has been said on this subject in the Introduction. Like everything else that we are accustomed to call "natural," the question of natural shape is complicated, and it is far from being as "natural" as we assume. There may be shapes in nature but we do not necessarily know what they look like. We have to learn them as we learn to recognize sounds, to understand what they mean, and how to use them ourselves. We acquire this knowledge before the age of awareness. We cannot recall the process, and assume therefore that it was "natural"—supposedly innate. By bumping into them and barking our little shins, we teach ourselves that certain objects are cradles and beds, tables and chairs. We learn to name fire and water, cats and dogs. Out of doors, certain shapes are animals, others are houses and trees and ponds, and others again are vehicles, etc. We learn not only to recognize and name familiar shapes while we ourselves are unaware that we are learning, but in the more favoured parts of the earth we learn to recognize in the same unconscious way the *representations*, pictures, of these and of even less familiar objects.

The shapes given by form are a different matter, for form imposes its own patterns on the shapes in nature, just as the tailor and dressmaker, and hatter and shoemaker do on our bodies, or indeed that something superhuman wherewith Athena endowed Ulysses in order to fascinate Nausicaa.

It is rare to see shapes as naked as they may be in nature, for we cannot help seeing them arrayed, as it were, by art. This raiment is transmitted with the art with which it is identified, with which in fact it is one. Like all dress, it is a matter of cut, that is to say of pattern and proportions, and silhouette, which, allowing for slight changes in kind and quality of trimming and number of buttons, goes on unchanged even in our time for decades, and in the past went on for generations.

It is these petty variations that are easily affected from the outside, but no more alter a style than a new condiment, introduced from the East Indies into Europe, has radically altered Italian and French cooking.

On the other hand, no imported style remains unaffected in the land where it is adopted; and if English tailoring and French dressmaking look more natural on the bodies of inhabitants of Turin and Teutoburg than of Tokyo, it is not only because the two former are anatomically closer to their north-western neighbours than are their Nipponese co-religionists. It is also due to the fact that the universal language which London and Paris fashions speak was learned much earlier in Turin and Teutoburg than in Tokyo. Fashion, after all, is a kind of speech and will be talked less and less well the farther it has travelled from its origin, as pidgin English along the China seas nowadays, and likely enough, Greek spoken at the time of Milinda in Bactria.

Fashion knows no frontiers except those of a civilization, which is very obvious to-day since, far beyond our pale, our fashions reach the classes that partake, or aspire to partake, of the joys and sorrows, the essence and intimacies, of our civilization.

To-day wherever Parisian dressmaking goes, Parisian fashions go also, with variants due not to the proportions, cut, or even ornament, but only to the greater or less degree of incompetence, or to the resistance of local materials employed either because the Parisian was not available, or because the dressmaker wished to introduce a bit of local colour. And just so in antiquity Hellenistic types, proportions, and patterns for all animate and inanimate objects, as well as Hellenistic spacing and arrangement, reached as far as any ray of Hellenistic civilization, and beyond political frontiers.

So long as these art shapes and patterns, no matter how exotic they may be, assimilate natural shapes, raw shapes, as it were, there can be no talk of foreign influence. In the realms of visual representation, Etruscans, Latins, Oscans, Parthians, Indians, Celts and Iberians, Numidians and Sarmatians were Hellenized.

An art is affected by influence only when its own moulds are altered by contact with another art, as certainly was the case with the arts of the peoples in touch with Greeks in antiquity, as is the case with those in touch with the French to-day. Just as little as Paris is affected to-day, except in passing trivialities, by foreign-born customers or students, so little in antiquity was the Hellenistic artist contaminated in essentials by Scythian or Sarmatian, by Sassanian or Bactrian employers and apprentices.

If any of these people were civilized enough to have art shapes of their own, surely it would have been the Iranians. Yet Mithraism, which for generations competed on nearly equal terms with Christianity, betrays in its imagery no element that is not late Hellenistic, unless it be the costume of the slayer, which is the same as that worn by Paris in all representations of his Judgement. Another Iranian religion, Manichaeism, which counted adherents among the intellectual classes, among others St. Augustine before his conversion, has in art left few traces of its existence—none, in fact, until the other day. Only in this century the sand-buried cities of Eastern Turkestan have yielded up miniature Manichaean paintings. These, however, differ in no respect from the Indo-Chinese frescoes of Buddhist import discovered in the same region. Nor is it likely that the illuminated books, for which Manichaeism was famous from the start (its founder Manes himself adorned his manuscripts with apposite illuminations), were different from what was being manufactured for other Hellenized contemporaries.

It is worth noticing that except in architecture Persia has in the course of history given few signs of artistic creativeness or originality. It is true that in our fifteenth and sixteenth centuries it refined on what came to it from elsewhere, but in the Achaemenean period its sculpture owed everything to Assyria and Ionia.

In Parthian and Sassanian reliefs, coins, and other faint

traces of illustrative art, everything is Hellenistic except what is due to the originality deriving from incompetence, and of course to costume, as for example the gigantic head-gear of the Sassanian King of Kings. Under Islam, Persia was subject first to the artists and artificers of Syria, themselves no more than flaccid late Hellenistic provincials, and then to all kinds of Mongol, chiefly Turki, invaders. Only towards 1500, as just said, does Persia, with Behzad and a few others nearly on his level, attain to an art of representation that is almost its own: elegant, refined, and precious as no other in inner Asia. It is limited to miniature painting, even when on the scale of extensive rugs. No monumental composition of that period has reached us.

The Iranians, if they had not disposed of imperial re-sources, might in antiquity have left us as little trace of artistic achievement as the Jews. Herodotus says expressly that "it is not their [the Persians'] custom to make and set up statues and temples and altars." There is to my knowledge no vestige of Mazdian iconography or composition. Zoroastrianism was probably as anti-plastic as Judaism, as little prone to indulge in graven images. Least of all was it likely to cultivate monumental landscape-painting for its own sake, seeing that elsewhere this art crept in as background only to figures, and it took centuries—twenty, in fact—before it began to have an independent existence. In China alone does landscape seem to have been practised as early as the end of our first millennium, that is to say five centuries at least before we Europeans took the same road. To speak therefore with Professor Strzygowski of a Mazdian landscape, to describe its character, and to discover its influence in the cloudlets of the apse of SS. Cosmas and Damian in Rome seems a bit fanciful.

It may be questioned whether any of the folk in touch with the Greek world had enough artistic energy to hit back and affect degenerating and disintegrating Hellenistic art. At

17. Hubert Robert: Roman Villa. Louvre, Paris.

18. Titian: Philip II offering the Infante Fernando to Victory.
Prado Museum, Madrid.

the bitter end, perhaps not earlier than our fifth century,
traces of such an effect can be descried.

Here let me quote Herzfeld, than whom there is no better
authority on Iranian archaeology: "There is no greater
caesura in the 5000 years of the history of the ancient east
than the period of Alexander, and there is no archaeological
object produced after this time that does not bear its stamp."
About Persian shapes with Greek form he says: "The result
is a hybrid art, if art it can be called, worthy to be studied
only out of scientific and historical, not of aesthetic interest."
(*Archaeological History of Iran*, Schweich lectures, 1934,
p. 52.)

Egypt itself, aesthetically the most creative except Greece
of the ancient lands, contributed little to Greek art, and that,
if at all, in its early archaic period when Argos and Athens
were taking first steps towards the mastery of the nude. As
for Phoenicians, Hittites, Mitannians, Hurrians, Carians,
Phrygians, they contributed birds and beasts, and fashions
in apparel, and particularly in ways of wearing the hair, to
the Proto-Corinthian and Corinthian ceramists and artificers,
but they contributed nothing to the grammar of Greek art.
Little else was to be expected; and none of these races, left
to themselves, created works of art as distinct from artifacts,
such as palaeolithics, mesolithics, and neolithics have scattered over the face of our earth.

There was among the various Syro-Mesopotomian nations
one people more gifted than the others during the centuries
immediately preceding the dawn of classical Greek art. That
people was the Assyrian. Yet it too had small influence upon
Greek figure art, for that art, like every serious effort at representation, was based on the nude. Now except the Egyptians, nobody before the Greeks attempted to master the
nude, and erect it into a canon. The Assyrians therefore, for
all their command of mass, action, and movement, transmitted to the Greeks little else but their version of the Egyp-

tian palmette, certain costumes and certain quadrupeds, real
and mythical. For the overpowering figures from Branchidae
and the landscape backgrounds of besieged towns on two
Lycian tombs remain, so far as we know, isolated instances
of contact with Assyria. It is not likely, I repeat, that the
other Asiatic people who put up so little fight against the
Ionian, followed by the more effective Hellenistic invader,
would have retained enough originality to react against Hellenistic forms, and to impose their own artistic ideals, if indeed they had any ideals as distinct from folkways.

The Phoenicians were, to use modern speech, "paste and
scissors" craftsmen, combining Egyptian, Babylonian, and
Assyrian motives in a facile way to adorn their export wares.
As for Hurrians and later Hittites, they closely imitated
Sumerian art, infusing into their products a ruffian brutality
of intention with no adequate execution, strikingly like what
the Etruscans did, when even more slavishly following Greek
models from early Ionian down to Hellenistic times. Of pre-
Hellenic Phrygia and Caria we know little in the figure arts
that could count as their own. They manifestly had nothing
to contribute except the originality of incompetence and,
perhaps, behind that, the resistance of crude craft habits. I
can discover nothing better in the late "early Christian"
Rabula illuminations in the Laurenziana of Florence, interesting archaeologically perhaps but devoid of artistic quality;
and I discover scarcely more in the kindred mediaeval Cappadocian frescoes, although they are of some interest to ico-
nographers, and still more to students of the pathology of
form.

On the shores of the Euxine the Greeks came in touch
with tribes of a certain degree of civilization. On the north
there were horse-breeding Scythians with sufficient wealth to
command the service of high-class goldsmiths. They dictated
the subjects, the costumes, and even the attitudes. The pro-

portions, the articulations, the contours, and whatsoever else means form, remained Greek.

It is the same on the Propontis, in Macedonia, in the Balkans, in the Adriatic lands, in Sicily, Provence, and Spain. It is improbable that in any of these regions, art, as distinct from artifacts, has ever been discovered which was not of Greek origin, no matter how disguised by costume or type, and no matter how degenerate. The Elche head, the finest ancient work of art hitherto discovered in Spain, is in spite of the high cheekbones, the long chin, the exotic head-dress and ornaments, an unmistakable Ionian masterpiece, and the so-called Iberian statues are crude imitations of its like.

Even the figure art of Egypt, multimillennial Egypt, could not resist, and under the Ptolemies its canon of the nude yielded to the Greek, and little by little discarded what was not Hellenistic except costume and attributes.

As the Graeco-Egyptian shapes survived only in connection with the gods and their worship, nothing remained of Egyptian arts with the disappearance of Egyptian paganism. As long as this paganism endured, and particularly in the centuries preceding the triumph of Christianity, the Nilotic cults practised in Rome brought their own iconography, their own attributes, their own ritual, costumes, and instruments; and these are so strikingly exotic that to this day the untutored person will scarcely notice that the nude bodies supporting these heads of birds and beasts, wearing these wigs and aprons, holding these ankhs and sistrums are already Hellenized.

Every religion that has an iconography, let alone an art of its own, sends it along with its missionaries as Papists and Protestants still do to-day, the first with a falsetto Italianate architecture, the second with a toy Gothic. Buddhism likewise carried its late Hellenistic iconography, so close in essentials to the imagery of the fourth and fifth Christian centuries, to Java, to Indo-China, to China itself.

The iconography of the Indian religions was so definite, so sure, so crystallized that it imposed itself even on China. Yet it owed nearly everything to the Greek invader.

The Jews and Visual Art

The Hindus, whom the followers of Alexander half succeeded in Hellenizing, were far wealthier and artistically more gifted than the poor highlanders who under the name of Judaeans then occupied the hinterland of the Palestinian coast. Neither they themselves nor their forebears possessed any kind of plastic or even mechanical ability. Their records say that for a great part of their heroic period there was no blacksmith in the land. The same records confess that when their *Roi Soleil*, their *Prachtkoenig*, wanted to build a temple to his god, he had to get not only the materials but the workmen from Tyre. Of this structure there is no trace, certainly none of any plastic object connected with it. But recent excavations have brought to light ivories that adorned the furniture of a palace in Samaria built for Ahab, the wicked King, who eight centuries later would have styled himself a philhellene. The representations on these ivories, and their workmanship, are Phoenician.

As a matter of fact Israel through the ages has manifested nothing essentially national in the plastic arts, neither in antiquity, nor through the Middle Ages, nor to-day. The coinage of their Maccabaean period is the poorest Hellenistic. If we may trust the reproductions of the ornaments in relief, on the base of the seven-branched candlestick to be seen in the Arch of Titus, that cult object was Hellenistic enough to have been made for Herod by Greek silversmiths. In later periods Jews imitated the art of the peoples among whom they were scattered, to the pitiful extent that they made use of art at all. Even in recent years when Jews emancipated from the ghetto have taken to painting and sculpture and architecture, they have proved neither original nor in the least Jewish. I defy anyone to point out in the work of Liebermann, Pissarro, Rothenstein, Modigliani, Messel, Antokolskij, Epstein, Chagall, or Soutine, anything excepting subject matter that is specifically Jewish.

The frescoes with Old Testament subjects discovered in a synagogue at Dura-Europos, are provincialized and distorted late Hellenistic, like all the arts of the "desert ports," as Rostovtzeff has illuminatingly designated such cities as Palmyra, Nisibis, Dura, and Edessa. Except for subject matter, costume, and paraphernalia of ritual there is nothing more Jewish in them than in the pictures of the Liebermanns and Modiglianis of to-day. Whether the authors of these frescoes were Jews or Gentiles, we cannot and need not know. As painters they were Hellenistic, as in his humble way was the painter Eudoxius who signed a fresco in one of the Jewish catacombs in Rome.

It is likely that wealthy Alexandrian Jews had their copies of the Septuagint illustrated. Seeing that there existed no Jewish art, they must have employed Hellenes or completely Hellenized Jews. Even before Philo they had identified Jehova with Zeus wielding the thunderbolt, the builders of the Tower of Babel with the Titans, and other Hebrew fables with Greek myths. Philo himself applies to Jehovah epithets taken over from the Hellenes, such as "saviour," "benefactor," "giver of victory," "dispenser of wealth," the "greatly generous." It is hard to believe that this type of Jew, who, no longer understanding Hebrew or Aramaic, probably prayed in Greek and certainly read the Pentateuch and the Prophets in that language, would have cared for a Jewish art if it existed. His visual imagery would have been as Hellenized as the mosaics of St. Mary Major in Rome, which indeed may reproduce Alexandrian illustrations of Israel's epic.

It was the same in the Middle Ages and the Renaissance. The calendar pages of Byzantine manuscripts gave the East and South European Jews the models that are still current for marriage contracts and other legal documents. Illustrations to Jewish books in the Latin world are not too rare in the fourteenth and fifteenth centuries, and are invariably as Gothic as any other designs of the same centuries in the same country. Those done in Germany are, as everything Jewish in those regions has always been, exaggeratedly Teutonic. In like manner illuminations for Hebrew texts made in the Quattrocento in Bologna or Parma, Modena, Reggio, or Ferrara are exaggeratedly Emilian.

The Jews like their Ishmaelite cousins the Arabs, and indeed perhaps like all pure Semites (if such there be), have displayed little talent for the visual, and almost none for the figure arts. The art of Mesopotamia, including the basins of the Euphrates and Tigris and their extensions, is of Sumerian and not of Semitic origin. Thus not only are Assyrian and Hittite, as well as all Babylonian, sculpture non-Semitic, but the same is the case with the Semitic empire of the West, Carthage, where every artifact that can claim to be a work of art is Greek. To the Jews belonged the splendours and raptures of the word. Hebrew literature not only has afforded inspiration and comfort to Christian and Mohammedan but has fashioned or reshaped their instruments of expression. The Old and New Testaments, the second more specifically Jewish than even the first (which down to the Exile is Israelitish as distinct from Jewish), are behind and under and in Christianity and behind Islam if not in it. I use the words in their cultural and not in their doctrinal sense. Christianity brought about the Judaization of antiquity—the greatest revolution our history has registered.

Apart from its late Hellenistic theology on the one hand and its Madonna and saint worship on the other, Catholicism in its ritual, its feasts, its phraseology, even its ecclesiastical organization and hierarchy is so overwhelmingly Jewish that it may well be regarded as a detribalized and universalized Judaism.

The ancient world had lost its pattern of the universe, and its vision of human destiny. The Jews alone retained a scheme, simple, clear, and plausible, which could appeal to the perplexed, the disintegrated, the despairing. The world has not got over it yet, so little in fact that to-day (1938) three empires are attacking it openly or furtively, brutally or sneakingly, but, for the present at least, with doubtful success. By the fifth century of our era, the Hellenistic world was so Judaized that its living literature, while retaining the roots, grammar, and phraseology of Greek, was getting Hebraized. It could not be otherwise, seeing that the ritual came straight from the synagogue with its Biblical sentences, Biblical readings, and continual psalm-singing. The references, the appeals, were not to the glories of their own past, but to Hebrew worthies, Hebrew history and lore. The word "Hellene" ceased to have an ethnic or even cultural sense, but was getting to mean "pagan." There were still grammarians of course, and the learned were still reading Homer and perhaps Plato, although more likely Proclus, and for them Nonnus manufactured an epic, as much a hothouse product as the Mahabharata and Ramayana of the Indian pundits. For the same learned, in ever diminishing numbers, in ever obscurer circles, epigrams were being forged that like the verses of a Panormita, or Sannazzaro nearly a thousand years later, some of us can still enjoy with pleasurable satisfaction.

Pretty trifles, the visual equivalents of these epigrams, with identical mythological references, continued for centuries to embellish ivory boxes and silver dishes; but living art was dedicated, it would seem, entirely and wholeheartedly to illustrating Jewish song and story.

Nevertheless one can discover no trace of any Jewish art

shapes or of any specifically Jewish iconography in the remains of late Hellenistic imagery in Christian use. That could not have been the case if Jewish art patterns existed at the time. There was no question of any but Hellenistic patterns and artists, and had Christians looked around they would have found none in late antiquity to replace them. They were the only ones surviving, no matter how debased.

Debased indeed, but not owing to Christianity alone or chiefly. Christianity was not the direct cause of the decline in the arts of visual representation. Indirectly the low economic condition of its earliest adherents militated against art. For the most part they were denizens of slums, indifferent to art, scarcely aware of its existence, and, as can be seen in catacombs and cemeteries, they could afford to employ only the humblest and least expensive of artificers.

Then there was the fanatical hatred of the anti-Hellenic Jew against everything that might entice him away from his bleak abstractions and the passionately fervid, aggressive, and exasperated affirmation of his monotheism.

This primitive mentality, unimaginative, noumenal, and in a sense pretheistic and so accused of atheism as it infected the upper and finally the uppermost classes, which were already tainted by Stoicism, continually tended to turn them away from that love of the body and its more delicate and noble activities which underlies the feeling for visual art. It was the cause of an ever diminishing interest in the nude and, yielding to the pressure of this anti-Hellenic puritanism, ended in a horror of it. The nude was no longer studied, and without a mastery of the nude, no art of figure representation can thrive. It may be objected that worldliness cannot be extirpated, that so late as the sixth century many senatorial families remained powerful and able to enjoy life. Most of them, however, must have belonged to the part of the ruling classes that, having never been more than half humanized, found too much satisfaction in the tougher ani-

mal enjoyments to care for the attenuated ones offered by
the ideations of art. Between the ascetics and the never quite
debarbarized gentry, clients for artists grew fewer and fewer,
until the last of them disappeared.

It may be objected that I ignore differences between the
art products of the various nations I have just mentioned.
In the connection we are dealing with here, small differences
are of no importance. From the point of view of form they
are slight, and pertain to quality rather than to style. It is
only in the realm of illustration that national characteristics
can manifest themselves. On these I have dwelt enough already to make my meaning clear. My tendencies towards
universalism and timelessness have disinclined me to dwell
on differences that seem slight, compared with wide and
deep resemblances, and have inclined me to look for the
same human quality in every individual. And furthermore to
erect the same qualities into ultimate standards and to appraise societies as well as individuals by the extent to which
they have possessed these qualities.

I am indeed prone to be impressed by resemblances rather
than by differences. The first are patent, and so manifest as
to be taken as a matter of course. Except in rare cases the
differences are superficial. Deeper ones have to be looked for
with deliberate and minute attention. When discovered they
are more amusing than serious, more like the flash of a fire-
fly than the light of an illumination. In fact, but for language, the distinguishing marks of the different nationalities
are so faint that they have to do all they can to reinforce
them. The same holds true of their art products.

The question of influences, although chiefly a concern for
students of the histories of commerce and transport, or the
ticklish question of the indebtedness of one so-called race,
really one language group, to another, does have a certain
interest for the art historian as well, although a limited one.

It is reduced to the inquiry as to what happens when decline sets in. Is it due chiefly, if not wholly, to external causes or to internal ones, as, for example, the diminution of creative energy leaving only eruptive forces free to carry on their disintegrating activities from within?

What I have in mind is well illustrated by the controversy over the origin of later Roman artifacts, like jewellery with inlay of garnets, coloured pastes and glass, semi-precious stones and enamels. Riegl would have them to be a native invention to which art had sunk by 400 A.D. and supposes that the more humble of them, buckles, clasps, brooches, and safety-pins, were mass products manufactured for wide distribution within the Empire. In the forty and more years since Riegl wrote, material has been brought to light proving that his thesis was wrong and that the products in question were brought in by the barbarians from the north and east who were infiltrating, settling, and finally dominating the greater part of our world. It went so far that in Italy smart youth affected the long hair and costumes of the Goths, and in Byzantium Sassanian dress and finery.

It should be the business of art historians to ascertain whether at a given date, say the beginning of our fifth century, the ancient world had already sunk so low that only showy childish art pleased it.

Nevertheless if Riegl turns out to have been wrong as an archaeologist, he remains a great art historian, for he was the first to employ a rare intelligence and method in investigating change of taste, and how it was brought about. For art history, we cannot too often repeat, deals more with what was enjoyed and admired at a certain period, than with the question of where it originated and where it was produced.

In this instance, however, the conclusion led to the generalization already made here, namely, that it is only when a style is in utter decay that other modes of representation gain influence. Waxing Greek art could assimilate foreign notions in dress and ornaments, while in our fifth century, Hellenism was already so enfeebled that it could no longer prevent the masses from slipping back to puerile and barbarous preferences. The decline in figure arts, however, was not due to external influences, but entirely to interior reasons referred to repeatedly in this essay: the disappearance of creative artists and the survival of mere artisans who, reduced to successive copying, and deprived of leadership, sank back to primitive geometrical patterns, vertical and frontal designs. This phenomenon seems to characterize, in our European world at least, all moments of serious disintegration, as has been the case with us from the beginning of art nouveau at the end of the last century to the so-called abstract art of to-day.

The Originality of Incompetence

In connection with Iranian art, whether Achaemenean, Parthian, or Sassanian, I venture to speak of the "originality of incompetence." To begin with, the notion of "originality" that has meant so much, so increasingly in the last two hundred years, scarcely existed prior to the first dawning of the so-called "Romantic period." Indeed, it would be interesting to know whether as a category, and as a quality, it was recognized at all; whether it is not rather a by-product of the idea of genius as something Niedagewesenes—something that had never existed hitherto, never had been seen or heard of before—as a visitant from another sphere, bringing otherness and ever more otherness.

A young Dürer, a young Leonardo, a Raphael, a Michelangelo, or a young Rembrandt or Velasquez, or even Greco, did not go to his master and say: "Come, teach me quickly how to be as different, as unlike you as possible." If he thought at all, he hoped that he soon would imitate his master so well as to be mistaken for him. If he read the Gospels he would have made his own the saying (Luke VI, 40): "The disciple is not above his master: but every one that is perfect shall be as his master." If it were not so, how shall we account for the fact that it is so hard to distinguish between the earliest works of an artist and those of his teacher? There are still pictures and drawings which some attribute to Verrocchio and others to Leonardo, some to Perugino and others to Raphael, some to Giorgione and others to Titian. I am taking examples out of a field I have tended; but I could give innumerable instances from other fields, where it is still so difficult to distinguish between master and pupil, and could cite examples out of other arts and other schools. None of these could occur if the pupil were not the docile animal he begins by being, if he is both industrious and able.

Only when lazy or incompetent, only when he has not been able to learn what the master has been trying to teach him, and was unable to imitate the master in every respect, does he show originality at a too early stage of his career. In the past, the poor devil did not pride himself on it, or expect a brilliant career to follow. He could not help himself. He had to put up with this kind of originality as the deformity it was. It has taken our time—with its tendency to hail as a good everything my own generation regarded as evil —to discover originality in the distortions and absurdities resulting from mere incompetence. Recent German-minded writers have tended to speak of incompetence as deliberately thought-out styles dictated by entirely different *Weltanschauungen*, based on independent *Einstellungen*.

We can rest assured that if the Greeks who worked for the Achaemeneans at Persepolis, for the Parthians at Ecbatana, and for the Sassanians at Seleucia had any native apprentices, these apprentices thought only of identifying themselves with their Ionian or Hellenistic masters. So did Etruscan and Roman artificers. When it came to the pupils of these pupils, they fell under the inevitable law of successive copying—inevitable because of inattention to the source, namely, draughtsmanship. Now the law of successive copying is that the progressive degradation of the copy ends in something as remote from the original, something as distorted as Irish or Armenian, Christian, Cappadocian, or mediaeval Mesopotamian figures—original, indeed, but with the originality first of incompetence, and then of self-satisfied unawareness.

It has been the case at all times and in all places that the farther away from the generating centres of art, the more incompetent, the more distorted, and the more "original" the product. Only it must be the native product and not the work of an artist born, bred, or trained at the centre. If the sculptures of the so-called late Etruscan style are inferior to most of those found in the city of Rome, it is not due to the superior taste or talent of the native craftsman in the capital but to the probability that the latter was not a Roman but an immigrant, an import from Greece. If Rome could have afforded him as little as Volterra, and been reduced to her own genius, the art discovered in that imperial city might not have been much finer.

We can thus take it for granted that when a work of a high order in the Greek mode appeared anywhere in the ancient world, it was done by a Greek (in training at least), whether it be the Elche head referred to already, the Veii Latona and Apollo, or the goldsmith's work done for Scythians and Sarmatians. Likewise in the Romanesque and Gothic ages we must suspect that French-trained craftsmen carved the finest figures, statues, reliefs, or capitals of columns anywhere out of France, be it in Hungary or Spain, Scandinavia or Germany. In the last-named land, native students have been proving that the noblest statues at Bamberg were done by a sculptor who previously had worked at

Rheims. It is my private idea that one could go to Burgos, or León, or Compostella, and point on the one hand to the sculptures done by Frenchmen (by which I mean artists wholly trained in France) and on the other hand to those made by Spaniards. By way of justifying my private notion and to show that I am not blinded by prejudice, I add that it never occurred to me to suspect that the Puerta de la Gloria at Santiago or the sculptures at Naumburg and Meissen—in their own way such marvellous achievements—had been conceived and executed by Frenchmen.

Indeed, one might take a map of Eurasia and, fixing one leg of a pair of compasses at Athens towards 400 B.C. or on Paris towards 1200 A.D., swing the free leg in ever wider curves; if the map was large enough to permit indications of the principal works of art in this territory, we could perceive that the influence of the creative centre diminished with the extension of the free leg of the compasses. In other words, that the farther a place was away from the focus, the feebler were the rays that reached it and the less effective the results. Artifacts would tend to have less and less of Greek quality in antiquity or of French quality in the Middle Ages, the farther from Greece or from the Île de France they were produced. So certain is this conclusion that, whenever a masterpiece is discovered at a distance from the centres, one must inquire whether it was not the handiwork of itinerant Greeks or Frenchmen. Villard de Honnecourt in his sketchbook tells of his activities in far-away Hungary. We know that in the fourteenth century Étienne de Bonneuil and his Parisian companions gave the plan and began to build the cathedral of still more distant Upsala. We may be sure they were but two of many French architects of a high order called to distant parts, as in later centuries Italian architects found their way to Moscow, to Agra, and even to Pekin.

Teams of Greek and then of French artificers of sufficient number to train natives were responsible for the provincial arts of late antiquity and of England, Spain, and Germany in the Middle Ages. In antiquity one had to go as far as Gandhara to discover in type, proportion, or expression touches not due to mere incapacity for copying the model; in the Middle Ages, only as far as Germany and Italy, countries which retained traditions of their own, Othonian in the one, antique in the other, strong enough to modify what they adopted.

Peripheral Art

Different from provincial is marginal or peripheral art as practised by artisans with no artistic training, who copy the copies of copies that reach them with the last ripples from centres like Athens or Constantinople, Paris or Florence. The products of these cultural frontier districts are as a rule so crude and so helpless and childish as to make us ask whether they were due to the beginning or to the end of an art movement.

Frontiers change with the changes taking place in the centres of civilization. Thus Etruria and Picenum along with the estuary of the Rhône were for generations and generations after about 800 B.C. the western outposts of the Mediterranean, that is to say of Assyro-Egyptian, Phoenician, Rhodian, Ionian, Peloponnesian and Attic art; just as in the twelfth century of our era Cantabrian Spain was an outpost of Cluny and Saint-Denis. The best that we find in those regions was either imported or done on the spot by immigrant artists, Greek or French; the next best by the direct apprentices of these artists.

Speaking of North Syrian sculpture of 1000 B.C., Moortgat (whose *Bildende Kunst des alten Orients und die Bergvoelker* I happened to be perusing while writing this) says that it was so crude both in drawing and in composition as to have been taken for primitive and consequently dated as early, with the implication that it was the product of creative genius and not of provincial or even marginal imitation. I recall Professor Capart saying that in Egypt many stone objects that were for the same reason prized as pre-dynastic, were rustic imitations of much later things, originally executed in bronze.

A frontier art, or, as we shall often speak of it, a marginal or peripheral art, owes its characteristics chiefly to lack on the part of its artificers of proper training, training in the most essential requirements of the arts of visual representation, by which I mean chiefly the drawing of the nude. Long before the political frontier had shrunk away from its farthest extension and started creeping back to the source of power, long before Rome failed to exercise its political authority on the Tagus, the Rhine, the Danube, or the Euphrates, the inhabitants of these peripheries had either grown too impoverished to employ oecumenical artists and their direct pupils, or too barbarized as well as too superstitious to appreciate them. The latter would seem to have been the case, for the Palmyrene Rothschilds surely had the means to employ Greek sculptors, as they had for calling Greek painters to do their frescoes. Evidently the native stone-carvers, mere makers of images that were nothing but graven, enjoyed the preference.

Self-satisfied incompetence on the part of the artist, complacent indifference if not enthusiastic approval on the part of the public, characterizes an ebbing civilization, leaving little but wreckage and refuse interspersed among the proud ruins of once noble cities. The surviving denizens salute every destruction, every distortion, every successful attempt to lower what is left of past splendour to their own level of debased and crippled intelligence. They grow delirious with approbation, as we do now over the anti-art successes of painters and sculptors of the day, and over the wholesale

19. Agostino di Duccio: Angels. Templi Malatestiano, Rimini.

20. Velasquez: View of Villa Medici in Rome. Prado Museum, Madrid.

demolitions going on before our eyes in the most conspicuous centres of what had once upon a time been our spiritual
homes; while we are enraptured with buildings that disclaim
any purpose but that of being as responsive to our animal
needs—to our comfort, that is—as the cave was to the severely utilitarian requirements of the neanderthaler.[1]

In other words, as a civilization shrinks, the peripheral or
marginal region gains upon the interior until it finally con-
quers the centres, reducing Babylon and Memphis, and
Thebes of the hundred gates, to deserts, Athens and Antioch
to small market towns, and Alexandria to little more than a
fishing village.

The art that once was barely good enough for the precarious frontier is now all that the former capitals can
achieve. The field-marshals, the generals, the captains of the
various arts have gone. Even the non-commissioned officers
have scattered and disappeared. Only a straggling militia of
mere artisans remains, retaining nothing of the hierarchy
of the arts except the conceit that seems to adhere so ob-
stinately to the skin of the humblest painter or sculptor.

On the crumbling cliffs of the Euphrates, at Meskene, I
encountered a full-blooded Arab who was an itinerate maker
of graven images. I asked him to show his skill by making
one while I waited. He answered that even Allah in his paradise could not improve on the image he would produce, and
proceeded to chisel on a stone slab the outlines of a seated
and, of course, draped female. It was in the Mesopotamian
formula, that we see on Rhages bowls and kindred ceramics,
as well as in the illuminations of that region, and has not
changed in the last seven hundred years except to lose what
little quality that particular convention ever had. At the end
of half an hour he had finished. His self-complacence knew
no bounds. Not even Rodin in the midst of his literary admirers, as we knew him after 1900, could have enjoyed

[1] Written in 1938.

greater satisfaction. Had there been Bedouins standing around, they no doubt would have bleated an admiration as heartfelt and as intelligent as that of our own amateurs in the face of the latest distortions of shape, the latest kaleidoscope of colour, or the most inextricable enigmas of pattern and composition to which we are treated to-day.

Between these young, although no longer so very young friends of ours, and the Bedouin, the difference in material things is little less than infinite and all to the advantage of the first. In the realm of taste they are more nearly on a level; and I should be at a loss to say which stood the lower.

Peripheralism or marginalism (if we may use these terms) is due to the abandonment of the artisan to his own devices, freed from the inspiration and control of the artist. It can occur at any time and in any place, as indeed we see to-day in Paris and London and New York.

But the artisan's devices do not carry him far or forward. He falls back on his sloppy habits of execution, while in visualization he returns to the crude shapes and infantile patterns that have taken root in his mind, because they were more accessible to his feeling and more suitable to his hand than art based on intellectual training. Thus certain Greek patterns of the geometric period have stuck to Albanian and other Balkanic embroideries down to our day. Peasant art, when it is not as primitive as children's toys, has remained Romanesque through the whole of Latin Europe, although in a childish, crudely simplified way. Until the other day the Jewish *Bondieuseries* one saw displayed in shop-windows of the Viennese ghetto had an even cruder Byzantine aspect.

It is useless to think of lands from which civilization receded so utterly as from ancient Hellas till three or four generations ago, or coastal Asia Minor to this day. The early eleventh-century mosaics of Hosios Lucas are no more indigenous to Phocis than those of Daphne were to Attica.

Both must have been done by artists from Constantinople.
Greece had as good as ceased to be even peripheral and later,
under Turkish rule, ended as entirely barbarous.

Rome

And the city of Rome! It suffered almost no destruction
at the hand of the barbarian, but by 600 of our era had
nevertheless sunk from the secular position of attracting the
best artists of the civilized world, and was now huddling
close to the outskirts of Byzantine influence. In architecture,
too, like the meanest peripheral towns, it was not ashamed
to use fragments of ancient buildings crumbling for lack of
care. Sculpture disappeared and painting was reduced to pictographic daubs. Presently Greek anchorites, in their mission-
ary zeal, advanced to this outpost of the Byzantine Empire
and, nestling into the substructures of the least ruined part
of what had been the palace of the Caesars, began to adorn
them with frescoes, some of which are works of art. There
are layer upon layer of them as elsewhere in the Orthodox
world, and they went on being painted for generations and
perhaps for centuries. Nor did the Carolingian revival, which
again gave Rome some political prominence, affect its art.
Rome was too far from Aix-la-Chapelle and Rheims and
Tours; and the painting of those centres as reflected in
illuminated manuscripts had little to teach Romans even in
their degradation. For attenuated and stringy as decoration
and almost empty as illustration though the mosaics in the
apses of S. Maria in Domnica and of S. Prassede may be,
Carolingian art produced no figure compositions to compete
with them. They are Byzantine, and it must have been their
authors and other Greek painters who inspired Desiderius of
Monte Cassino, and later educated the one great artist of

note that Rome ever produced, I mean Pietro Cavallini. For be it remembered that the only other artist that Rome through the ages, ancient and modern, can claim as its own is Giulio Pippi, who although the only Italian painter mentioned by Shakespeare, is but a mediocre one, artistically corrupt and corrupting.

With the transfer of the Papal Court to Avignon and the consequent disappearance of the camp-life prosperity that its presence brought, art almost vanished from Rome. So when a hundred years later the Vatican began to be itself again, and to build and decorate, it found no artificers worthy of the name. Rome had returned to being marginal—this time, however, not to Greece as in antiquity nor to Byzantium as in the earlier Middle Ages, but to Tuscany and its Athens, Florence.

Yes, what Athens was to the ancient world, Florence has been to ours. But for Florence, Italy might have had a more infantile and perhaps more expressionistic art, more like Rhenish and Danubian than the Italian we know. Yet vital and expansive though Florentine genius was, its radiance grew curiously feebler as it darted southward. It scarcely reached beyond Umbria and even there with diminished warmth, while its rays fell but sporadically on Naples and Palermo. No doubt masterpieces like those of Donatello, Desiderio, and Rossellino in Naples were responsible for the sculpture of Giovanni da Nola and Santa Croce. The strange thing is that no ray from Florence lit Rome directly; for Antoniazzo called Romano was not a townsman but an Umbrian. Rome was thus within the Tuscan margin, but artistically not even marginal, for she produced no artists. They had to be imported. And imported they were, first from Florence and its dependencies, then from Milan and Bologna, and finally from Naples—that Naples which, except for the sculptors just mentioned, had till the seventeenth century so little art of its own.

Roman Art

What has been said about Rome and the arts overlaps what remains to be said about the term "Roman art." There was no such thing as "Roman art" at any time, no more in antiquity than in more recent times. In the Middle Ages, to be sure, there was, as we have just seen, a Roman artist whose work has come down in still legible form, Cavallini. He, however, owed as little probably to native sources as Giulio Romano three centuries later. Cavallini owed everything to the Byzantines, Giulio Romano as much to the Umbro-Florentines. In antiquity Rome was culturally Etruscan to begin with, then the capital of a more and more Hellenized great power, and finally the administrative centre of a world Hellenistic in all but the roots of language, and in inveterate local manners and superstitions. This administrative centre drew to itself, as such centres will, a disproportionate, an exorbitant share of the wealth of the world that enabled it to spend magnificently on embellishing itself, as indeed was done later by the administrative centre of an even vaster if less civilized empire, the St. Petersburg of Catherine the Great and Alexander I. As the Russia of that time owed everything, except perhaps its nielloed snuff-boxes from Twer, to Italian and French architects, sculptors and painters, so undoubtedly did Rome to artists from Greece and the Eastern Mediterranean. One of the rare signatures found in Roman painting is of a Seleucos, on a fresco of the Farnesina. He was surely a Syrian Greek and not an Italian.

We may use the term "Roman art," as we used until lately the term "Roman school," when we mean Florentines and Umbro-Florentines like Michelangelo and Raphael, Pierin del Vaga and Salviati, Jacopino del Conte, Vasari and their followers, who worked in Rome in the Cinquecento; or as

we still use the word "Gothic" although nobody now believes with the youthful Goethe that this generous style owed
anything to the Goths. We may use it for convenience, but
with the understanding that the art of later antiquity, that
is to say of the period of Roman rule, was as Hellenistic as
if Rome had never existed. The Hellenistic craftsmen working on the banks of the Tiber naturally had to consider local
exigencies, as the French and Italians did on the shores of
the Neva, but I discover more to betray Russia in the works
of Rastrelli or Batoni or Lampi, than I can feel to be
specifically Roman in any artifact made in imperial Rome.

It would have occurred to no Roman to claim that his
people made an original or serious contribution to art. The
elder Pliny's account is anything but brilliant; and as for the
noblest of them all, the most cultivated and the most sensitive, the poet Virgil, in lines that every schoolboy knows,
with his "Tu regere memento," leaves it to others to hammer
out bronze statues that will look as if they breathed, and to
carve in marble faces that look alive. He proclaimed what
Augustus and the finest Romans thought. They never
dreamt of imposing a "style Empire." That was left for a
Napoleon, an Italian, to be sure, and the most fascinating in
history, but head of one of the most artistically creative peoples the world ever has known since the Greeks.

Early Christian Art

So much for the present about the term "Roman art."
And now for another term, "early Christian art." It must
have come into use when all European art from the disappearance of Hellenism down to our day had been designated
as "Christian," to distinguish it from the antique or "pagan."
It would follow that the first generations of these craftsmen
would be classed as "early Christian." Soon, unhappily, the
term exuded, as it were, the notion that it had, contents

apart, a Christian character, different from the work done at the same time for people who had not yet been baptized, or seen the light of the Gospel. And thence no doubt arose the further delusion that the carvers of sarcophagi, the daubers of funereal signs and symbols, were necessarily Christians.

The facts were quite other. The humbler Christians, like the slaves or freedmen that most of them were, could afford to employ the least expensive only of craftsmen, the ones we find working in the earliest catacombs and in such a cemetery as that of the pagan "lower orders" recently brought to light at the mouth of the Tiber. With time, the ghetto and the servile Christians gave place to "Romans"—another question-begging term. For, except in citizenship, who and just what was a Roman by the second, let alone by the third, fourth, or fifth century? The wealthier and more cultivated among them were, as we have seen, completely Hellenized, except for language, and employed Hellenistic artists (since there were no others), who presented them with a world of visual shapes and forms more Greek than the most successful of their new religions was Hebrew. Indeed, the figure arts, let me say once again, did more to infect Christianity with Hellenism than all the writings of nostalgic Church Fathers and Doctors like Clement and Origen. Even the central image of the new cult, the Saviour, was visualized and carved into the shape of a youthful Olympian. Numbers of sarcophagi were produced in Rome which are distinguishable only in subject matter from those carved at the same time for equally well situated persons, who remained faithful to their ancestral worship. Nor are we concerned with the question of the origin or of the religion of the artificers, among whom there were, as Tertullian tells us, Christian makers of idols. The form of these as distinct from their contents is late Hellenistic and, as form, differs infinitesimally from kindred products of the same date, all over the less barbarized part of the still nominally Roman Empire of the West, as well as over the relatively intact East.

We may continue to use the term "Roman art" on the understanding that we connect nothing of a racial, national, or cultural notion with it, but only a temporal one, namely of something happening while Rome held sway over the Graeco-Latin world; so we may continue to use the term "early Christian art," knowing all the while that this was late Hellenistic art in the service of early Christians.

The same holds true of the arts derived from the Greeks who, settling some generations after Alexander in and around Gandhara, furnished Buddhism not only with its shapes but with its iconography as well, in the same way that late Hellenistic art was fitting out the Christian Church. Let me quote here from René Grousset's attractive volume entitled *In the Footsteps of the Buddha* (page 186), about the relative indifference of art to its subject matter, whether world-abandoning or world-loving. "And yet to the untrained eye was there so great a distance from the Buddhist art of the Gupta workshops to the Hindu works of the Mahratta country? Is not the triumphant Shiva of the caves of Ellora or of Elephanta once again one of those Bodhisattvas to whom we were introduced by the painters of Ajanta as well as by the sculptors of Borobudur? The bodies are just as harmonious, as graceful as those of yore, but free henceforth from all idea of renunciation, recovered from their pensive disillusionment in order to plunge straight into the heart of things, into the intoxication of life, by turns mystic and sensuous."

Mediterranean Art

I take it that this term designates art that had its roots on the shores of the Midland Sea and its hinterland. It would include the art of Egypt to the second cataract of the Nile and beyond down to Meroë; the art of the Near East at least as far as to the Euphrates; also the art of Hellas to the

Roman Limes in the North, to the Sahara in the South, and, on the North-East, to the Crimea and the Azov Sea. Not only does this hold true for antiquity and the Middle Ages, but for more recent times. Thus all European art down to this day, with the exception of Gothic in its hour and of the Netherlands in theirs, remains Mediterranean. That has been secured by the Italian Renaissance, against whose ever present influence rebellion is now raging. We are still the heirs of Greece and Judaea and are carrying out their ideals. We are still living in antiquity.

Hellenistic Art

The term "Hellenistic" covers the art that after the conquest of Alexander captured the entire Mediterranean world and its hinterland as just now defined. Only the influence extended much farther than even this definition would imply. We have seen that Buddhist art, practised in what are now Afghanistan and the Punjab and Java, is fully as Hellenistic as the so-called Christian art prevailing in the West. This influence was not soon lost. Gupta sculpture shows abundant signs and traces of this indebtedness, more perhaps than the contemporary figure arts of the Latin world; but too little Greek by that time remained in either to justify its being regarded as still Hellenistic. On the other hand, if I had my way I should abolish the word "Byzantine" and replace it with "mediaeval Hellenistic" to designate the art of the Greek-speaking world, down at least to the sack of Constantinople by the Latin barbarians.

Problem of Personality

There remains a problem that no student of any branch of history can afford to ignore, the problem of personality—of the individual, I mean, and his contribution to the whole, to the City of Man, and to our specific concern, the City of Art.

One cannot utter many words without betraying a metaphysical attitude, and without an affirmation ethical as well as aesthetical, not to say political. I have no affection for an abstract entity like "society" or "state," or any enlargement or reduction of these. I believe that man's aim should be to enable the individual to realize the best in himself, with due regard to what he owes not only to others as individuals but to these individuals as a community. I believe that a proper House of Life can be kept going and improving on those terms only, and not by those of a myth called "state." It is a myth which ultimately means irresponsible bureaucracy resting on fraud or fanaticism and ending in violence and the exploitation of the community for a governing gang's own ends —whether these ends be the relatively harmless ones of self, or the far more dangerous ones of power. The individual at best has small chance. Between his animal impulses and the discipline and training, the "conditioning" he is submitted to in order that he may control them, there is little room for the education of his private ego and the cultivation of its most specific and perhaps, in the long run, most creative possibilities.

Except as its clown and jester, society does not encourage individuality and the state abhors it. Nevertheless if "inglorious Miltons" exist, it is because they have been mute. History knows few Chattertons, but many whose genius was recognized with small delay. For genius as distinct from talent means creative reaction against spiritual as well as material environments, and its unavoidable by-product is newness. And newness the public cannot hold out against.

I need not insist that the personality we are concerned with here is primarily the artistic one, and is revealed in the works that have come down to us, with graphic and not verbal representation. I mean, for instance, that even in the case of a Michelangelo, we must not let his verses influence the reception we give his sculptures and paintings. His letters and sonnets may afford a better understanding of the man, of his inhibitions, ambitions, and intentions, but they never helped me to identify myself with his visual design, to become the statue or painting he fashioned, nor have they made it easier to lose myself in ecstasy before them.

Personality like originality in art is characterized in the first place by unlikeness to what has been done in the same field just before. There are three principal ways of attaining unlikeness. One is through the incompetence we have touched upon already. The other through despair of producing, with the shapes and patterns created by current problems, anything that would take the fancy of art critics, dealers, and collectors on the look-out for mere otherness. There is a third way, and that is to carry a problem of form and design further than it has yet been carried.

The first method may lead to quaint and rather attractive absurdities of provincial art, as we see in so much German and Spanish and out-of-the-way Italian sculpture and painting from the outlying regions of Umbria and the Marches, Istria and Liguria.

The second method is having its day just now, led by artists who could have produced splendid academic work, which, in this moment of proletarian tendencies, few would hear of, and fewer still buy.

The third has been followed whenever a problem was being worked on, till it found a solution so complete that there was nothing more to be done with it, except to repeat it competently.

Creative originality, individual genius, can thus manifest itself only when it finds a problem that it can carry forward towards a solution. It may, like a Guilhamus working at Modena in the twelfth, and a Masaccio in the Florence of the early fifteenth century, sow the seed or, like Michelangelo, reap the harvest but, as with literal and not figurative harvesting, seed and soil and season leave little room for waywardness. The freak experiment produces disaster only, as we see in the case of one of the most gifted of artists, Leonardo, in his "Last Supper." Satisfactory creations like the ceiling of Michelangelo and the Stanze of Raphael, carry tactile values, movement and space composition to the fullest flowering of which they are capable. The artistic personalities of these two geniuses coincide with the phases of the problem in which they found themselves involved. How much, and to what a degree that was the case may be inferred from the fact that neither could make headway against the momentum that was hurrying him towards the grossest exaggerations. Death alone saved Raphael from ending as a Giulio Romano, a follower who acts as if under a post-hypnotic suggestion. As for Michelangelo, he lived to paint the dyspeptic, overtrained athletes who fill his Wagnerian "Last Judgement" and the inflatedly heroic figures of the Pauline chapel.

We read at S. Maria dell'Anima in the epitaph of Pope Hadrian VI, "*Quantum refert in quae tempora vel optimi cujusque virtus incidet*"; which may be paraphrased as follows: How much the genius of even the most gifted depends for its effectiveness on the time in which it appears. The *virtus* of a Hitler or of a Stalin in 1875 for instance would have been as guiltless of their country's blood as the village Cromwell's in Gray's "Elegy." In art it is the same. Can we imagine that Raphael could have arisen in our twelfth century or a Michelangelo in the Trecento, any more than a Picasso or a Joyce in the audacious but still rational "Eighteen-nineties"? As in life we are earth-bubbles, peculiar to one particular spot, so in art we are twigs that can shoot out from only this or that branch of the tree which has been growing since the dawn of human consciousness.

Mankind has always been haunted by an interest in the time factor, not only in human history but in the individual's destiny as well. What else is astrology, which crops up so universally in moments of uncertainty and trouble, but the "subconscious" feeling that so much depends upon the kind of world one is born into?

Little room and few occasions remain for the manifestation of individuality. In art it appears mainly on the crests of creative energy. In the hollows it is apt to disappear.

In the field with which I happen to be best acquainted, Italian painting of the Renaissance, our chief effort during the last seventy years has been to detach and isolate the individual artistic personality from those that preceded and those that followed it. Our successes have been notable. Instead of recognizing it on the crest only, we have learnt to follow it up the wave while it is gathering volume, and down the other side as it is merged into the work of imitators. A telling example is Giovanni Bellini. A few decades ago he was admired chiefly, if not indeed solely, for a few altarpieces and some Madonnas painted between say 1480 and 1506, a career of some five and twenty years. After sharp oscillations of the pendulum between "contractionist" and "expansionist" critics, students have temporarily settled down—students never settle down more than temporarily—to the inclusion of a large number of works earlier than 1480 and a considerable number later than 1506, some of them equal if not superior to those previously admired. Not that these pictures had been wholly ignored. The great Pietàs of Rimini and the Brera from Bellini's earlier years, and the fascinating "Bacchanal" as well as the captivating "Lady at Her Toilet" of his last hours, so to speak, were known to exist. They either were not admired and loved as we love and appreciate them now, or they were misunderstood, as was so conspicuously the case with Rio writing about the "Bacchanal." Bellini's earlier paintings used to be ascribed to Mantegna chiefly, but also to Pollaiuolo, to Alvise Vivarini, and to Dürer. Nor was a single portrait attributed to him, whom we now recognize as one of the masters and creators of portraiture. As for his latest achievements, many of us in my time used to ascribe them to Basaiti and Bissolo, to Rocco Marconi and even to Cariani.

The same was the case with Botticelli. Only pictures in the spotlight were counted as his, the "Primavera," the "Birth of Venus," the "Magnificat," the Uffizi "Adoration," two or three portraits and as many Madonnas. Works we now regard as among his earliest and best were ascribed to Fra Filippo, to Filippino, to Ghirlandaio, to Pollaiuolo, and the earliest of all were disregarded or unrecognised. To this day there is no unanimity among scholars, and some reject what others accept.

Even Michelangelo's artistic personality retains ragged margins to the present day. There are hardly any of his earliest marbles that are not being questioned; and there is no agreement about paintings like the uncouth but sublime "Deposition," or the too charming "Madonna with Angels," both in the National Gallery. Likewise with Leonardo; not many are of the same mind as to where he begins and Verrocchio leaves off; as to where he leaves off and Predis or Boltraffio or Melzi begins. And Raphael—till the other day few were inclined to believe that the lower part of the "Transfiguration" and the Barberini "Fornarina" were his rather than Giulio Romano's; and far from settled is the problem regarding Giulio, Pierin del Vaga, and Francesco Penni, the share of each in the later frescoes in the Vatican and elsewhere in Rome. Then what shall we say about the unexpected leap forward, the "sport" in art to which we attach the name of Giorgione There is no softly gliding transition from Bellini to Giorgione as there is from him to Titian. One would suppose that the glamour of his fame and the enchantment of his four or five indisputable paintings would save his reputation from becoming the dump that it still remains, despite the effort of Morelli and his followers. Not only is every kind of cigar-boxy prettiness foisted upon it, but his finest creations, like the magical "Fête Champêtre," are tossed hither and thither, to Sebastiano, to Cariani, to Titian. Nor, in fact, is it easy to say where Giorgione leaves off and Titian begins.

This uncertainty is not confined to my own special field. Think of the fierce discussions that have been going on about whether a masterpiece of the highest order like "The Mill" is or is not by Rembrandt, and think of the many portraits and groups that have come to rest as a Velasquez or a del Mazo only after long oscillation to and fro. And the question of Van Eyck—were there really two or only one? And is Hubert a myth? Then who was the Flémalle Master, not perhaps a parallel to my "Amico di Sandro"? And, as that temporarily useful construction proved to be an early phase of Filippino, so would he of Roger van der Weyden? One could fill page after page with instances. And I do not take into account copies and forgeries so admirable that they try the expert's mettle and morals.

As for antiquity, who shall say what precisely was the artistic personality of Myron, of Phidias, of Alcamenes, of Praxiteles, of Lysippus, or of Scopas, not to speak of the great painters of those centuries whose names only have come down to us. Needless to say, it is not in the visual arts alone that this uncertainty prevails. In our Bible what questions of authorship, of interpolations, of dates! Where is the precise line of demarcation between the first and the second Isaiah, and between the second and a possible third? What epistles of Paul are authentic is still far from agreed upon. In philosophy how disentangle Leucippus from Democritus or Socrates from Plato? Controversy is still rife touching the authenticity not only of this arch-philosopher's letters but even of his dialogues, the Menexenos for instance, or the Hippias Major. In literature we have the exasperating problem of the Shakespeare canon. And what of the Homeric one? In my time this last has undergone a complete reversal and it is not likely that it is final. In music I am told that chorals and cantatas hitherto accepted as Bach's now turn out to be by Byrd and Purcell and others.

If personality, individuality, originality were as pronounced as it is usually assumed to be, how is it that in the instances cited, and the thousand others that could be enumerated, we find it so difficult to tell where one personality begins and the other ends? It would seem that the only answer to this question is that in art as in all other human activities, the communal, the universal outweighs the individual and particular to such a degree that but for hero-worship, mythology, hagiology, and propaganda, which inflate and distort things out of all relation to facts or to results, the most original genius rarely leaves more than faint permanent marks on the field of his activity.

Originality (if we may revert to it in passing), as a quality to admire and appreciate, is looked for in young emergent artists of our own day, not in those who have already achieved fame, and still less in artists of the past. This is due to a craving on the part of the public, not for a new way of seeing or hearing but for a new expression of well-known things—a visual, verbal, or musical venture, not to outlast a season and not rude enough to stand in the way of a still more recent novelty. Even in Dante's time the public deserted a Cimabue for a Giotto. In our so swift-moving age, a painter to escape oblivion must attempt to renew his manner once a year at least. He keeps his reputation on no safer tenure than the Priest of Nemi, the priest who "slew the slayer and shall himself be slain."

Artists take to originality from the moment that they begin to despair of exercising their respective professions within the terms and limits of their art; and I am speaking of the real artist, not of artificers who are out for success and publicity. They behave like fish out of water, like animals out of

21. Titian: Education of Cupid. Villa Borghese Gallery, Rome.

22. Detail from Pompeian Fresco. Villa dei Misteri Dionisiaci.

their element, and the greatest of them, like the aged Michelangelo in sculpture and painting, like Wagner in music, lash about like "Moby Dick" and give vent to their tragic tension in a pathos that transports and inebriates but leaves an after-taste of rhetoric rather than art.

So much for the individual and what at best he can contribute. On the other hand, at no period, no matter how early, has anything been done communally by a clan, tribe, or people in the mass. It is the individual—nameless, unrecorded, but the individual—who composed folk songs and ballads and epics, each contributing his individual gift, that now and again amounted to genius, to the genius of a Homer. It was individual craftsmen who painted at Altamira and Knossos, and individual builders who built and carved the noble remains of classical antiquity and the marvels of our Middle Ages. Although each builder contributed his originality of mastery or incompetence, few of their names have reached us, and fewer still have any meaning. Of mediaeval stone-masons we have any number of names. They leave us indifferent because we are in the habit of regarding architecture as an anonymous if not impersonal art, where individuality does not count.

Interest in individuality is a relatively recent phenomenon, except for the few classical centuries. The first ten or eleven centuries of our own era have few names to offer, and these only at the beginning.

Originality and individuality would seem to accompany inventiveness in technique and shapes, the illustrative and instrumental elements in the work of art, rather than the decorative, the more essential and more permanent. The grammar of the arts and quality undergo little change through the ages and, as we have seen, are not greatly affected by extraneous influences.

Thus newness, originality, individuality, would not seem to count so much in art as to be beyond question. In a history of art which is neither a history of technique and invention nor a series of biographies of artists, the personal, the individual side of things must not be exaggerated. Still less should matters of mere newness or originality be given undue prominence. Priority and the controversies as to who was the first to paint, carve, write, or sing in such and such a way have neither artistic nor ethical value. Nobody boasts of having been the first to suffer from the Black Death, or the bubonic plague, or the economic pestilence, as destructive as both these hellish visitations together, that has been raging since 1930.

In many ways art history would be blessed if it could ignore names altogether. It would then be easier to expose and get rid of the innumerable irrelevancies which now encumber it—whether technical, biographical, iconographical, or the still more vexatious metaphysical, theological, and Freudian irrelevancies which are a mere pretext for writing about art in a way that leads not towards but away from feeling and understanding it.

The history of art should be more concerned with problems than with personalities. Problems are solved piecemeal. Out of each of these pieces one would make an artistic personality, regardless of the individuals who embody the quest —unless indeed the career of a single individual coincides with the process of settling that particular piece of the problem which it is possible to achieve in a given time, place, and circumstance.

The nude, for example: Pollaiuolo and Michelangelo may be taken for cases of this rare kind of coincidence, when an individual, from start to finish, coincides with the segment of a circle, the complete solution being that circle. There is also the problem of magic that Giorgione introduced into painting but was prevented by an early death from solving, leaving it to Titian to pursue it. Titian went on with it, and his longevity permitted him to complete and one may say to exhaust its formal possibilities. Here we have two individual human beings, but only one artistic personality. So in a sense with regard to space composition, Perugino and Raphael constitute but one artistic personality. On the other hand, the man Bellini may be said to have had three distinct personalities: an early one till about 1475; a middle one till after 1500; and a late one. The second scarcely results from the first, and, in turn, does not necessitate the third.

This idea cannot be developed further here. May I be excused from adding that it has, from the beginning of my activities, been latent in my approach to art history. It accounts for the attempt to construct a myth like "Amico di Sandro," for the way I have traced, regardless of documentary testimony, connections between one painter and another, as well as for my growing indifference to the individuality of the mere executants of a pattern which they would faithfully copy, if incompetence of mind and hand did not prevent them. Individuals and their names are a serious and vexatious handicap, but we cannot ignore them, seeing how instinctively we are interested in other human beings. It is so easy to identify ourselves with them, seeming to partake of their lives, their successes and their failures. We do not readily forgo this pleasure, and we insist on personality, where attainable. When thinking of them we seldom avoid a tendency to romanticize them, a tendency based often on the puerile notion that the artist was from cradle to grave living the art he was producing. We imagine that the artists must have looked like a composite image of their own figures. The facts are different. The greater the artist the less he looked it and the more normal, ordinary, and even commonplace was apt to be his workaday life.

Names are for further reasons almost unavoidable. They are a program, a vision, a hope. The names Giorgione and Dürer, Blake and Cézanne set up all sorts of specific anticipations with regard to any work ascribed to them. And this, by the way, is the reason for demanding an impeccable connoisseurship, so that we may not be frustrated and misled in the experience. There is a humbler but more imperative reason why we may not dispense with names. It is that without them it is almost impossible to make things subjects for discussion, for conversation. It would be as much a handicap to try and talk of nameless artists as it would be to talk of birds and beasts and flowers and trees and minerals without being able to name them.

However, as these names are soaked with every kind of recollection and association, setting up expectations regarding objects bearing these names, there is danger that the expectation will discharge itself on any object to which a given name is applied. Thus the appellation "Roman temple" liberated Goethe's enthusiasm for the first he ever saw, the commonplace one at Assisi. Shelley likewise discharged all his romanticism on the temples of Paestum, but he spent most of his admiration on the so-called "Basilica" or "Temple of Juno" and had little left over for the incomparably finer temple designated as "Neptune's." Endless cases of the kind could be cited. It will suffice to mention Pater once more. No other writer has distilled and transvased the essence of a Botticelli or a Giorgione as perfectly as he has. Yet when it came to the individual work he was as ready to admire and enjoy a merely Giorgionesque picture, or a Botticellian studio product, as an autograph.

It may be asked how it comes to pass that a person who can penetrate to the inmost heart of the great master can yet fail to distinguish between his real work, the creation of both mind and hand, and the mere imitation, or studio version. It is a disconcerting and even alarming question which haunts the mind and at times makes us wonder whether the à peu près of the "near Giorgione" or the "near Botticelli" is not good enough for verbal artists discoursing about the visual arts.

For the man of letters, a Pater, a Ruskin, or even a Burck-hardt, the à peu près may suffice. It is neither near enough nor exact enough for the critic, for the student whose aim it is to make of himself an instrument of precision in the appreciation of works of art. Unless the historian of art is in the first place such an instrument, he cannot write history; for without full understanding and delicate appreciation a work of art cannot be evaluated or dealt with as an event in the history of art.

National Art

After all that has been said, the reader can infer without prompting what should be thought about the epithet "national" in connection with art. The term applies to illustration alone as this has been defined here, and to decoration only in instances where a certain purely qualitative peculiarity has become attached to the products of a certain region or community. Thus we may speak of Italian scale or proportion, and of the kindred Italian feeling for space, because since antiquity no other people has enjoyed these gifts and profited by them to anything like the same degree. How petty the detail of the Houses of Parliament in London, as was noted long ago by Taine, of our skyscrapers in New York —or even of Versailles, as compared with almost any edifice in Florence, Rome, or Venice dating from the twelfth century downward. The gigantic need not be grand! In the same way we can expatiate on the craftsmanship of the French in general and of the Parisians in particular, if indeed this craftsmanship has not perished in the course of the new Thirty Years' War—let us hope not Hundred Years' War—which started in 1914. And so until the de-regionalization of trades and crafts that has accompanied and outspaced the cancerous growths of political nationalism, every important district, every considerable town in Europe was distinguished for some specific thing which it could produce better than any other place and to which, therefore, its name was apt to be applied; e.g., "Irish linen," "French cabinet work or bronzes," "Bohemian glass," "Sheffield plate," "Viennese leather ware." All or nearly all are gone, except perhaps tailoring in London and women's clothes in Paris.

Then there are regional and national characteristics with regard to the subject matter, the content as it is generally called, but in our vocabulary the illustration. Although interesting and even important in other fields, as, for instance, in the history of sentiment, these traits have as a rule less and less specifically artistic value, the more they please the insensitive masses which respond only to what can pierce their skins. They enjoy emphatic, inflated, violent presentation only.

In the visual arts this kind of illustration, whether in illumination, metal relief, sculpture, or painting, has been cherished by the Germans from the Othonian period to our day. In recent decades it has found language with which to glorify its own aberrations in the terms "expressionistic" and variants of that word.

We may say then that the epithet "expressionistic" applies to most Teutonic art, and also to Spanish carving in the fifteenth century, which was overwhelmingly "Nordic" in origin, and to Spanish painting of the same period. Spain in her sickly moments has been singularly submissive to German winds of doctrine, not only in art.

The English, on the other hand, from the Heptarchy down have tended to the belief that the Muses need not be served, as Jacob served for Rachel, but can be scolded, pulled about, and forced to proclaim as a genius any dauber or scribbler. The English have had a tendency to ooze prettiness. It makes its first appearance in the manuscripts and bone-carvings of the Anglo-Saxon period, is held in check for a

time by Norman—I mean early Romanesque—austerity, to
burst into full flood with ripe Gothic. The English, like the
rest of us, defend most gallantly their weakest positions. One
of their less defensible ones is the castle of visual art, with
its innermost keep, monumental design. They are rather
peppery when their ability to hold it is questioned, and are
apt to establish claims to ground disputed between them and
the French. To drop metaphors, they would annex Gothic
sculptures, illuminations, and pictures to which their title is
not clear. One might propose as a fairly accurate test that,
within a given design or pattern, common to both sides of
the Channel, the prettier specimen is likely to be English.

I have no belief in permanent mental and spiritual characteristics, or in inherited instead of traditional qualities serving to differentiate one language group from another in the
white race. I am not even sure of permanent tendencies. Are
they more than tradition, ingrained habit, and self-laudation?
What is there in common between the Germany of Goethe
and the Germany of Goebbels? Nothing but the roots and
stems of their common language. For I doubt whether many
abstract words retain for the one the meaning they had for
the other. Likewise among the French, Lamartine and Hugo,
Leconte de Lisle and Sully-Prudhomme, Baudelaire even,
and Verlaine, masters of poetic clarity and directness, have
given place to versifiers who glory in occult cryptic diction.
What is left over of the puritanical, Sabbatarian, Bible-
breathing, squeamish Anglo-Saxon of my youth? Nowadays
you would have to look for him among the wild folk of our
Southern states or beyond the Caledonian Canal.

Long existing entities like Germany and England, and still
more the Orthodox and Roman Churches, have a right to
declare—the Churches that their iconography has inspired
art even as their liturgy has influenced literature, and the
nations that their folkways, traditions, and costumes have
kept artists treading paths laid out for them so long that

they can tread no others. Nothing of that kind can be claimed for sculpture and painting that pretends to be "democratic" or "authoritarian" or "totalitarian." Mathematics and the other sciences may be used for all sorts of democratic purposes, and remain not only neutral but uncontaminated. Artillery and aircraft are as ready to serve their captors as their producers. It is the same with art. The paintings of the Mexican Rivera, for instance, do not suggest any theory of society or government. They only distress one with the sight of ugliness and would-be representations of hatred. Art is perhaps as unsuitable for propaganda as cannons for churning butter, but could it be used for that purpose, it would be as indifferent to the beliefs and politics of those who employed it. I see no reason why proletarian regimes, whether red or black or brown, should be so eager to write themselves down as Calibans in art, and to identify themselves with misshapen figures, with exhibitions of ignoble rancour, or shoddily theatrical manifestations of the lust for power. Thersites was mentally and perhaps morally the superior of Achilles, but art could not deal with his look, his voice, his gesture. Homer has pilloried him for ever.

Art as art, not art for art, must be life-enhancing. Art tends to prefer subject matter which does not defeat that purpose. It wants to represent people better made, healthier, happier, more graceful, more distinguished, nobler, more heroic than we are, not the opposite. Art cannot put up with excess and pretence, with boasting and strutting, whining and cursing. Art cannot lie.

The Effigy and the Portrait

If what has been said and implied so many times in the above pages be accepted, we must be frank and conclude that art loves to represent the élite of birth, of talent, but on condition that this élite has the adequate and suitable physique—*le physique de l'emploi.*

If British art has not been too strong on the side of decoration, it has made up for it, in a measure, by its success in that interesting and valuable realm of illustration, the effigy. It is that which turns the Royal Academy show into a spring fair. The public comes to admire the effigies of the men and women which the year's painting presents for their emulation.

I speak of an effigy rather than a portrait, because the portrait is the rendering of an individual in terms of decoration, and of the individuality of the inner man as well as of his social standing. That is what Rembrandt, for instance, did supremely well, particularly in his last years. The effigy, on the other hand, aims at the social aspects of the subject, emphasizes the soldierliness of the soldier, the judiciousness of the judge, the clericality of the clergy, the self-importance of the business or professional man, the fashionableness of the woman of fashion, the clubableness of the clubman. Every frequenter of the Royal Academy draws inspiration from the effigies of the successful people in his own as well as in other walks of life. The exhibiting artist knows no better. In fact the more he sees what his public thinks it wants to see, the more it admires, honours, and rewards him. Is he not its executing hand? The chief requirement, however, is that the effigy shall be of persons who in themselves and in their setting are life-enhancing. With rare exceptions this has always been so, and not in England alone. The portrait as distinct from the effigy makes its shy appearance early in Egypt, but in our world not before Hellenistic times. Then the question becomes complicated by the increasing use of the death-mask, especially in Rome. This produces an individuality of mere shape, furnishing information about the subject, while, more often than not, it has as little art value as any other mechanical reproduction: say, the ordinary photograph. In the thousand years between 450 and 1450 of our era, the portrait, with extremely rare exceptions, vanishes. Even the effigy disappears almost completely, to come to light occasionally in the least individual shape possible, in representations of sovereigns in the overadmired Carolingian illuminations, in tomb sculptures, in rare portrait statues like the Angevine Charles in the Roman Capitol, or in the early fourteenth-century Ranieri del Torrina at Casole d'Elsa, and frequently in sepulchral brasses. Only in the fifteenth century, with Van Eyck in the Netherlands, Masaccio and Pisanello in Italy, does portraiture begin to revive and create more real portraits than perhaps had ever existed before. Yet for reasons of many kinds, the effigy prevails over the portrait, and the more a portrait is like an effigy, the more popular it is. Witness the wild enthusiasm for the later Sargents, and even the more discreet admiration for the frank effigies of Bonnat or Laszlo.

Photography

A certain prejudice still lingers in the public and even among experts against photography. We have travelled far from the days nearly fifty years ago when the then "new criticism" was received with the sneer that it depended on the "photograph and the foot rule." Yet an apologetic tone is not rare to-day among those who use photographs. It is therefore well to discuss briefly the legitimate, desirable, and certainly necessary use of photography, despite the abuse to which it is liable.

To begin with, we must discard the notion that photography reproduces an object as it is, as the objective "itness" of anything. There is no such thing. The average man supposes that if the camera gives him an image of a thing corresponding to his own way of seeing it, that image is an exact, albeit two-dimensional, reduced and colourless counterfeit. He has never been told that his way of seeing has a long history behind it, utilitarian, practical, cannibal even. He takes it for granted that he sees "reality," that is to say something outside himself, corresponding exactly to what he sees.

Seeing is as much an acquired art as speaking, although no doubt easier to learn. Until the other day, when the wide diffusion of illustrated weeklies and dailies, followed by moving pictures, began to establish a sort of visual Volapuk or Esperanto, there were on the earth several visualizing groups, as there have been and still are different linguistic ones; only the visualizing groups are more closely interrelated and of wider extension. Until less than two centuries ago the Eurasian continent and North Africa from the Atlantic to the Pacific had but five groups: the Latin-Christian, the Orthodox, the Islamitic, the Indian, and the Chinese. There were contaminations at meeting points as between Latin and Orthodox in Polish Galicia, in the Balkans, and in Crete; between Indian and Chinese in Tibet, in Eastern Turkestan, and Nepal, and in all the further Indies. Two centuries ago the average person in one of these groups would not have understood the visual representations of another group. Even now we are pretty much at sea outside our own group, and do not find it easy to evaluate achievements in another one. We are apt either to under- or over-estimate them, according as we are scrupulously honest with ourselves, or subject to snobbish contagion. The mere fact that an object is Indian or Chinese, Negro or Maya will rouse antipathy or enthusiasm, without regard to the intrinsic quality of the particular object. This would scarcely be the case if we were as familiar with the imagery of a given group as we are with our own. In our own group we judge the individual object on its merits, and do not write it down as beautiful or ugly because it does or does not belong to a class; just so we judge our own kith and kin on their individual merit and do not think of saying: "What can you expect of a German, a Jew, an Italian, an Irishman"—to mention the European groups among us most exposed to abuse.

Here let me point again to the blamelessness of visual as compared with verbal representation. Visualizing differences have never yet been, nor are likely to be, used to park people off into herds called nationalities. Language, on the contrary, is the only foundation still remaining for the citadels of those who would play the cannibal towards their alien neighbours.

To return to photography after this excursion, it would help us to see more than our own eye sees if the camera were the impersonal recorder it is supposed to be.

The camera is an instrument in the hands of the photographer, and he, being human, is apt to be a careless, mediocre, and naïvely prejudiced operator. At best how are you going to induce him to see in his camera what he does not see with his eyes—that is to say, with the mind behind the eyes? The eyes without the mind would perceive in solids nothing but spots or pockets of shadow and blisters of light, checkering and criss-crossing a given area. The rest is a matter of mental organization and intellectual construction. What the operator will see in the camera will depend, therefore, on his gifts, and training, and skill, and even more on his general education; ultimately it will depend on his scheme of the universe, and on what he wants and expects to get out of it. For which reasons it is as difficult to find a student of sculpture satisfied with a photograph not of his own taking, as to see a picture restorer, or book illustrator, or stage actor, who is satisfied with any but his own private interpretation.

This is a danger against which we are rarely warned. With due attention to lighting, and by posing the camera at a given angle to the object, you can, within limits, make it reproduce the aspect of the same object that suits your momentary purpose—honourable no doubt, but with a strong private bias.

To counteract this, the remedy is to consult photographs made by other operators as well, and by as many others as possible. If this is not possible, procure a photograph done by an expert operator who has no theories of his own, nor indeed any with regard to the object he is taking except a technical one.

The farther away from the figures in the round, and the nearer to the lowest relief, the easier the problem grows, just because the object is less and less exposed to distortion by lighting. Other troubles are to be looked for, as for instance the extreme difficulty of reproducing transitions from emphatic to gliding outlines, or the suppleness of a contour, as distinct from an outline.

This carries us over from the relief, no matter how flattened—"*stiacciato*"—to the drawing, whether it be done with the graver, pen or pencil, silverpoint, lead or chalks. Where this drawing is helped out with washes and pigments, it begins to present the obstacles to exact reproduction that we encounter in painting.

The task of photographing a painting is almost unsurmountable where it is a question of preserving the values, relations, and transitions of colour. In other respects it is easier, ever so much easier, than of objects in the round or high relief. Nevertheless the results are seldom satisfactory. This is particularly the case with paintings of quality, and by the greatest masters. Experience would urge me to say: The poorer the picture, the better the photograph.

Photography is thus branded as a not too reliable servant, one in fact which will be more ready to flatter the whims and even the vices of the critic-operator than to rectify them. Photography, at best, is an instrument in the hands of the manipulator, and an uncertain instrument at that.

Yet we cannot dispense with it. Memory is inadequate to the task of calling up the detail required for comparison, and in our work comparison is everything. It may be said that archaeology, like all other studies pursued with a scientific method, is based on comparison. It is constantly comparing unknown with known, uncertain with certain, unclassified with classified. Nor is it only a question of memory, in the sense that memory is unable to furnish the necessary details. It is a fact, of which long experience alone will fully convince one, that the photograph brings out not only details but aspects of objects that escape our notice. When the work of art is present one cannot avoid enjoying it as a whole and may even identify oneself with it to the point of self-obliteration, and thus fail to work up interest in detail, or lose the capacity for coping with it. Not so before the photograph, or rather photographs. There, training and habit turn one automatically into the scrutinizing observer and close investigator, who is not easily dazzled by some effect that at the moment appeals irresistibly.

I am not ashamed to confess that I have more often gone astray when I have seen the work of art by itself and alone, than when I have known its reproductions only.

Nowadays I hesitate to come to a conclusion about a work of art without submitting it to the leisurely scrutiny of photographs. The more photographs of the same object, the better. Each contributes something of its own, even prints from the same negative that should be identical. Better still when done by different operators, particularly when it is a question of objects in the round or in high relief.

Nor should manual reproductions, drawings, I mean, and every kind of engraving, woodcut or lithograph, be discarded as too subjective. Subjective they are, but scarcely more so than photographs taken by scholars and artists who willy-nilly reproduce what they want to see. These interpret no more and no less than does the draughtsman; and if the latter is a gifted scholar and artist, as was Viollet-le-Duc for instance, or Ruskin, his sketch may be a revelation.

Needless to say, in some cases the so-called mechanical

reproduction, the photograph (which is far from being a merely mechanical one), yields results so unsatisfactory, being almost undecipherable, that its outlines have to be traced on transparent paper by an expert hand and superposed over the reproduction. That is notoriously the case with the palaeolithic paintings in caves like those at Altamira, where (until recently at least) the undulating surfaces and the lighting reduced photography to all but impotency. Similar reasons make repoussé work and reliefs in metal, certain barbaric coins and medals, brooches and other ornaments hard to decipher in the photograph, and lead one to bless an interpretive drawing.

What has just been said about photographs is based on the supposition that the student is at home with original works in the style of the school and artist he is studying. Without this preparation the photograph can serve little better than an acquaintance with flattened and dried specimens can help the botanist.

These paragraphs on reproduction of works of art may be concluded by a few words on the photographic impressions produced by Röntgen, violet, and other rays. They are now the fashion. Impoverished museums starve themselves to install up-to-date radiographic studios, fitted out with every up-to-date contraption and contrivance. Mechanical devices are the forlorn hope of those who have little faith in trained observation and educated feeling. But these various rays are anything but merely mechanical in the sense of being foolproof. They too can be made to yield results that suit the operator. I have seen exactly opposite ones obtained by two different experts. Let us admit that the various rays may be instructive to students of technique and cleaning and restoring; it is doubtful whether they are of serious assistance in establishing authenticity or in analysing a work of art as a creation or revealing how it was conceived by its author and how carried to completion. That must be done chiefly, if not solely, through the examination of his drawings. For the rays can only penetrate. They cannot peal off stratum after stratum and spread them before our eyes as if they were sketches placed alongside of each other. They cannot, because, except in the case of a few tempera pictures where the design is completely thought out before painting begins, the dabs and daubs and blobs of pigment are apt to be so hastily dashed down, and get so mixed up, that like stain upon stain they make little sense. When a figure does make sense it does not necessarily bear relation to the finished picture. It may belong to one started on the same panel or canvas and dropped.

Craftsmen seldom waste material. We find Michelangelo using up scraps of paper on which there were accounts or notes or sketches done decades previously. We have sheets of paper with drawings unrelated to each other, done at different periods of Michelangelo's career, and even by later artists into whose hands these sheets fell subsequently. We have learnt to separate them and to keep them in watertight compartments, as it were, instead of letting them run into each other. The ray experts are still too excited over their discovery to be concerned about its limitations. Drawings have the advantage just mentioned that they are not superposed but juxtaposed, so that each in most cases shows up separately and distinctly. If we have enough of them they can give an idea of the conception and gestation of the work of art. The adequately trained student can decide which are earlier, which later, and which were discarded as idle fancies. By these means he can construct a series that follows stage by stage the development of the design to its successful completion.

The technique likewise seems revealed clearly enough on the surface if it is in a fair state—clearly enough for the historian of art, if not for the historian of technique. Thus, to take an instance, the naked eye can easily perceive that

23. Greco-Phoenician sixth-century Bust found at Elche.
Archaeological Museum, Madrid.

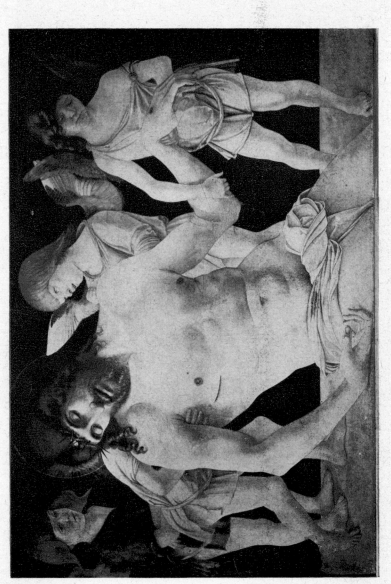

24. Giovanni Bellini: Pietà. Municipal Gallery, Rimini.

Lotto's technique is derived from the Vivarinis and not from the Bellinis, and that in Titian there is something of Gentile Bellini.

I speak here of these rays in connection with art history. It is another matter for the craftsman who hopes to discover just how a given picture was painted, and still another for that pathetic failure in art, the "genius" with no talent, in quest of the "secret of the old masters."

Art History and Art Practice

Must the art historian practise the art about which he is writing, practise it to the extent at least of understanding its technical problems and difficulties?

There are still painters who will not allow that any but other painters can understand their painting, as the sculptor Falconet attacked Winckelmann, who was not an artist, for writing about art. In 1777 Herder defended the critic against the artist with almost the same terms and the identical vocabulary that we use to-day.

Have these painters created their models that sit or stand or act for them? Have they created the animal and vegetable kingdom they so frequently make use of for their pictures? Have they shaped the hills and valleys and coloured the groves and fields and the infinite variety of cloud effects of which they compose their landscapes? How can they speak of these, comment upon them, criticize them, they who have not made them! They are generally naïve enough to say: "We are only painting what we see." But painting is their language, and every picture is a commentary, a criticism, an interpretation of what it represents. The painters and the artists in general may retort, "But we do study the anatomy and physiology of the animals we are going to paint; we have mastered geology, botany, and meteorology." Permit me to

ask how much scientific anatomy and physiology Polycletus
or Myron or Phidias had learnt? How much geology, botany,
or meteorology Titian or Rembrandt knew, or Ruysdael,
Claude, Turner, Constable, or Cézanne? They probably had
no more expert knowledge, no other experience of their
models, than is yielded by zestful concentrated observation
guided by a certain species of intelligence.

That precisely is the case with the critic and his relation
to the work of art.

One can be of two minds about it. The practitioner of an
art is apt to overestimate solutions of problems that absorb
him, and the overcoming of difficulties that trouble him.
Furthermore, the excited interest in technique that possesses
the kind of person I have in mind is apt to make a crank of
him. Thus I have seldom known a picture restorer, certainly
not a British or American one, who was capable of a sound
judgement about the technique (or the art quality) of the
painting he was victimizing.

As the interest that this essay may inspire is more likely
to reside in its autobiographical glimpses than in anything
theoretical or "scientific," let me venture to recount an experience of my own.

I had the privilege for years of frequenting the studio of
the least alarming, the most learned, the most competent restorer of Italian pictures that ever came my way. Few have
known what Luigi Cavenaghi knew about the technique of
the old masters. He restored hundreds if not thousands of
their works, and, in order to do so, inquired into the way
they were painted. Yet again and again I saw him puzzled in
the presence of a panel he had not seen before, and uncertain whether it were done in tempera with oil-glazes or with
oil alone. I found him hesitating in the presence of pictures
I knew to be forgeries. On the other hand, he could suspect
forgery where there was none. Once upon a time I gave him
a Bellini to restore. He kept it, as was his wont, for years.

One day, unexpectedly, he appeared with the panel, and told me he was sorry, but he did not like to touch it because it looked like a forgery. I was not perturbed, confident that it was genuine. I asked Cavenaghi whether he had brought the wherewithal for cleaning the picture. Yes, he had. "Very well, then, if it is a forgery let us see how it was done." He set to work and got off the stupendous carriage varnish that in England used to be applied to every Italian Quattrocento panel, and there came out an almost intact old picture, every touch betraying the delicate brush of Giovanni Bellini.

How is it that Cavenaghi with his technical experience had been wrong, and I, an utter ignoramus in such matters, right? Partly, no doubt, the potent "turtle soup" of British varnish, with which he was not too familiar, had led him astray. Perhaps there is more to it than that. Perhaps dwelling too much on the *how* a thing is done is not the surest training, the best preparation for appreciating *what* is done. Possibly one who familiarizes himself with the artistic personality of an old master, and has learned to identify himself with most of the creative ways of the same master, is less likely to go astray. Nowadays, I must hasten to add, forgers themselves seem to have learned the hidden ways not only of technique but of style as well.

Thus a few years ago a Botticelli was submitted to me. I reacted instantly to it as to a forgery. The dealer protested, begged to be allowed to leave the picture with me as long as I liked, and was confident that I would go back on my first impression and end by agreeing with him that the picture was genuine. I kept it and studied it for months together. I got an expert to examine the technique. I myself applied every stylistic test to it. No attempt, whether technical or stylistic (in the narrower sense), to demolish it succeeded. The farther I went the more cumulative the evidence that it was an old picture and a Botticelli. Nevertheless I remain convinced that it is a forgery. The hands are the hands of

Esau, but the voice is the voice of Jacob, of the trickster, the faker. No matter how meticulously he has carried out all the Morellian precepts—the shape of hands and ears, the folds in the draperies, the drawing of the hair; no matter how foolproof his technique, I no more believe that its author was the Botticelli I have lived with for so long than I should mistake for my wife a woman of the same shape and complexion, who had put on her clothes and ornaments, and even learned to imitate her gait, her gestures, her smile, and her speech.

CHAPTER V

ART HISTORY SPECIFICALLY

ART HISTORY, unlike political history or the history of any
other sequence of events over and past, enjoys the advantages and suffers from the drawbacks inherent in every
attempt to write about activities still operating, problems
still unsolved, and people still alive. No matter how much
one has learnt to delve in archives and to delight in deciphering and publishing documents, and thereby bringing
some point of the past nearer, and making it look brighter,
and ourselves feel warmer toward it; no matter how much
we enjoy reading history in the raw as mere res gestae—
chronicles of wasted time—or in the shape and form of literary works like Herodotus or Tacitus, Voltaire or Gibbon,
Michelet or Macaulay, Treitschke or Carlyle, such history
deals with what is dead and gone and treats with events that
are over and past, and individuals who are no more; and
speaks of things that we cannot experience, but only hear
and read about. Their influence to be sure is not spent, but
even the most gifted historian seldom succeeds in tracing it
in the world of to-day. Art history on the contrary has to do
with masterpieces still with us, still appealing, as living entities, as manifestly active energies. To one who has taken
the same trouble to learn the repertory of shapes current in
the different visualizing families of mankind as he has taken
to acquire their verbal languages, the whole world's art is
either wholly alive and contemporary or wholly dead. We
may fancy that we can learn about the life of the past from

written sources, but no written record can help one to imagine what a visual art was like of which no examples survive. We can frame no idea of its specific qualities, nor even of its shapes and patterns. Our only approach to it is through the tradition that it bore a likeness to an art that has come down to us in adequate examples, as is the case with some of the greatest names in antiquity. To take an instance: What did a mural painting by Polygnotus look like, or an easel picture by Apelles? The vases decorated by younger contemporaries of these masters may offer some vague idea.

The deciphering of inscriptions, the perusal of documents and diaries of events afford little incentive to *imitation*.

In things human it is not what exists or what happens or what is done that counts, but what is believed about them; in other words, their myth, their personification. Personification serves the need for making ideas, principles, and causes life-enhancing. Without this there can be no enthusiasm (which is the product of life-enhancing identification of self with something else), and without enthusiasm there can be no corporate action. Yet it is impossible to get enthusiastic over an abstraction without personifying it. Nowadays, for some of us, personification suffices. In the past it could not stop there, and went on to anthropomorphization, as is still the case with most of us. The mythopoeic process is analogous. Every life-enhancing personality became a hero in the mythological sense. Every permanently life-enhancing personality was a god. The most life-enhancing personality conceivable is God.

Myths, no matter how absurd, are in the nature of art, and life-enhancing as is all art. We cannot help searching for parallels from which to obtain justification, draw inspiration, and receive illumination for the present and give it glamour and respectability. One could cite hundreds of instances in the past when people went so far as to gain credit for their own writings by attributing them to a famous prophet, legislator, poet, or hero of old; to Homer or Orpheus, to David or Solomon, Isaiah or Enoch, or Virgil or Merlin. To take instances out of the last hundred and fifty years, and confine ourselves to visual art only, what style as it pushed away from its predecessor has not found its justification and inspiration in the past? "Empire" in the art of the Augustan age; the Romantic in Monreale, the Alhambra, Belém, or the Sainte Chapelle; François I in the châteaux of the Loire; art nouveau in Egypt or Crete; to-day's style in Negro sculpture, and to-morrow's in Papuan plasticity and Peruvian featherwork.

The business of the art historian is to rise, not above unchanging values, but above preferences instigated by the fads, stampedes, and hysterias of the moment. He must overcome private prejudice and dandiacal exclusiveness, and learn to appreciate successive styles first for their intrinsic merits, no matter how slight, and then for their living value in a humanistic scheme of life.

A style, we have concluded, is a constant and unassailable way of seeing things, and the history of the arts of visual representation should be the history of successive ways of seeing the world and all that therein is—the history in short, of styles.

The history of literature has for generations been written as an account of successive ways of imagining the life one would like to live, and of the attempts to explain these modes by theologies, philosophies, and pseudo-sciences. The history of music likewise is being studied as a succession of penetrations and discoveries in the realm of sound, deepening as well as enlarging our auditive universe and our capacity for enjoying it.

Every other type of what has been hitherto considered art history should be subordinated to this one purpose. Research is valuable to the degree that it helps to reconstruct the elements and fragments of a style in the way that classical archaeology has done. Connoisseurship in the last hundred years has brought to light again the almost wholly submerged styles of Quattrocento painting and sculpture in France and Flanders, in the Rhine and Danube basins, but perhaps the greatest resurrection of all has been that of the Tuscan and Veronese artists of the fourteenth century and the Florentines and Venetians of the fifteenth. The history of technique also has made valuable contributions, and I for one owe a debt of gratitude to a book that taught me much that even to-day others would do well to learn—I refer to Charles Eastlake's *History of Oil Painting*. And at this hour many would profit by reading the illuminating treatises of Denman Ross and of Daniel Thompson. It is right that the formative stages of a style should be adequately considered. In no case, however, should the art historian let himself be beguiled, by zestful indulgence in these ancillary occupations, into believing that he is writing the history of art. Least of all should he fritter away his energies and our attention with tricky questions of origin. Origins should be traced back so far only as, within the present horizon of intellectual activity, they are relevant to our specific preoccupations. They take their interest from the entities of which they attempt to study the beginnings. The tendency of recent decades has been to forget this. We grow more excited over the palaeolithic layer, and the neolithic slum, than over that masterpiece of Iotinus and Phidias which for twenty-three hundred years the world of culture has worshipped under the name of "Parthenon." We must not forget Chartres in its splendour, while searching for its embryo.

Historians of some centuries ago could not compose the history of their home-town without going back to Adam and the Creation, or at least to Noah and the Flood. As an admirable English essayist has said recently, the fruits rather than the roots should be the object of our attention and admiration. Interest in the roots is more often than not a trait of that skyscraping pedantry which characterizes so much of the automatic pecking of brainless "research fellows," in our myriad schools of useless knowledge.

Research does not write history. It only furnishes material for history. Some of it is poor, friable stuff, of little use as building stone, and scarcely good enough as rubble for stopping a hole.

The value of research depends upon the field where it is carried on. In the realm of classical Greek and of Italian Quattrocento and Cinquecento art, the most mediocre adept may dig up an inscription, or a fragment, or a coin out of the ground; or discover a document in an archive, or a signature on a picture; may make elaborate statistics of the number of times in the art of the Middle Ages Our Lord blesses with three fingers, how many times with two and a half, and how often with two only; or how frequently St. Catherine has her wheel and St. Andrew his cross to right, or again to left. Research is of less and less consequence, when the art with which it is concerned is peripheral, sterile, with no fecundating effect anywhere, as is the case with most of mediaeval Catalan Ligurian as well as with almost all later phases of East Christian art. Micrological pursuits along those lines lead no further than the bees in the anecdote of the king who wanted a story without an end. A wayfarer offered such a tale and began by saying: "Once there was a beehive, and one bee went in, and then another bee went in, and another, and another." He went on till the weary king asked whether the story could not be proceeded with. "Not till all the bees were in." "And when was that to be?" "Never."

Art history, if it is to be more than one way among others of keeping adolescents of all ages out of mischief, must avoid being too curious about the less significant schools of art, schools based largely on successive copying, and leading nowhere, as is the case with late Gothic, with much of the so-called early Christian, much of Carolingian, most of the too numerous illuminated manuscripts from the inferior scriptoria of the Othonian and later periods, and with much mediaeval Florentine and Sienese, not to speak of more provincial painting, over which I myself have wasted so much time, and by example induced others to waste even more.

Art history is the story of what art has created, of the problems that it has had to solve before producing what it did; of what it could achieve and transmit; to what spiritual needs it gave expression, thereby bringing them into the field of consciousness, what technical or psychological handicaps prevented it from yielding better fruit at given moments. It should tell what art shapes were presented to the public from age to age by artificers and artists; how related these objects were to one another, how lit and how coloured. The public itself can only accept or reject. It cannot invent, nor can it be credited with expecting anything definite. Yet it is not quite passive. In historical times at least, it has never been entirely deprived of choice, limited as that choice may have been. Even in pre-dynastic Egypt, the individual's means and perhaps his taste decided whether his knives should be of bronze or obsidian or flint, with the slight variety of shapes necessitated by the differences in consistency and colour of the material employed. To-day the choice seems limitless. It only seems so; for in matters of art we have no desire to get away from a convention we have accepted with or without a struggle. We make small effort to know the other conventions, assuming that they are numberless and no concern of ours. Yet they are not numerous. They are in fact few. Two or three stepping-stones and you have crossed over from Bouguereau to Dali. How like each other these painters, and all between them, will look some day! Think how easily any tourist learns to recognize that a picture is a *"primitif"*! It means that certain pictures painted in Italy and Catalonia, France and Flanders, Rhine and Danube lands, have for us to-day a something in common that unites them, despite divergencies of character or quality. And yet to their contemporaries the separate schools or the individual artists must have looked no less different from each other than ours look to us.

Bicci di Lorenzo and Masaccio, Bicci's son Neri and Fra Filippo, Cosimo Rosselli and Botticelli—what painters of our last hundred years have been further apart than those coupled contemporaries cooped up together in tiny Quattrocento Florence? There was in far-away China at the same time another convention, farther apart still, so far apart that the few Europeans who had access to it could have made much of it. It might have said little more to them than a page in the Devanagari script says to him who has not learned to read or understand Sanskrit; for, as we have had occasion to assert again and again, one has to learn art representation as one learns any other language, even one's mother tongue.

It is therefore rash to talk, and write, and lecture about the art of a given time as being not only the complete but the necessary expression of that time, as being *Geistesgeschichte*—the shibboleth of recent German art history— the story of mind or spirit in general. As a matter of fact the art of a period expresses only what its practitioners can manage to say, and that depends not alone on their individual genius, on the condition of their craft, and on their preferences and curiosities, but on their talents as well. Talent is a matter of using and improving the means at hand, the instruments, the technique one has acquired at school, and perchance perfected. The man of genius without this inherited capital would be almost as badly off as a prophet without tongue or pen. Even a Blake could not do without the achievement of the past; but having had no proper teachers to allot him his share in it, he had to snatch it for himself, and ended by pouring his honey and his lava through forms moulded by Fuseli and Michelangelo together—a strange brew.

No art, nor yet all the arts combined, can hope to give in one moment or period of time adequate expression to the goodness and nobility that are latent in man, and to all that genius can discover and order and use for the House of Man that is ever building and ever rising, despite the brutish propensities of our animal nature.

It is the business of art history to describe and interpret the shapes and compositions presented to various human societies for their admiration and instruction: distinguishing those that still rank as works of art from those that are little more than mere artifacts, and objects of curiosity; to dwell lovingly on the first and glide rapidly over the others, handing over some of the last to the ethnologist for further investigation. Art history should try to discover how various modes of representation were received by the communities to which they were offered; which of those modes became established for generations or even permanently; which were only passing fashions; which gave satisfaction to the most advanced circles of a given society; which on the other hand to its less noble groups; above all which way of seeing contributed most to building up our own stock of images as well as their becoming in themselves classic, that is to say ever contemporary. Art history should go further and try to see what correspondence there was between the visual representations and other expressions of the life of a period, literature for instance, music, the stage, as well as philosophy, political theory and conduct, and of course religion. In short, the study of successive modes of seeing can be used as a document, and as a most informing document in the general history of humanity.

By way of illustration let us take Raphael and Titian, who still hold central positions in the world of art. Against the second I have never heard of rebellion. The admiration for the first, excessive at one time, has suffered a certain decline in the last hundred years; but one by one painters and critics are creeping back to kneel before him. It would be worth while to inquire not only into the modes of seeing that preceded and shaped both these great masters—which in a sense has been done fairly well by this time—but also what it was in their respective styles that made them so quickly reach the position they have held ever since.

Art creates masterpieces which are first and foremost a revelation and a joy; after a while they become and stay on as a light, a guide, a model. Art, moreover, teaches us to feel and see what, left to ourselves, we who are not artists have not seen and perhaps never would see. Take for example new kinds of beauty in our own fellow men and women. Who has not noticed the sudden emergence of a type of woman with which we had no previous acquaintance? Some painter or sculptor has created it out of pure fancy, you would think. But, lo and behold, you begin to see it everywhere, not only in the drawing-rooms of the select but on the street, in trains, in buses. How is it you never saw it before? It could not have sprung up over-night. It was always there but, unaware of being noticeable, was not thinking of how to manifest its qualities. The artist, aided by dressmakers, hatters, and hair-dressers, revealed it to itself.

In my youth it was in Old and in New England the kindred Rossetti and Burne-Jones types that we admired. This was followed by others, inspired first by Botticelli, and then by early fifth-century Attic types, the first rediscovered Korae of the Acropolis. Later the hard, smart Sargent women conquered Boston, then New York, to end as the idol of imperial London. Then appeared in all fashionable Anglo-Saxonia the "Gibson girl" with her male companion, both sartorially elegant, socially *blasés*, and spiritually empty. Nor was society in Paris unaffected by the washerwomen and ballet dancers of Degas and the male and female apaches of Lautrec and Forain. In the second Reich men and women succeeded in looking as haughty, as would-be distinguished, languid, and leering, as Lenbach painted them.

It is the same with nature. One may well ask what enduring masterpieces the Impressionist painters created. But what have they not opened our eyes to see in the colour of the world! It used to be limited to blues and greys, vegetable and bottle greens, yellows, reds, russets, each separated from the others almost as stones and garnets in a setting. The Impressionists taught us to see shades of rose, of purple, of vermilion, to enjoy the sonority of malachite greens and the flute notes of cobalt blues (if I may be allowed to use these analogies), and tints which we can attempt to describe only in their resemblance to apples, peaches, apricots, oranges, and lemons. And who earlier saw, and was aware of seeing, transparent and even coloured shadows, to appreciate the beauty of the lichen on tree trunks, of the fallen leaf and the splinter on the road-side, not to speak of the translucent reflections of the floral world.

Did not the sportsman who happened on Sir John Millais painting "Chill October" look over his shoulder and ejaculate, "Come, come, my man, we all know that fields are green and skies are blue. Don't let's have any nonsense." Now Millais was far from being an Impressionist, yet what he saw was beyond what even a sportsman, presumably an observer of nature, could or would see.

As a matter of fact, we keep learning to see not only from earliest infancy but through the rest of life. Only once out of the nursery and still growing, it is art that teaches us. Perchance we are but at the beginning of the revelation. We cannot conceive what, if annihilating catastrophe does not intervene, artists will teach us to appreciate in nature, and still less can we imagine what masterpieces of creative genius the future reserves for us: no more than even an Ictinus and a Phidias, when building and decorating the Parthenon, could have surmised Chartres and Rouen and Rheims and Amiens and Beauvais; no more than Pompeian painters of backgrounds could have foreseen the landscapes of Rembrandt, Ruysdael, Claude, or Cézanne.

If the history of art is to be an interpretation of what shapes, what forms, what compositions humanity from generation to generation, from decade to decade, has been privileged to see and to live with, it follows that we must in historical periods diminish our interest in the individual artist and ignore him almost as we do in prehistoric art. The lives of even the greatest geniuses as well as the history of their achievements we must leave to biographers, and the more readily as even the Michelangelos and Caravaggios and their like never so completely dominated their contemporaries as Alexander and Napoleon and other men of action dominated theirs. The story of an artist's activities plays a much less important part in the art of his own day than the story of the man of action. Thus it is by no means easy to separate biography from history in the case of the individual who more than any other changed the entire aspect of Mediterranean politics, culture, and civilization. To this day, twenty-two centuries after his death, we still divide the past of the world between what preceded and what followed Alexander the Great, exactly as we cannot help dividing recent history into before and after the first World War. But it is not so with even the greatest artists. It is certainly desirable for us to know Michelangelo, but most of his close contemporaries in Italy itself pursued their way, unaware of his existence. There is no inkling of him in Giorgione or the younger Titian, or indeed in any Venetian much before the middle of the sixteenth century. In the north, Dürer betrays scarcely any acquaintance with him, and Holbein less. On the other hand, what important person contemporary with

Alexander, or Napoleon, or Caesar could remain untouched? The boast of a Catullus that Caesar meant nothing to him is a confession of the opposite, that in fact he meant much.

Yet men of action turn more and more into cloudy myths if they are remembered at all; whereas the artistic as distinct from the civic personality of the painter, the sculptor, the architect, the writer, lives on through his extant works. The influence of these works may operate increasingly for generations after the physical death of their creator. Nobody in Michelangelo's lifetime, not even Tintoretto, owed so much to him as did Rubens in the next century. His shapes, his action, his spacing were still living forces in the nineteenth century, not only in France but even in Pre-Raphaelite England, as was manifested by Alfred George Stevens. Or think of what Burne-Jones owed to Fra Filippo Lippi and to Mantegna. To-day, have not the most admired painters of the hour gone back to Piero della Francesca and to the hitherto so obscure Tura and Ercole Roberti, neither of whose names had lodged in an artist's mind for centuries.

It is, then, the extant works that count, and not the biography of the artist. These extant works make up the artistic personality, as distinct from the civic, biographical personality; and this alone is of vital interest. Anecdotes, associations, anything and everything that is not clearly revealed in the extant works is irrelevant, and retards our coming to grips with them.

Artistic personalities are equivalent to distinct modes of seeing, and are something in the nature of a sport. Who will deny that this sport can manifest itself as genius? What is genius, in our field at least, but creative reaction against its begetters and teachers? Yet for us all that counts is the manifestation that has won through, that was never obliterated or, if so, was easily revived. In art history, as in the course of all other events, there is room for a certain play of the unexpected, of the unpredictable. Should we have had the Michelangelesque without Michelangelo, the Giorgionesque without Giorgione, the Tintoretto, the Velasquez, the Rubens way of seeing without the temperaments of these individual personalities? The expected course of Florentine art should have ended in the Sansovinos and in Andrea del Sarto, not in Michelangelo; and the Venetian Quattrocento painters should have ended in Basaiti, in Bissolo, in Catena perhaps, possibly in Palma, not in Giorgione and his successor Titian.

Something new, something never seen before, was placed before the eye of a public astonished and fascinated by Leonardo. His vision of things was popularized by scores of pupils, followers, and imitators not only in Italy but in the Netherlands, in France, in Germany even. Yet there is no agreement as to what this genius conceived and carried through with his own hands.

It would thus seem that the great master's vision could be so transforming, could stamp itself so deeply upon all within its range, that its revelation might be communicated by imitators no less than by the creators' own hand.

As a matter of history and experience, what the cultivated public cares for is not the Life of Life that can be kindled in us by the artist's touch alone. It cares for his vision, and this it gets as well in the Leonardesque as in Leonardo, in the Bellinesque as in Bellini, and so on. And finally the public cares for the heart, for the central idea, and these they find in the followers of the great masters, but carried further, simplified, and pre-masticated, as it were, in a Luini, for instance, rather than in Leonardo himself. It may be observed without cynicism that Luini gave the most cultivated public of recent generations, led by Ruskin, all of Leonardo that they could stand. Ruskin did not hesitate to exalt Luini's Lugano "Crucifixion" "as for all religious art qualities the greatest picture south of the Alps or rather in Europe" and thus placed him far above the Florentine magician.

The popular attitude towards art, its indifference to everything but prettiness and brightness, is illustrated by Pseudo-Francesco Fiorentino, a collective name for a concern where copies chiefly of Fra Filippo and Pesellino were turned out in great numbers, brilliant in colour, enamel-like in effect, but almost devoid of the transitions which modelling requires to obtain tactile values. I am told that one of Pesellino's masterpieces was turned down by museum after museum in America, because they could not appreciate the difference between it and a copy from the factory above mentioned. Do we do better? No doubt, but at what expense! In the case of Leonardo, connoisseurship compels me to believe that he had a hand in Verrocchio's "Baptism," that not only the pretty angel, but much else there that is not so pretty, is his; that the subtly unpleasant bronze David ascribed usually to Verrocchio may be largely his; that the hideous Madonna of the Hermitage and the somewhat simpering one of Munich, as well as the rather empty "Annunciation" of the Uffizi are from his brain and hand. Or let us take Corregio. His artistic personality has profited little by the rediscovery of early efforts before his genius took wing. In most instances the search for the sources of a great master's vision has led to our finding them, but to the confusion of the vision. Has a coherent understanding and feeling for what is essentially Botticelli's style been made easier, now that we have traced him to the kitchens and cellars of Verrocchio and other cooks and brewers of doubtful portions and potions?

It is not the fumbling, not the tuning of the instruments that avails but the complete expression, and in the arts of visual representation it is the most crystalline, most unprismatic that counts—not the Raphael who hardly can be distinguished from Perugino, as in works for Città di Castello, or from his own apprentice Giulio Romano, as in the Barberini "Fornarina" and the lower part of the "Transfiguration"; but the Raphael of the "Madonnas," from the "Granduca" to the "Sistina," and of the frescoes in the Stanze. That is the vision that, in the four centuries and more which followed, few have failed to love and to yearn for as an ideal state of being.

The history of art, then, as distinct from the history of techniques and biographies of artists, should be a record of successive although not always continuous modes of representation. What counts in actual experience is the kind of representation—grace it with the name of vision, or exalt it by calling it a revelation—the kind of world which is offered to our eyes by means of graphic design. This, admitting their own modes of expression, applies to the other arts as well: to literature, to music, and to her twin sister, architecture. What, for instance, is Rousseau but the name for a particular, coherent, and in its time revolutionary way of feeling about society as a whole? What are the Romantics who succeeded and the Naturalists, Realists, that followed fast and faster! In music, the complete laicization of it connected with the name of Mozart, that took place toward the end of the eighteenth century, left it open for Beethoven to make us feel both the wistfulness and longings for a full and noble life, and the baffling deficiencies of our own nature standing in the way of attaining it, and enabled a Wagner to bring home to us the inexorable fatality that leads the most magnificent life-enhancing energies to frustration and tragedy.

We need not insist that the public as well as writers on art have had in mind a style and a quality rather than a civic personality when they speak of a given musician, poet, or visual artist of the past. In essence the word "Raphael" was not different in meaning from the word "Renaissance" or, as our great-grandfathers used to say, "Roman school." One referred to a certain kind of pattern, a certain kind of mood, a certain quality of being just as much as did the others.

Not that I would encourage the abuse of the German idea of Volk—happily not to be translated and still less domesticated in plain English. Folk, as folk, has never originated, never created anything. Folk is at best a term for an abstraction subsuming a number of individuals belonging to what is supposed to be the basic layer of society. When something is created by it then it is the gifted individual sprung from that mass, in other words, a sport, who invents it, not some mystic body uttering the messages of the Earth Mothers. The individual counts immeasurably more in the evolved and perfected phases of art. We cannot exaggerate the contribution of a Giorgione, a Dürer, a Rembrandt, a Watteau. Nevertheless the greatest innovators among them have as individuals affected but slightly the scroll wherein is registered the way in which, through successive ages, a society feels, perceives, and records what genius has enabled it to see.

An effort to write about art in this way was attempted some fifty years ago by the Viennese Alois Riegl in an elaborate essay, the title of which in English might be *Late Roman Arts and Crafts*. As the artifacts there discussed have no spiritual content, no exhalation of uplift, it has not been translated into a Western language, although I know of no other publication, in our field, more indispensable to thoughtful students. So much has been discovered, discussed, classified, and dated since its appearance that many of its results and even contentions can be set aside. The purpose, the direction, the method, remain.

The relative modesty of the material studied, and the fact that no names of artificers are connected with it, nor even the precise region where it originated, makes it easier to accept a non-personal and almost non-local treatment. The contention is that the artificers and artists of late antiquity grew increasingly tired of form, increasingly indifferent to shape, but more and more addicted to colour, and more still

to the play of light and shade; furthermore, that they rev-
elled in abstract space, and in composition completely de-
tached from backgrounds whether of landscape or of architecture, and existing, as it were, in infinity.

One need not accept all of this, and I confess that the
proposition about space leaves me sceptical. But the fact
that a gradual change came over the arts, parallel to the
change in religious sentiment that culminated in the triumph of ascetic ideals, is beyond dispute. Indifference to a
worldly civilization revolted against the glory and splendour
of Hellenism in favour of Judaic other-worldliness, in combination with the Coptic-Alexandrian life-weariness that
characterized Christianity.

Riegl had many unconscious precursors in the last few
centuries, since Vasari. Close to our time he was anticipated,
but only in half-conscious fashion, first by Burckhardt in his
work on Italian architecture, which he would have wished
to be a history of evolving and changing shapes and patterns
that were not of a representational order; then by Goodyear
in his fascinating *Grammar of the Lotus*; and finally by the
book this *Grammar* inspired, Riegl's own *Stilfragen*, dealing
as did the *Grammar*, but more intellectually, with the history of ornament. Wölfflin, the most disinterested and most
constructive of surviving workers on art history, in his *Classical Art* comes nearest in awareness to Riegl, but never
reaches the same full and deep sense of the problem. Let me
take the occasion to declare my own indebtedness to his two
books on classical and baroque art.

Chronology

From the foregoing pages it would seem that in an unconscious way the educated classes, as distinct from archaeologists, connoisseurs, experts, and other specialists, have al-

ways felt that the art of the past was a record of what, at any given moment, the public was offered to contemplate and enjoy, as well as what it ended by retaining. We must accordingly realize more and more the necessity of the right sequence of the phenomena. Hence the preoccupation with chronology, not in art history alone, but in all historical questions, whether of literature, abstract thought, music, science, and of course in the shape and form of politico-military events as distinct from their incidents and unpremeditated results. It has become a preoccupation which, on the part of unskilled labour, takes on grotesque shapes of micrologistic pettiness. In our studies, as in Roman law, one should not forget the maxim *"De minimis non curat praetor."* Squabbles are going on about the dating within a day or two of this or that brush stroke in Michelangelo's ceiling, about this or that chisel mark on one or other of his marbles. In our studies where events are seldom crucial, seldom watersheds in the streams of history, pedantically exact dating is not called for. In the case of the individual artist, it may be wiser to do what was attempted in my lists of "Italian Painters," namely, to indicate which of their works were early, which mature, and which late. The exact sequence of events is of prime importance; for it is only in their proper relation that we can hope to understand them as events, to enjoy them fully as creations, and to press out of them the elixirs that refresh and strengthen. For the past is our own autobiography, and that of every humanized, that is to say cultivated, individual. It is also, when not romanticized and mythicized, the humus of the future. The past, moreover, should furnish a sense of the potential, of the momentum and direction of every activity in the present. So-called spontaneous manifestations of energy, in any field, are apt to resemble mere explosions, mere flashes—no matter how brilliant and alarming. For unearthing the secrets of the old masters nothing is so necessary as to make sure one is pur-

suing the right vein. Without the chart furnished us by an
adequate chronology, that is not possible. It must be adequate but not more than that. If too minute it may be as
confusing as a map overcrowded with detail.

Successive Attitudes Towards Works of Art

More and more, then, is it borne in upon us that it is the
succession of styles, modes, or changes in interest, direction,
and taste, and not individual artists, no matter how gifted
each in his own way, that form the backbone of art history.

The autonomous value of the work of art once fully understood and not misused as a slop-basin for the expressionistic
writer's outpourings, there is every reason for treating it as a
document in the history of feeling, taste, and thought. Nothing is more profitable for this purpose than to pursue the
fortunes of a masterpiece from the moment of its creation,
through all its phases of glory as well as of occultation, down
to the present day. The study of its vicissitudes, the changes
of attitude toward it, the ups and downs of appreciation,
and the reasons for these changes are matters which should
claim attention as a serious part of our pursuits. Thus far
little has been done and energy is wasted on the study of
the flea that bites another flea, or on the meaningless reconstruction of Catalan and Italian polyptichs in which the
patron and the frame-maker had all the say, and the artist
nothing. As yet research along these lines has scarcely been
attempted, and my proposal to various American universities
to encourage it has been ignored. In a satisfactory way it
has been done but once, in a monograph on Correggio by
Silvia de Vito Battaglia (R. Istituto di Storia dell'Arte,
Rome, 1934). In perusing that volume, which sets out to be
a mere bibliography, we can acquire a fair notion of what
Correggio meant to people in the course of the last four

centuries. That is *Geistesgeschichte* but it is based on facts, and not evolved out of the vapours of current wishful thinking.

Interest in the past is so closely dependent on the problems of the present, that as the present changes, both its specific curiosities and its way of looking at works of art change. That rather than the discovery of new materials, valuable as they may be, is the reason why the history has continually to be rewritten.

Heraclitus would have it that we cannot dip twice into the same stream. What is there that we can exactly repeat, seeing that neither within nor without are we and our universe the same for two consecutive seconds? Still less can we enjoy or appreciate or understand anything the same way twice.

In the realm of mind and heart five years may be the measure of a generation. From one to another generation the changes may not seem striking; but after a not too protracted lapse of time, our reaction toward a creation of the past begins to be increasingly different from what it was in those who first enjoyed it. This feeling is continuously changing, but so imperceptibly that it takes special gifts to perceive it, and advocate a turn of taste or an alteration of attitude.

In the verbal arts, whether as pure literature and history in general; or as wisdom among all Orientals from Egypt and Judaea to India and China; or as philosophy written by the Greeks and ourselves, their descendants, from Plato and his precursors to Kant and Bergson, the changes from epoch to epoch have been the object of illuminating study. Thereby the contribution of each generation has been ascertained both for its intrinsic qualities and for its effect on succeeding periods, which found in the original contribution a delight, a stimulus that previously had not been felt, not even by those for whom it was first created. In the same way we should study the visual arts: first as to what they meant to those for whom they were created, then as to what they mean to ourselves now, and finally as to what interven-ing periods have got out of them. In that way we become aware of the work of art as a permanent possibility of in-spiration and enjoyment; while at the same time its varying effects upon successive generations help us to understand in what way these differed from one another.

Recommendations

Now let me briefly make two or three recommendations beyond those made already.

Art history of every kind, not only of visual but of literary and musical art as well, is apt to pay too much attention to the "why" and not enough to the "how." The "why" is no doubt a more exciting inquiry because it never can get be-yond mere guessing, impelled and coloured by the preju-dices and passions of the day. But the "how" can be ascer-tained in a way that will persuade most students to agree as to its probability.

The economic factor should never be lost sight of. I do not refer only to the conditions of a society as a whole, but to those of the individual, or the group, that orders an arti-fact of any kind. In the same place, at the same time, the quality of art produced must always have depended, as it still does, on how much some one is able or willing to spend. I have previously referred to the case of the paintings and stuccoes done for early Christians in Rome, as well as those of the Isola Sacra outside Ostia, where freed-men, slaves, and other humble folk were buried; and have spoken of how their art was conditioned by the circumstance that they could afford only the humblest artificers. I could call up instance after instance in Quattrocento painting where the painter would from the same cartoon produce a number of versions, more or less autograph, but varying so much in ornamental effect as to suggest no other reason for the difference than that the painter was paid more for the one than for the other.

As I am revising this (September 1946), the "Gates of Paradise" by Ghiberti are being cleaned. It turns out that they were gilt. Andrea Pisano's door for the same Baptistery has a heavier gilding. Probably this means that in the interval Florence had got less rich. In Siena as well as in Constantinople the gold-ground paintings and illuminations get poorer with increasing impoverishment.

Having just referred to the relation between artist and client reminds me to protest against the absurdity, so current in romantic art history, of taking it for granted that it was the painter or sculptor who was responsible for the subject matter of his work, and of proceeding thereupon to draw conclusions touching the artificer's character, private opinions, and predilections. As a matter of fact, it was the employer who gave his orders as he would to a carpenter, tailor, or shoemaker. The artist could be creative and personal to the extent of his natural and acquired capacity, but always within the conditions imposed by the person who gave the order.

I protest against yet another fallacy, that happily occurs more often in books on architecture than on the arts of representation. Historians of architecture are apt to confine themselves strictly to existing buildings and the written documents concerning them. Here too the economic factor must never be forgotten. For instance, some historians will tell you that Romanesque art had its origin in districts where Romanesque buildings are still spread most thickly. More likely those places were too poor or, perhaps, too indifferent, to rebuild in Gothic or later styles. As a matter of fact, Romanesque lingered on in the less prosperous, more outlying parts of Île-de-France, or in Poitou and the Vendée and in the more out-of-the-way districts of Spain. In that country only a few great cathedrals were not rebuilt in

the Gothic style. In France the wealthier regions did likewise. I cannot recall many entirely Romanesque cathedrals
in Normandy, Picardy, Île-de-France, or Burgundy. Many an
abbey failed to be rebuilt in the Gothic style, which means
that the monastic communities were no longer as wealthy as
when, regardless of expense, they built Cluny, Vézelay, or
St. Benoît-sur-Loire.

The same fallacy is still playing havoc with histories based
on those documents only that happen to have come to light.
Their authors are like the students of architecture who would
scrupulously refrain from speculating on how some Egyptian, Greek, Roman, or mediaeval building looked when
complete, and do not even admit that such an interest is
legitimate or, as they call it, "scientific."

Protest against the theory of milieu, so virulent in my
youth, is no longer necessary. It may perhaps still serve to
produce the opposite of what Taine and his school expected.
The classical instance is Perugino, the most Arcadian of
artists, but living in the most turbulent and sanguinary town
in Italy and himself an assassin. (Do not we hear of the
sentimentality of Sing-Sing prisoners and how they are
moved by virtuous characters in plays performed for them?)
Art more ecstatic than in early fifteenth-century Siena the
Western world has never seen. Yet Siena at that time was
notoriously sensual, ribald, and factious. Let me take a more
recent example and draw attention to the case of Copley as
described by James Flexner in his entertaining and instructive book on America's old masters (The Viking Press, New
York, 1939). Brought up on a wharf with foul shipping close
at hand and rowdy sailors on shore, this served only to inspire Copley with horror of the sea, and a loathing of wild
or merely disorderly conduct and bad manners of any kind.

For kindred reasons, ages of absolutism like those of Louis
XIV and the nineteenth-century Tsardom can produce great
art or literature or both. It may be that it is to escape from

actuality, like Claude and Poussin in France, Perugino and Raphael in an Italy of big and little tyrannies. Prosperous, free peoples do not need escapes and may produce fewer masterpieces.

Now a final word about connoisseurship. If, as Napoleon is supposed to have said, history is a fable agreed upon, connoisseurship is a guess that passes unopposed; not because the guess is reasonable and plausible, but that students end by getting bored with a given problem and drop it with ironical silence. The unprofessional might be shocked if he learnt how many of his favourite masterpieces of antiquity and of later periods pass under names that remain unchallenged because nobody is sufficiently interested to challenge them.

I sometimes wonder, thinking of connoisseurship, whether a day may not come when it will seem as futile to discuss the attribution of works of art as it now seems to wrangle over the attribution of sacred relics. Yet as we may go on reverencing relics for what they meant for centuries to good people, so many a mediocre picture, say the Barberini "Beatrice Cenci," may continue to interest us for the cult it enjoyed once upon a time, rather than for intrinsic qualities that we no longer perceive.

Significant Events in History

A few more paragraphs about history by way of appendix. History is more than a chronicle of the past, an account of any and every kind of thing that happened through the ages. History narrates the ordered succession of significant events, and significant events are those events that have contributed to making us what we are to-day.

So for us Europeans, wherever now residing along the ever diminishing spans of this planet, what happened in antiquity outside the Mediterranean basin and its hinterlands is almost without import. There were artifacts in India before Mesopotamians, Achaemeneans, and Greeks, following each other, brought their arts with them. No doubt there was art in China, and masterly bronzes, jades, and stone-carvings were produced for two thousand years at least before Buddhist missionaries brought Hellenized Indian art to China, thereby stimulating its people to a creativeness in the field of representation that they had not attained before and, left to themselves, might never have achieved. Northern barbarians contributed much that was ornamental to early Romanesque. Artifacts of sorts, some of no small intrinsic interest, are spread over the earth's surface from western Kamchatka to Singapore, from Greenland's icy mountains to Patagonia's stormy capes, in Africa and on the islands of the sea! But even the arts of China and of India, remarkable and deeply human as they are and with histories of their own worthy of every attention, are not history for us Europeans. Only to the extent that we influenced and affected them, and they influenced and affected our arts, should they find a place in our history. Their contribution to our arts is modest, reduced, as far as China is concerned, to little more than a few textile patterns in the late Middle Ages and to chinoiseries in our eighteenth century, and nothing worth mentioning has come to us from India. Besides possible influence, faint enough on fourth- and fifth-century relief and sculpture, I recall only the way certain male figures sit, with one leg tucked under the thigh and the other hanging down loose, which we come across once in a great while in the fourteenth-century illuminations.

In Europe itself art history must avoid what has not contributed to the main stream, no matter how interesting, how magnificent in itself. It should exclude, for instance, most German and even Spanish and Dutch art. It should dwell less and less on Italian art after Caravaggio, and end altogether by the middle of the eighteenth century with Solimena and Tiepolo. Except for Ribera, Murillo, Velasquez, and Goya in Spain, and Schongauer and Dürer and Holbein in German lands, the painters of these countries are neither in the main line of development nor of universal appeal to cultivated Europeans. As for Dutch painting, its achievement is immense and with the old, old Hals, the old Rembrandt, and the exquisite Vermeer, it reaches unsurpassed heights in portraiture and genre. It remains nevertheless doubtful whether any one of this great trio contributed much to modify the course of European art—much more than we see and suspect in English portraitists like Sir Joshua and the landscape painters of the Norwich school. Still less can British portraiture lay claim to a prominent place in the history I have in mind; and except for Constable the same is true of British landscape, much as one must admire the achievements of both.

The artists just mentioned, excepting perhaps Schongauer and Hals and Constable, owed more to their Italian precursors and contemporaries, and thus come into our history. Then how conceive Velasquez without his indebtedness first to the followers of Caravaggio, and later to Titian and Veronese? There is little painting in Spain, from Ribera to Goya, that is not Italianate. Dürer and Rembrandt and Vermeer owe less, though enough to bring them into the main stream, but the first two might have grown to their full stature without Italy. About Vermeer I am not so sure.

I will now venture to jot down a skeleton outline of what should be the history of the figure arts among the Mediterranean and Atlantic peoples.

Egyptian and Mesopotamian, leading up to archaic Greek. Mesopotamian, generating all art phenomena of nearer Asia, including Hathi, Hurrian, Hittite, Armenian; of Northern as well as of Central Asia, as Ordos and Siberian and influencing pre-Buddhist Chinese. Egyptian and Mesopotamian together generate Phoenician and early Cypriote.

Creto-Mycenaean, Greek whether archaic, Hellenistic, or Christian down to 1400 A.D. By that time so-called Byzantine art is mummified into rigid patterns in Greek and Balkan lands, and into pietistic prettiness in Muscovite territories.

Etruscan, Italian of every region, and Roman of every province are offshoots of Greek art in its successive phases, with local variations due to native incompetence. From about 500 to 1200 of our era, in fresco and panel painting from Wladimir in northernmost Russia to Cádiz in southwestern Spain, from Bergen near the Arctic Circle to Sicilian Trapani, an almost uniform morphology and iconography prevailed. It is at times palatable in the Orthodox Christian world, and generally distressing in the Latin part of Europe, with the exception of Othonian art in Germany, and of somewhat earlier schools of drawing and tinting at Winchester and Tours, and sporadic masterpieces like the frescoes of San Vincenzo al Volturno under Monte Cassino, the crypt of San Clemente in Rome, and the ceiling of Saint Savin in Poitou. Toward 1100, however, a revival destined to be continuous began, both North and South, not only in painting but even more vigorously in sculpture. Thenceforth sculpture in the North advanced to the glories of Toulouse, Saint-Gilles, Moissac, Chartres, Rheims, Amiens, and, at an early date, started a movement in northern Italy which, joining in Tuscany with the classical genius of Niccolò Pisano and the Romanesque sturdiness of Arnolfo (despite the regression caused by the Gothic distemper spread by Giovanni Pisano, the Michelangelo of the Trecento, which fatally weakened sculptors as well as painters), reached its culmination in the first half of the sixteenth century. Nor was its force fully spent before the middle of the eighteenth.

In North-Central and in Western Europe an independent movement away from Gothic towards Renaissance started about 1400. In actual manifestation it seemed at times more calligraphic, more tossed about than ever, but was already nothing more substantial, and to return to the vertical from attempting to drape with flimsy draperies a clothes-horse, if so much diagonal, and to give the head and mask more modelling and verisimilitude. This phase, called in painting the "International style," threatened to prevail all over Europe for about fifty years after 1400 and might have ended, but for the victorious resistance of the Van Eycks coming from Bruges and of Donatello and Masaccio from Florence, in an art as merely ornamental, diagrammatic, and conventional as the Japanese of those and later times. Thanks to the geniuses just mentioned, Tuscans lost no time in overcoming this menace, and even Franco-Flemish art took a direction, gained a vision, that not only made possible the masters and masterpieces of the fifteenth and later centuries in the Lowlands and France, but, with the continuous assistance of Italy, led straight to the learned Poussin and the continued glories of French painting down to Degas and Cézanne.

We must distinguish between European history of art and the history of art in each European country. Much that is interesting locally, and legitimately cherished in Germany and Spain, in Holland even, some of which, like Dutch landscape, possesses intrinsic qualities of the most varied order, has poured but little into the stream of European art history. It may be argued that well into the middle of the nineteenth century the Ruysdaels, and Rembrandt, and their constellations influenced European painting, except in the Norwich school, much less than the Carraccis and Domenichino, although the artistic value of these last is not for one moment to be compared with the poetry, pathos, and passion of the Dutch. No more than the Spaniard Velasquez did these great Dutchmen affect the art of their foreign contemporaries. It took the nineteenth century to rediscover them, although even then as inspiration, stimulus, and justification rather than for guidance. Indeed, revived and rediscovered admiration seldom attains the effect of immediate and continued influence.

Exotic Arts

In order to avoid misunderstanding, let me say emphatically that for their high merits, I value the various art manifestations that I would not include in my history although I should not discourage the study of their own local development, of what they meant to their countrymen, and what they mean to us from the time that we discovered and began to understand and enjoy them. Yet it is better to leave German, Dutch, and Spanish art to be studied in detail by the natives of these provinces. If they exaggerate the achievement of their artists, and the value of their own erudition, surely the labourer is worthy of his hire. We can disregard their estimates and pick and choose what is for our soul's good, as well for the delight of the moment.

The question of the exotic arts is more complicated. I do not so much have in mind the creations of peoples and tribes living in what we are still pleased to call "a state of nature," Africans black and brown and ash-coloured, Polynesians and Melanesians, as of the nations with civilized histories like East Indians, Chinese, and Japanese, Islamitic Persians as well as proto-historical tribes like Central Americans, who remained neolithic or bronze-age until a few centuries ago.

Compared with our art of the last sixty centuries with its endless variety of subject matter, of material, of kind and quality, every other art, Chinese included, is limited. I had the good fortune to be one of the first to feel the beauty of the various exotic arts and to encourage collectors and dealers and amateurs to give them attention. Chinese art in particular fascinated me at a time when a connoisseur like

Salomon Bing refused to believe that it existed at all apart from porcelain, lacquers, and chinoiseries.

Even Chinese, by far the most valuable of all the arts from beyond our pale, can offer students of visual representation its landscape only, as an achievement that our painters have not equalled or surpassed—its landscape so scenic, so contemplative, so nostalgic, so different from the cartographic Flemish and Italian landscapes of the Quattrocento or the increasingly naturalistic ones of the seventeenth-century Dutch, English, and Flemish, culminating in Cézanne.

The exotic arts soon weary. As is the case with Yogi theosophies, Mazdanianism, and similar appeals, it is craving for mere otherness that draws us to them rather than any unique superiority of their own. Nor can we devote ourselves with advantage to intensive study of them. For one thing, we cannot admit that the visual art of a people can be fully appreciated without an intimate acquaintance with its language, literature, thought, and history. Feeling vaguely their incapacity to appreciate Chinese art as art, the philologers have made it the subject of mere iconography. Against this a protest has been already made by Yukio Yashiro, the one student from the Far East who knows our methods, comprehends our values, and yet as a Japanese possesses all that is necessary to understand Chinese art as art, and resents its degradation to mere subject matter as we resent similar treatment of Greek and more recent art.

How quickly one comes to an end of Byzantine art that has so lately been rediscovered! Its repertory is limited in extent: paintings, whether mosaic, fresco, panel, or illumination; and still more in ivories, enamels, textiles, and other artifacts. It is precious, refulgent, monotonous. It ends towards 1200 as a gorgeous mummy case enclosing the embalmed remains of a dead art. Little more can be said of Islamitic Persian and all "Arab" arts, despite the exaggerated importance given recently to both. They must eventually find their place. But it will not be at the centre of the stage. The art of every people is now accessible in original examples brought from everywhere to everywhere, and reproductions of it coming nearer and nearer to perfection are to be had at smaller and smaller outlay. The starved craving for visual satisfaction is being at last stilled, even surfeited. What with the current illustrated papers which reproduce not only recent and contemporary artifacts brought back by explorers; what with the increasing material that the world over is being almost daily recovered from the past, it would not be surprising if a revulsion followed from the lust of omnivorous looking, from the panoptical pell-mell miscellany with which we are gluttonously indulging ourselves to-day.

To me, and to those like-minded with me, such a revulsion would be welcome. It is in fact taking place at present and accounts for the rebellion against classical shapes, for the cult of the distorted, the incongruous, the absurd, and the return to the geometrical. Ultimately this revulsion may lead to selective seeing and permit us to guide and train the specifically gifted to distinguish between art and artifact, between illustration and visual information, between creation and imitation. It may lead us to descry on what level of culture, or material civilization, any object gives satisfaction, and to differentiate the gratification of mere curiosity and research from satisfactions that are systemic, tonic, and artistic.

Far from being mere display of data, with perhaps no other principle of order than a geographical or chronological one, art history is in a position to profit by all the criticism, the biography, the documentary and scientific research that can be brought to bear, provided the selective principle of value remains in watchful control.

History, we are agreed, should not be a mere chronicle, mere data, mere *res gestae*, mere events as events, no matter what their nature or purpose. Nor yet should history be exploited and abused as cabalistic lore whence to extract justification for the absurdities and passions of the hour. History is a narrative that facts cannot disprove, and like every other art, including every phase and form of literature, it must be life-enhancing, life-expanding, life-intensifying. History achieves this, just as tactile values, movement, and composition do in the visual arts, by retracing the processes of action, making us aware of and causing us to linger over its significant moments and vital articulations. Instead of passing them by, or totally ignoring them as we do in our workaday life, history should lead us to recapture the past at those points that we most gladly recall and enjoy, in the same way that as individuals we delight in being suddenly flooded and overwhelmed by memories of our earliest and most zestful years, when each of us was discovering life as "stout Cortez" discovered the Pacific, a universe of magic, mystery, and unlimited possibilities.

In other words, art history is called upon to present not merely what artifacts a given community at a given moment was offered to look at, what it greeted perhaps with excited curiosity, what it approved and disapproved, what it got used to seeing and liking, and ended by defending against invading novelties. That is not enough. Like politico-social history, better called human history, art history should not dwell too much on waves of fashion, winds of doctrine, or the maunderings of primitivism, but should pick out and present the most life-enhancing moments, dwell among the permanent acquisitions, and make them accessible and intelligible. Seeing, however, that art history deals, not with the events that are over and done with, irretrievably and forever, but with creations that are still with us, it should be its business to explain the value, the importance, the transcendance even of the greatest moments as they are still represented by sovereign masterpieces. Other surviving artifacts must be subordinated, and dwelt upon, if at all, in so far only as they serve to connect moments of splendour and lead up to them—as well as, unhappily, away from them. Thus ultimately real art history and real art criticism turn out to be all but identical.

Only we should try to keep clear and distinct the history of humanity in general (which comprises all other branches of history) and art history. We should stick to art, and not run off the track into cultural, economical, sociological, religious, and literary fields—at all events not without knowing what we are doing. We should do so only while gathering materials with which to illuminate and interpret great masters and specific masterpieces.

In the course of the book to which this essay is a preface we shall be investigating what happened to the visual arts, and particularly to the arts of visual representation, during their decline, when they lost first form, then composition, and finally shape itself. We shall pursue this process to the almost total degeneration of representational art into the flaccid puerilities and crudities of the period designated, in various parts of what was once the antique world, as Coptic, Merovingian, Saxon, Lombard, Croatian, etc. We shall pursue it with interest, with alacrity even, but with care not to hypnotize ourselves into illusions about the artistic value of the phenomena engaging our attention. We shall not lose sight of the fact that we are absorbed in the study of art not in health but in disease, in other words that we are investigating the pathology of art. As in all declines, we shall come on moments of seeming arrest and even convalescence. They will grow rarer and rarer, till finally, when all seems over, a real improvement begins, continues, gathers strength, and leads to recovery. Then, and then only, can we hope to find increasing promise of art as distinct from artifacts, and products of permanent—I mean intrinsic—value, apart from interest accruing from their setting in place and time. Then our task will lose the irksomeness of a disagreeable but imperative duty, and turn into the happiness that accompanies creative activity and the hope of unchecked advance.

CONCLUSION

Readers who have followed me thus far may say: "The writer bases his notions, prejudices, and discontents on the arts derived from the Greek, and always with a turn to the plastic, a preference for the linear, a search for the contour, just as his inspiration flows from pure Hellenism and his yearnings reach toward it."

I should not defend myself too vigorously against this charge. I would wish to have it understood, however, that by "Hellenism" I do not mean the condition of society between twenty-five hundred and fifteen hundred years ago. I have in mind rather the attitude toward the universe, the approach to life, the cherished values and aims of the thinkers, artists, and men of action of those ten centuries in the Greek-speaking world. Hellenism is not a fixed state of things but a path, a way, a reaching out towards a humanity that is as remote from chaos as it can succeed in soaring above and beyond "nature." It will never rebel against "nature" through nihilism or despair, as ascetic religions have preached, setting up unrealizable ideals and unpractical standards. Hellenism does not deny or even decry the animal in man. It would humanize him.

Art, in the widest sense of the word, is the instrument Hellenism has used and would use for that purpose. All the arts, poetry, music, ritual, the visual arts, the theatre, must work singly and together to create the most comprehensive art of all, a humanized society, and its masterpiece, the free man: free within and free without, ready in Goethe's untarnishable words to live manfully in the whole, the good, and the beautiful.[1]

The art which, never disobeying its own laws, endeavours to fulfill this mission is normal, is classical. It is the standard art towards which we Europeans in the course of history have always turned back after no matter what occultations, declines, aberrations, and rebellions. Nowadays we are in the midst of a decline which, like all cultural declines, ignores its symptoms and euphorically imagines that it is revolutionizing the world when it is merely playing the infant, kicking, screaming, and smashing, or daubing and kneading with paint and clay. Each admires his own products ecstatically, and each believes that he is initiating a new epoch.

European art in direct line of succession from the Greek, that is to say classical art, is what it is because after thousands of years of groping, mankind, headed by the Hellenes, succeeded in discovering what channels of expression, what moulds of form corresponded best with our anatomical, physiological, and psychological make-up.

As long as man has two eyes, two ears, two arms, and two legs, but one set of vital organs, one heart, one stomach, and so on, he will tend to return to a mean, to the classical, no matter how much like the Chinese dwarf he may wobble backwards and forwards, to right and left.

You can cast off each separate masterpiece created by the arts in recent generations or the whole of the sixty-odd centuries during which art, as distinct from artifacts, was being created. You can perhaps succeed in ridding yourself of all remembered concepts, facts, ideas, of the recent as well as of the remote past. You can throw overboard every mental heritage that consciousness has prized. When you have done so, where are you? What has become of you? You remain

[1] "Im Ganzen, Guten, Schönen resolut zu leben . . ." *Gesellige Lieder, Generalbeichte.*

incapable of uttering a word that has not its roots buried
deep in the remotest past. You cannot open your lips without being used as a mouthpiece by myriads upon myriads of
the dead. You are little more than a disk recording the reproducing traditions that no awareness can fathom, traditions
deposited during countless thousands of years in your anatomical and physiological structure, in your tissues, in your
nervous and glandular systems. Yet you fancy that you are
free to start afresh as man did hundreds of millenniums ago.
In that remote age he had to fight only against other wild
beasts, and the figments of his own brain. Now he must walk
the treadmill of mechanical forces that he himself has con-
structed but from which, now that they dominate him, he
cannot wrench himself free. He may yet live to regret the
ease with which he threw away the conscious traditions that
were operative in humanizing him. He may come to sigh
for what it was to have been an American, an Englishman,
an Italian, a Frenchman, a German in the years when our
civilization seemed so secure, and its foundations dug so
deep into the past, that we could not imagine their being
shaken.

To sum up this essay in a few words:

History is the story of how man is being humanized.

Art history is the story of what art has contributed to
that end.

No history can be written without axiomatic values, consciously manifested, or unconsciously assumed.

Values cannot exist without a valuer. We know no valuer
but man.

Human values depend on our physical make-up, on the
way our brain, belly, and members act, and on the demands
made by the needs, appetites, and impulses they give rise to.
It is with these we have to treat if we wish to come to any
understanding of values. Metaphysics, logic, optimistic or
pessimistic constructions, philological nightmares, historical

fairy-tales have little influence on the essentials of human nature, on its cravings, its ideals, its satisfactions. Mankind's ultimate aim is satisfaction, yet not satisfaction on any plane, but on the highest plane attainable at a given moment by individuals capable, through gifts as well as numbers, because of their quality as well as their quantity, not only of inspiring but of leading the rest of mankind toward the desired goal.

INDEX OF NAMES

INDEX OF SUBJECTS

257